The Poseidonian Chora

Archaic Greeks in the Italic hinterland

Mikels Skele

BAR International Series 1094
2002

Published in 2016 by
BAR Publishing, Oxford

BAR International Series 1094

The Poseidonian Chora

ISBN 978 1 84171 472 1

© M Skele and the Publisher 2002

Typesetting and layout: Darko Jerko

BAR Publishing is the trading name of British Archaeological Reports (Oxford) Ltd.
British Archaeological Reports was first incorporated in 1974 to publish the BAR
Series, International and British. In 1992 Hadrian Books Ltd became part of the BAR
group. This volume was originally published by Archaeopress in conjunction with
British Archaeological Reports (Oxford) Ltd / Hadrian Books Ltd, the Series principal
publisher, in 2002. This present volume is published by BAR Publishing, 2016.

Printed in England

BAR
PUBLISHING

BAR titles are available from:

BAR Publishing
122 Banbury Rd, Oxford, OX2 7BP, UK
EMAIL   info@barpublishing.com
PHONE   +44 (0)1865 310431
FAX   +44 (0)1865 316916
www.barpublishing.com

Monte Calpazio from the Temple of Hera I.

Acknowledgements

The list of people and institutions that have made this project possible is a long one. Funding for field work in 1990-1991 was provided by a University Fellowship and a Steinberg Fellowship from Washington University. The American Geographical Society made its archives available; Figures 12-14 are reprinted here by their permission. The trip to Milwaukee to examine their archives and several trips to Paestum during which the groundwork for this study was laid were supported by the School of Social Sciences, the Office of Research and Projects and the Office of Contract Archaeology at Southern Illinois University at Edwardsville (SIUE).

This work began as a doctoral dissertation; I cannot imagine having a better or more distinguished dissertation committee. Sarantis Symeonoglou, the chair, allowed me great latitude to pursue my research in whichever direction seemed appropriate to me, and at the same time offered firm guidance at the times when I needed it. The other members of my committee, Robert L. Thorp, Patty Jo Watson, William I. Woods, John Griffiths Pedley and Ross Holloway each contributed valuable criticism and support. Professors Pedley and Holloway, with their depth of knowledge of the study area, provided particularly helpful comments and suggestions; if I did not always follow their advice, it may be put down to my native stubbornness.

In Italy, Giuliana Tocco, the Superintendent of Antiquities for the Province of Salerno, provided invaluable assistance. Marina Cipriani, the director of the Paestum Museum, and Gianni Avagliano, the vice-director, not only gave me the run of the museum and the archaeological park, but helped identify some of the material recovered during the survey of the Capodifiume.

The excellent profiles and illustrations of the Capodifiume survey material were made by Julie Harper, and Mike Hemmer weighed in with his considerable cartographic skills at the eleventh hour to produce Figures 9, 15, 16, and 17.

There are two people, however, to whom I owe a special debt of gratitude. The first is William I. Woods of the Office of Contract Archaeology at SIUE. It was Bill who first introduced me to Paestum, and provided many opportunities to revisit over the years. Without his constant support and generosity it is a certainty that this project would never have happened. The other is Mario Mello of the University of Salerno, whose depth of knowledge of the regional ancient history of the Sele Plain is matched only by his warmth and generosity. Our many long discussions are the source of much that is in this study; it was he who suggested that the Capodifiume River might be an appropriate focus for a systematic survey.

Finally, I thank my wife, Peg Simons, whose patience, forbearance and encouragement have bordered on the saintly throughout the many crises that have attended this project.

TABLE OF CONTENTS

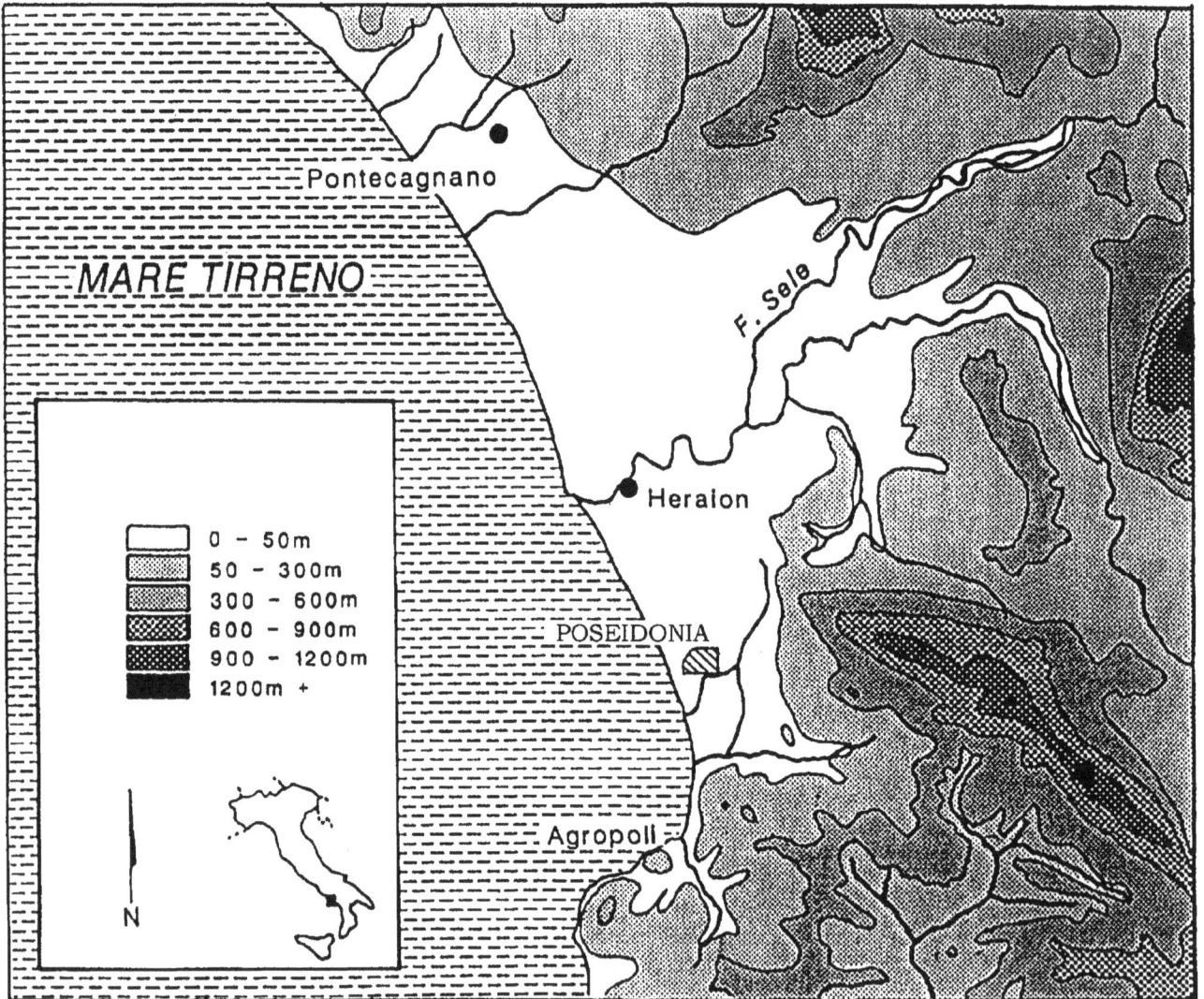

Pontecagnano

MARE TIRRENO

F. Sela

Heraion

POSEIDONIA

Agropoli

0 – 50m
50 – 300m
300 – 600m
600 – 900m
900 – 1200m
1200m +

N

Chapter 1
INTRODUCTION

Research goals

The goal of this study, as apart from its method, is to bring to bear evidence from as many sources as possible in an effort to understand the nature of the relationship between the Greek settlers of Poseidonia, founded at about the turn of the sixth century BC in the Sele Plain in modern Campania, Italy, and the Italic peoples indigenous to the plain. The Greek city flourished from its foundation until about 400 BC when it came under the control of Lucanians from the nearby Apennines. The city continued to thrive until late antiquity, when it was largely abandoned, apparently in response to malarial conditions. Ironically, it was this situation which preserved many of its monuments until its "rediscovery" in the late eighteenth century; since then, in one way or another, it has been the focus of much scholarly attention.

Until very recently, however, most of this attention has been lavished on the great monuments of the ancient city, especially its three well-preserved temples, and on the rich cemeteries, including the unique frescoed tombs, and sanctuaries outside the walls. This is entirely understandable given the orientation towards the acquisition and analysis of objects endemic to early classical archaeology, and the abundant field offered by Poseidonia-Paestum. Unfortunately, many of the anthropological questions of interest today were left unexamined, and much of the evidence is gone forever, although much remains salvageable. Insofar as the relationship between Greeks and Italics in the plain has been considered at all, it has been assumed by many that it was characterized by a military dominance of the Greeks over the natives, and that the resulting situation was one of tension, if not outright hostility. In any case, regardless of which side of the issue has been advanced, no specific studies of the situation have been initiated up to now. The present study examines the hypothesis that not only was the relationship cordial during the 200 year tenure of the Greeks, but that indigenous groups actually collaborated in the founding of the city.

The chorographic approach, as defined below, is particularly well suited to addressing this issue. Only when all of the evidence is evaluated within the context of the ancient landscape can a judgment be made regarding the social contract among the various peoples in the plain.

The scope and method of chorography

In its strictest sense, the term "chorography" refers to a description of a culturally and geographically coherent area in all senses relevant to the way it functions as a recognizable unit. The concept has a long, if checkered, history in the discipline of geography, where it was associated with a kind of particularist approach that signalled a retreat from environmental determinism in the early part of this century (Sauer, 1941; Smith, 1989). In classical archaeology, however, where descriptions of the particular constitute the overwhelming majority of the literature, the approach represents a broadening, rather than a narrowing, of scope. In spite of the dubious connotations that the term itself may have acquired in modern geography, it remains a useful mid-level tool in the study of ancient cultures, for while there have certainly been studies of these cultures on a broad scale as well as on a site level, there remains a gap between the specific and the all-encompassing. In my application of the concept to archaeology, I have integrated, to the degree possible, studies which have been traditionally treated separately, such as physiography, literature, economics and archaeology. Quite apart from the essential idea of treating a city and its *chora* as a whole, it is hoped that this methodological synthesis, in contrast to the usual collection of unconnected specialist reports, will clarify the picture of that whole.

Central to the approach is the concept of landscape, in the sense that includes not only the physical area, but all of the people on it, their interaction with it and their culture as a whole. Indeed, it is this synthesis that has inspired the blending of traditional disciplines, so that the physiographic reconstruction, for example, is based on archaeological as well as geomorphological evidence. It is my contention that the separation of these approaches in the past has led to a fragmentary and less than complete understanding of the dynamic between culture and place.

The chorography of Poseidonia

The inseparability of *polis* and *chora* is by no means a new idea; it has been remarked by writers from Homer on down to modern archaeologists and historians. It is a fact, however, that the understanding of this essential unity has rarely affected archaeological methodology in studying the Greek city-states, at least until very recently. There has, of course, been a long tradition dating back to the late 1960s of regional studies in archaeology, particularly in Mesoamerica and in the Middle East (Hole et all., 1969; Flannery et all., 1971; Adams and Nissen, 1972; and many others). These approaches differ, however, from chorography in two ways: urban centers (where they exist) and their surrounding coutrysides are essentially treated separately, even when a close relationship is acknowledged; and the scope of the study areas, especially in mesoamerica, is generally much broader geographically and narrower theoretically. Both differences stem to a large extent from differences in the areas being studied, but also to differences in the goals of the studies. The goal of chorography, although it includes settlement patterns, microenvironment analysis and other considerations characteristic of regional studies, is basically culture history. Other regional studies tend to focus on more theoretical issues, such as the rise of agriculture or incipient nucleation, or on the settlement patterns in much larger geographic areas. It is my contention that chorography provides an essential link in the empirical foundation for more theoretical studies in the world of ancient Greece and Italy, where there has traditionally been very little between descriptions of narrowly defined sites and broad generalizations.

Even now, the popularity of regional studies in classical archaeology owes more to economical considerations than to theoretical commitment; archaeological survey is inexpensive compared to full scale excavation, and yields a satisfying amount of information for a relatively low expenditure of scarce funding. The result has sometimes been a rush to survey without a clear understanding of the goals appropriate to the method, and consequently without a clear method (Skele, 1996). There have been outstanding exceptions: the Metaponto and Croton surveys (Carter and d'Annibale, 1985) are admirably focused, and the Boeotia survey (Bintliff, 1985) is a model of sampling procedure; the thoroughness of the Minnesota Messenia Project (Rapp and Gifford, 1985) is legend. More recently, the Argolid Exploration Project (Jameson, et all., 1995) stands out as very near the ideal of the present study, but on a larger scale.

Even when survey is appropriately used, however, it remains only one tool in a chorographic approach. In the Sele Plain there have been surveys of varying degrees of usefulness, including one along the Capodifiume River conducted as a part of the present study (see below).

Similarly, geomorphological studies of several kinds have been conducted previously in the Sele Plain, but always with respect to a specific problem, and seldom, it seems, with much communication among the directors of the various studies. Complicating the issue is the framework of geological time scale within which such studies are conducted. Archaeologists almost always need far greater chronological resolution than geologists are accustomed to, or, indeed, can provide. The present study combines a compilation of extant geomorphological evidence with relevant archaeological data, air photo interpretation and ground observations to attempt

to achieve this resolution. Historical records, including ancient literature, are taken into account, not as primary evidence, but as signposts for the interpretation of other evidence. In this way, a kind of micro-chronology unusual in geomorphological studies alone is approached.

Similar methods are used in establishing demographic patterns before and during the two centuries of Greek control of Poseidonia. Once again, the ancient literature is used as a guide, and previous archaeological work, in the Sele Plain and elsewhere, is re-examined and applied to the question at hand. Although there are some difficulties stemming from the divergent goals of the excavators through the years, an enormous wealth of evidence exists when taken in the context of the whole, allowing new interpretations of much of the data available. Previous surveys in the Sele Plain are also consulted, although there are problems associated with the goals and methods of these, as we shall see. Finally, a small intensive survey was conducted along an important waterway flanking the city.

The Capodifiume survey

The Capodifiume survey consists of an intensive systematic survey of the Capodifiume River from its source at the springs of the same name to the modern autostrada that runs about one kilometer East of the ancient city of Poseidonia-Paestum (see Fig. 4). Thirty one survey units along a 200 meter corridor straddling the river over a distance of about five kilometers, and sixteen control units away from the river, were investigated in an effort to shed some light on the extramural land-use in the plain throughout antiquity, but particularly during the Greek tenure; that is to say, the sixth to the end of the fifth centuries BC. The ideal would be a systematic survey of the entire Sele Plain, where sites are disappearing almost daily under the plow and bulldozer, but the usual constraints of time and money required the considerable narrowing of the field; for the present study, the extent of the survey was deemed sufficient.

The Capodifiume River was chosen for two reasons. First, it is a relatively small and easily definable area with clear topographic integrity; second, it was desired that the area chosen have the potential to address specific problems.

The upper course of the river ties together two locations of importance throughout the prehistory and history of the area: the Capodifiume springs and the ancient site of Poseidonia itself. That the shelf of travertine on which the city sits has historic importance is self-evident, and the Gaudo cemetery to its immediate North attests to its significance before then. As for the reliable and highly productive springs, apart from the visible Roman remains sinking into the pool, we know of a Hellenistic sanctuary on its bank and a Villanovan cemetery nearby, as well as numerous casual reports of the remains of lithic cultures scattered on the adjacent hillside. The spring pool lies directly below the heights of the promontory upon which sit the ruins of medieval Capaccio Vecchia, a site which, for all the tantalizing suggestions of ancient material there, has yet to be investigated systematically. It is somewhat surprising that no significant Greek presence has been reported there, considering that the city was named for Poseidon and protected by Hera, to both of whom springs and mountains were of more than passing interest.

The river itself must have been important to all the tenants of Paestum throughout its history, since it was the closest reliable source of great volumes of fresh water, the Romans having even diverted its course in relation to a moat around the city that had existed in one form or another since the fourth century BC. One might expect to find rural dwellings along such a feature.

In addition to its own merits for archaeological consideration, the Capodifiume runs more or less parallel to the entrance of the valley that gives access to the interior and, ultimately, the plain of Sybaris via Metapontine territory. Connections with the Vallo di Diano in the Tanagro drainage have long been noted; a road running just North of and parallel to the river from the Porta Aurea to the valley would surely give a more direct access than the confirmed ancient road leading directly East to the mountain slope (Fig. 11).

The area surrounding that road has been surveyed under the auspices of the Oriental Institute of the University of Naples, but more along the lines of reconnaissance than systematic intensive survey. Several sites were recorded; only two of them have a direct relevance to the present study. Indirectly, however, these new sites, along with some of the previously known sites in the area, have a strong impact on the interpretation of the Capodifiume survey, as will be seen.

More or less standard survey methods were used in this study. The boundaries of survey units were determined primarily by field boundaries, to allow ease of mapping in the field and to facilitate relocation for revisits by other investigators. Only fields with more than 30% visibility that were recently plowed or cultivated and rained on were surveyed. Since the survey took place in October and November, this was not a great limiting factor, although a dry period at the end of October and the beginning of November brought the project to a halt for a brief time, when I revisited a field with an artifact density of sixteen to twenty per square meter and discovered the material had become almost invisible with a light coating of dried soil. Some of the fields were freshly plowed and without crops, while others were planted in annual crops such as broccoli and fennel; these last were well cultivated between the widely spaced rows, and visibility was excellent while the plants were young. In all, it can be said that surface conditions on the fields surveyed were equivalent, despite the varying uses of the fields.

The actual survey method used was to walk each unit in parallel transects five meters apart, noting the artifact density and collecting possible diagnostic material. The idea was to collect a representative sample in the sense of presence or absence without regard for immediate identifiability; no attempt was made to hew to the proportions of different types of material in each unit. Architectural materials such as bricks or tiles were noted but rarely collected. The density of material in each collection unit was estimated by locating the greatest

density that covered an area likely to be reflective of occupation. In this case that was judged to be no smaller than about 400 square meters; in practice all the areas recorded were greater than that. A two meter by two meter square was then measured, and all of the material in it was counted and divided by four to arrive at the number of artifacts per square meter. Thus a density figure of 6-15, for example, means that within the collection unit there was a significant area containing that density of material; elsewhere within the unit, the density could be less. Under the circumstances, greater precision would be only apparent, given the constant manipulation of the agricultural surface.

In units of particular density or interest, a second or even third pass was made after the initial five-meter transects to assure thoroughness. A total of more than 750 artifacts was collected. These were washed, labelled and analyzed. As per expectation, the majority consisted of coarse domestic ware which is at this point not identifiable, but these were retained and stored in the depository of the *Museo Nazionale di Paestum* along with the identifiable material in the expectation that future study of this type of ware will make identification possible, expanding our understanding of the cultures represented in the collection units.

Fig. 4 shows the locations of the survey units and the density distribution of artifacts. The gaps along the river represent fields that were fallow, in pasture or otherwise presented inadequate visibility, with the exception of the fields immediately surrounding the springs, for which permission of access was denied by the land owners. No unit surveyed was completely devoid of archaeological material. Although many units displayed a deep chronology, generally one component was predominant, so that, within limits, the densities reflect the intensity of occupation.

The first thing that is clear from these densities is the general trend of relatively more material on the North side of the river than on the South, at least over the first three kilometers or so of its course. The bulk of the material collected in these units dates from the fourth century BC through Roman imperial times, although prehistoric material was also present in small quantities. In CS-1, CS-2 and CS-3 the presence of *impasto*, bits of daub, quartz and flint indicate a prehistoric presence. This material cannot be dated more precisely, since the pottery consisted of undecorated body sherds. The same is true of CS-7 and CS-11, which will be discussed in more detail shortly. This generally greater density on the North side of the river as opposed to the relative paucity of material on the South side reflects positively on the suggestion of a road parallel to and North of the river. Although the survey does not confirm the presence of such a road, it does strengthen the hypothesis, particularly in consideration of the fact that known sites on the other side of the river cluster around the confirmed ancient road there, and are conspicuously absent adjacent the river itself. Judging from the dates of the materials, this hypothetical road would have been most important from the fourth century on, although it seems clear that some sort of byway existed from prehistoric times as well; the relatively low quantity of material between these times (with one notable exception) would appear to indicate that the road was not used intensively in Archaic times. The exception is CS-11, where earlier material is represented by the rims of two amphorae: one a Corinthian type A dating to the late seventh-early sixth century BC, the other a Chiote amphora dating to the first half of the fifth. Other material collected from this unit spans the time between the Final Bronze Age to the fourth century BC; unfortunately, most of the artifacts are of the unidentifiable coarse domestic variety.

In terms of land use, the survey generally confirms the dramatic expansion of populations into the countryside during Lucanian times, but at the same time suggests that the earlier Greeks had more to do outside the walls than had been previously thought. CS-11 has already been discussed; CS-7 had some material from the fifth century, and CS-15 appears to represent a single-component site from the late sixth to the early fifth century. This last would appear to be either a substantial domestic site or an extramural sanctuary, judging from the kinds of materials recovered: cups, *olle,* loomweights and a variety of other domestic ware, but also an Ionic carinated cup and the foot of a fine Attic *skyphos*.

Among the results one might expect of a survey is the location of new sites. What constitutes a site in this context is somewhat problematic. In prehistoric contexts, for which the technique of systematic survey was developed, the definition is simple: a site is a place where there are archaeological materials, and its boundaries occur at the points where there are no more materials. In the Sele Plain, with its twenty six hundred year history of state-level society, this will not do. In this context, the definition of a site tends to be operational; it is a place where one would like to do some more investigation. Typically, areas with relatively high densities, or with a significant proportion of architectural material, or with an assemblage consistent with an identifiable function would qualify. With all its imperfection, I find this definition most useful for the current project. A list of such "sites" follows:

CS-4: Although of a relatively low density, a total of thirty five fragments of votive figures was recovered at this site, datable from the single fragment of a head *à côtes de melon* to no earlier than the fourth century BC. There was also a wide scatter of bricks and tiles. The range of artifacts from *impasto* to *terra sigillata,* however, suggests that perhaps the site has already been plowed under. There remains the possibility of investigations short of excavation: controlled surface collection and electromagnetic survey are two possibilities.

CS-7: This enigmatic site, located in the wedge between a medieval aqueduct and a modern one, may be the result of fill from elsewhere, although no record of it was noted at the local *Consorzio di Bonifica*. Materials are primarily Roman, including many freshly broken pottery fragments, but here also we have the presence of material ranging from prehistory to medieval times.

CS-11: This appears to have been occupied during the sixth and fifth centuries (see above).

CS-13: This site has a relatively high density, but is surely destroyed by now, since it was being pushed about with a bulldozer at the time of the survey. Materials generally date from the fourth century.

CS-14: This site was not collected, since it is identical to a site previously reported by the Oriental Institute survey, which recorded it as a rustic farmstead of Roman Imperial age, but also with some material dating as far back as the fifth century. I mention it because this site had the highest artifact density of any of the units examined by me; in fact, the only place I could find an equivalent concentration under similar cultivation was in the Eastern half of Paestum within the city walls. This factor, along with the presence of a large proportion of tiles and bricks, some of them deformed in the kiln, might lead one to re-examine its designation as a farmstead. The distance from the city, the proximity of the river and the huge amounts of material could be associated with a kiln for tile and brick production.

CS-15: I believe that this site has the potential of being the most rewarding of all the sites recorded in this survey, if indeed it is a domestic site, or possibly an extramural sanctuary. The high quality materials span the fifth century, and there are indications of earlier occupation as well. A critical factor is the relatively narrow chronological range, suggesting that much of the site may be intact.

CS-30: This site seems to be part of the Oriental Institute Site "C", a Roman villa, reported as a hundred meters or so East of the river; this survey extends its boundaries up to the river. Of interest is a line of travertine rubble cutting across the unit.

This list represents what might be considered sites in a traditional sense, and as such they are worthy of further investigation, excavation if possible. The traditional goals of excavation are perfectly valid, but in the context of a study of this kind, more care must be taken to glean as much information as possible. Ideally, the sites would be excavated simultaneously, or at least the results would be evaluated with reference to one another. Certainly greater attention than in the past must be given to the unglamorous coarseware, since only a secure chronology and functional analysis of this ware will permit full evaluation of the results of not only this survey, but any surveys in the plain, given that it constitutes the greater majority of artifacts present on the surface.

Apart from the location of sites, however, the value of this survey and others conducted systematically lies in revealing the intensity and distribution of occupation outside the walls of the city. In this case the Capodifiume corridor represents a sample of such occupation along an important waterway near the city. It is hoped that future surveys will complete the picture.

Chapter 2
THE SELE PLAIN BEFORE THE GREEKS

Introduction

The deltaic plain of the Sele River lies in a NW-SE crescent from Salerno to Agropoli, a distance of some 40 kilometers. Its Easternmost margins are delimited by the foothills of the Southern Apennines at a maximum distance of about 11 kilometers, and to its West is the Gulf of Salerno, the ancient Gulf of Poseidonia; to the South lie the hills of Cilento. These features have not only outlined but defined the nature of the Sele Plain, providing its substructure, contributing the material of which it is composed and shaping its morphology.

The mountains to the East are drained by three major streams apart from the Sele: the Picentino and the Tusciano to the North, and the Solofrone to the South. In addition, there are numerous small streams and an abundance of mineral springs rising from the lower slopes of the mountains, due to karst processes deep within these limestone mountains. The springs at Capodifiume give rise to the Capodifiume River, carrying highly calcarious waters past the walls of the ancient city of Poseidonia-Paestum, a fact which figures not only in the rise and success of that city, as we shall see, but its downfall as well; it was the altered drainage of the Capodifiume waters which gave rise to malarial swamps South of the city in late antiquity.

As the major rivers descend the mountains, they pass through Pleistocene gravels forming a broad shoulder beyond which the plain is filled with recent alluvium and travertine. The outcroppings of these gravels and of the contemporaneous travertines provide a secure boundary for the area of significant topographic change relevant to the period under study (Fig. 10). The stability of virtually all of the rest of the plain, especially in the Southern, Paestan, region, has been and continues to be the subject of controversy. While the ancient city itself stands on a secure foundation of Pleistocene travertine, elsewhere the plain is composed of alluvium, sand and recent travertine, complicated by rapidly forming calcrete. The course of the Sele after it is joined by the waters of the Calore, the position of the coastline at the mouth of the Sele and at Poseidonia in antiquity, the extent of the encroachment of the sea since antiquity and the effect of neo-tectonic activity on the level of the land relative to the sea have all been

passionately and eruditely argued; but if no firm consensus has been achieved, at least some significant headway has been made.

It is not surprising that so much attention has been lavished on these problems; they are central to the understanding of the ancient cultures in the area. Among other considerations, the existence of a harbor at Poseidonia, the location of the *Heraion* on the banks of the Sele relative to the sea in ancient times and the relationship between the environment and the decline of the city all rest on the ancient physiography of the area. Indeed, the nature of Greek land-use and the social contract between Greeks and indigenous peoples cannot be fully understood without reference to the physical environment in which they found themselves. It is impossible, for example, to determine the degree of Greek control of productive land without knowing its location and extent.

The physical landscape

The Poseidonian *chora* encompasses the plain South of the Sele River, which formed the ancient boundary between the Greek lands and Etruscan territory to the North, East to the Alburnus Mountains and South to the Punta Licosa, thus including steeply sloping limestone hills. The focus here, however, will be the plain itself and the foothills immediately surrounding it, since this is the area that will have provided the greater part of the agricultural production necessary (and so often overlooked) for the livelihood of the city.

Perhaps the most critical factor determining Sele Plain physiography is its proximity to the subduction zone of the African and Eurasian plates, creating a seismically active terrain circumscribed by faults and subject to a complex series of uplifts and depressions throughout its history, not to mention frequent earthquakes and the effects of the periodic eruptions of nearby Vesuvius. The whole of the Sele Plain as we have defined it, along with a considerable portion of the seabed to its West, comprises a graben subject to bradyseismic activity, the extent of which since antiquity has been a center of controversy for archaeologists interested in the reconstruction of the ancient landscape.

One of the more extreme views has been proposed by A. E. Günther (1964b: 909). Günther claimed to have seen evidence of holes bored by the marine mollusk *Lithodomus* to a height of approximately three meters above the present ground level in the columns of the temples at Paestum, and at ground level at the slightly higher Porta Sirena in the East wall of the city; he had also noted signs of ancient sea levels on the nearby cliffs of Agropoli at 11, 20 and 60 feet above present sea level. In a complex argument based on these observations and R. T. Günther's (1904) earlier estimate that the land surrounding the Bay of Naples had sunk some 17 feet since antiquity, A. E. Günther concluded that the Sele Plain had sunk 76 feet and then risen 61 feet since Classical times. This hypothesis, or one of several less extreme variations of it, enjoyed a certain vogue for a time, since it appeared to explain the decline of the city in a way that took into account the existing evidence of generally swampy conditions in the plain in late antiquity and beyond. Unfortunately, it did not stand up well to scrutiny. These extreme land movements were deemed to have taken place between the eleventh and eighteenth centuries AD and involved the whole of the Tyrrhenian coast, a state of affairs which, as pointed out by Flemming (1969: 47-48), would involve the flooding of much of 53 major Italian cities at the lowest point of the subsidence, including Rome, where St. Peters Square would have only just escaped inundation. Such a momentous occurrence would surely not have gone without mention in historical records. The apparent correlation with the Bay of Naples stems from a similar, but separate, graben comprising the Sarno valley (see Cinque *et all.*, 1987), but even if these massive changes are assumed only locally, there is evidence to the contrary. The supposed *Lithodomus* borings on the temple columns of Paestum appear to be no more than the natural pitting brought about by the weathering of the travertine of which the temples are constructed (Vita-Finzi, 1978: 61). Moreover, Flemming (1969: 49) notes that A. E. Günther's own published photographs of the temples show the controversial pitting over the entire length of the columns, and not just the lower three meters. Finally, recent geomorphological research has provided strong evidence that the sea never encroached inland in the area of Paestum after Classical times (De Wit *et all.*, 1988: 1619).

In spite of these objections, however, there remains considerable evidence that at least part of the Sele Plain is lower now than it was in antiquity, although not nearly on the order of magnitude suggested by Günther. Ciaranfi *et all.* (1981: 493) note the general subsidence of the plain coincident with the elevation of the mountains bounding it. Although they conclude that the plain is stable now, they stop short of indicating when the activity ceased.

The archaeological evidence indicates a slight lowering of the level of the plain on the order of one or two meters sometime between the third century BC and the first century AD. A small Hellenistic temple seaward of the South West wall of the city appears to have been abandoned at least by AD 79, judging from the layer of Vesuvian ashes covering the temple inside and out (Mello, 1967: 11-16). The abandonment was most likely occasioned by an expanding marsh created by factors impeding the natural drainage of the adjacent fossil lagoon, a spring-fed plain in ancient times. In modern times, the area is drained by artificial ditches. There is some evidence of Archaic construction at the site as well. Cipriani (1986: 57) notes the presence of architectonic material in the vicinity, but declines to interpret the evidence on the basis of the lack of a complete site report. This lends support to the idea of land becoming more or less abruptly unsuitable for occupation. Such a change need not have been brought about by catastrophic earth movement; a slow, gradual subsidence could have reached a point at which the dynamics of dune formation at the shoreline sufficiently altered existing drainage to bring about a marshy wetland. The process would have been abetted by a rising calcareous water table in response to the situation; in fact, de Wit *et all.* (1988: 1615) directly observed such a condition in the walls of a pit dug into the recent dunes.

In addition, eighteenth and nineteenth century reports of archaeological remains both in the gulf and on the shore correspond well to contemporary accounts by the fishermen of Agropoli of a long "wall" periodically visible in the water opposite Paestum (Voza, 1963: 227). Some have interpreted this as evidence of a port facility in ancient times, others, more cautiously, of at least a seaward shoreline.

This scenario is not ruled out by the geomorphic evidence, in the form of a series of auger borings immediately West and North of the city (de Wit *et all.*, 1988). The data suggest that not only was the area immediately seaward of the city lowered by a minimum of 1.35 meters and a maximum of 2.5 meters sometime between about 3000 BC and AD 79, but that this subsidence was greater locally than elsewhere in the plain. There is a distinct separation between the Paestum travertine and the Gaudo sequence adjacent and North, in terms of composition as well as differential subsidence.

De Wit and his colleagues offer two possibilities for the status of the ancient shoreline; both are based on the assumption that the marshy conditions for which the area was known in late antiquity and medieval times are normal, and that the period of Greek and Roman colonization represents an anomaly. This is based partly on the high concentrations of calcium carbonate in the waters of the area, a fact which has been noted since ancient times (*e. g.*, Pliny cvi, 228, or Silius Italicus viii, 580, among others). Calcrete formation at the coastal barriers would act to impede drainage in all but a few special circumstances.

The first model, and the one preferred by the investigators, follows from the premise that the subsidence seaward of Paestum began to decrease soon after about 1500 BC, when the waters of the Versilian transgression began to recede, but continued more slowly into Classical times. This would have resulted in an initial erosion of the coastal barrier at that location, leaving a low sandy beach, ideal conditions for the establishment of a settlement. As the sea level relative to the land continued to rise more slowly, however, progradation of the beach to the North and subsequent aeolian dune formation would "back in" to the area opposite the city, and the dune ridge would eventually re-form, causing the drainage problems leading to the abandonment of the Hellenistic sanctuary to the city's West. Under this hypothesis the ancient shoreline would have been slightly inland of the present one. The model is supported by the "apparent absence of the 79 AD tuff and palaeo-soils" in the sands of the present dune ridge immediately seaward of Poseidonia/Paestum (de Wit *et all.*, 1988: 1620).

The second model suggested assumes a constant rate of subsidence into late antiquity, with the result that the coastal ridge formed during the Versilian transgression, when sea levels were roughly 2.5 meters higher than today, would have remained intact; drainage would have presumably been maintained through human agency. At some point, then, perhaps the first century BC/AD, the Paestum travertine would have separated, causing the catastrophic release of water that had been trapped beneath its impervious surface. With the coastal barrier still in place, swampy conditions would immediately ensue. This model would involve a shoreline at or seaward of the present one.

Both models fit the confirmed archaeological evidence, with major implications regarding the position of the ancient shoreline and, hence, bearing on the problem of the existence of a port facility at Poseidonia. There is a range of possibilities, however, between the two. Whatever the actual rate of subsidence, it is the apparent local sea level which is the critical factor, and this complicates matters, since we have to take into account not only the vertical movement of the land, but also changes in the level of the water. In both models, the events described occur during a time when sea levels were fluctuating, the most notable occurrence being the Versilian transgression, generally dated from 3000-1500 BC. Thus the ancient shoreline and the extent of the coastal barrier depend on a very complex set of circumstances.

There are credible, if unconfirmed, reports of architectonic material encountered during the construction of a concrete walkway at the Lido just West of the Torre di Paestum (M. Mello, personal communication; Voza, 1963: 227). Unfortunately, future systematic investigation here is unlikely, if not impossible, due to the relentless construction activity in the interests of the tourist industry.

The reports are of "*blocchi squadrati*", indicating more than casual construction, which would support a shoreline at or seaward of the present one; in other words, a scenario leaning towards the second model. A complicating factor is the apparent absence of AD 79 tuff in the coastal barrier directly West of the city walls (de Wit *et all.*, 1988: 1617), suggesting that it was either not in place as late as that date, or that it subsequently eroded away and reformed later. At this point, only further research, both archaeological and geomorphological, can resolve the issue.

As with the immediate Paestum area, the geomorphology of the rest of the Southern plain is fairly clear until one arrives at the near-shore region, where it becomes, once again, maddeningly ambiguous. Brancaccio *et all.* (1986 and 1987) have identified four extinct dune ridges between the Sele River and Paestum, along with the present coastal barrier (Fig. 10). The earliest of these, the Ponte Barizzo

ridge, lies approximately seven kilometers inland, to the South of the bridge of the same name crossing the Sele and to the East of the SS 18 *autostrada*. At its highest elevation, it lies about 25 meters above sea level; isoleucine epimerization dating of gastropod shells in the deposits of this ridge yield an age of about 130,000 years, corresponding to the beginning of the Tyrrhenian II marine transgression of the Riss/Würm interglacial. Another dune ridge about 3.5 kilometers to the West of the Ponte Barizzo ridge, the Gromola ridge, rises to a similar elevation and can be related to the end of the Riss/Würm, about 100,000 years ago. In between the two is the undated Masseria Stregara dune ridge, which must have formed sometime after the Ponte Barizzo ridge and before the Gromola ridge. All three of these ridges, then, are firmly of Pleistocene origin, with the Gromola ridge associated with a Sele terrace that cuts a portion of the older Ponte Barizzo ridge. Implicit in these studies is an uplift of the Sele Plain on the order of 7-12 meters shortly after 100,000 years ago (Brancaccio *et all.*, 1986: 164-165). Of interest archaeologically is the implication that the plain North of Paestum and East of Gromola has been essentially stable during the entire period of interest. Any undisturbed sites located in this area should be intact; probability of deeply buried sites is very low, except where colluviation is a factor.

Seaward of the Gromola ridge, the situation is somewhat less clear. There are two major dune systems present, the outermost of which, the Sterpina ridge, is the current one and was still undergoing aeolian deposition until recently and displays no soil development at the surface. The chronology of this ridge is absolutely central to the reconstruction of the ancient shoreline, but presents some problems, as we shall see. The innermost Holocene ridge, lying approximately one kilometer inland of the present shoreline, is the Laura ridge; its dates are more secure, although by no means uncontroversial.

Brancaccio and his colleagues have obtained a date in the vicinity of 20,000 years ago for some gastropod shells from the underlying beach sands of the Laura ridge, but this figure may be dismissed out of hand, since it corresponds to the maximum glaciation of the Main Würm, a time when sea levels were so low that this part of the Sele Plain would have been well inland. The authors are quick to point out that the technique used, isoleucine epimerization, has a very low accuracy when applied to such young samples. They cautiously decline to say more than that the Laura ridge is not older than 30,000 years, a number which was no doubt chosen to include the possibility that the Laura dune was formed during the Tyrrhenian III transgression of the last Würmian interstadial. This would, however, involve a subsequent uplift of the plain on the order of 30-40 meters, and there is no corroborative evidence of such an event. De Wit *et all.* (1988: 1617), in fact, note the absence of tuffitic intercalations, with the exception of the AD 79 ashfall, in the Laura ridge that are present in nearby older deposits. A more probable date for the Laura ridge formation, then, is the second possibility suggested by the investigators: the Versilian transgression of 3000-1500 BC. Between the Laura and Sterpina ridges near the Sele, and behind the Laura ridge to a line about midway between it and the Gromola ridge are found fluvial deposits associated with the most recent Sele terrace, that is, post-Versilian.

If the Laura dune ridge was formed approximately 1500 BC, then clearly the most pressing issue in the reconstruction of the shoreline of some 900 years later is the precise date of the formation of the present Sterpina dune. There is, unfortunately, considerable ambiguity concerning the dating for this coastal barrier, although the available evidence suggests that it may have been formed as late as Roman Republican times. Interpretation of the Sterpina ridge is complicated by the extensive land improvement schemes of the late 1930s to the 1950s, especially near the mouth of the Sele. Pines were planted on the dune itself, which was levelled to eliminate low areas between five or six distinct cordons, and the low-lying retro-dune was at least partially filled in (Cocco et all., 1971:3).

There is evidence, however, that the present coastal barrier was in place at least by AD 79, in the form of a well-developed tuff from the Vesuvian eruption seen in the sequence just North of the Ponte di Ferro near the Porta Marina. This is somewhat problematic, being in the area where the Sterpina and Laura ridges converge, but without a clearly definable contact plane (de Wit et all., 1988: 1617). No current investigator, however, believes that the Sterpina ridge post-dates the Roman tenure in the plain. Pending further investigation, we must work with the probability that the first colonists found no coastal barrier seaward of the Laura dune.

The position of the two Holocene dune ridges figures significantly in interpreting the nature of the ancient mouth of the Sele River. The main controversy regarding this feature arises from a passage from Strabo (vi, 1, 1): "After the mouth of the Silarus [Sele] one comes to Leucania, and to the temple of the Argoan Hera, built by Jason." Today that sanctuary is found about 2.5 kilometers upstream of the present mouth. Either Strabo was mistaken or the mouth of the river in ancient times was, in some sense, considerably inland of its present location. We know that the Sterpina ridge was already formed by the time of the Vesuvian eruption of AD 79 and extends to within 500-600 meters of the present Sele; but the Northern end of the Laura ridge is lost in recent alluvium about 1.5 kilometers from the river. These features are consistent with the hypothesis that a broad estuary existed at the mouth of the river in antiquity.

Aerial photographs show traces of meander scars to the North of the Sele at its mouth, and features consistent with an estuary to the South. The meander scars may be interpreted as the remnants of distributaries formed as the estuary silted in, as it surely would have done in response to upstream deforestation as the population, and therefore the demands on the land, increased dramatically during the fourth century BC. Lagoonal deposits underlying recent landfill have, in fact, been noted in this area, although precise dates for the siltation process are lacking (Brancaccio et all., 1987: 54; Cocco et all., 1971: Figs. 1-2).

There is, however, no dearth of evidence that the mouth of the Sele is a topographical feature susceptible to change. The river empties into the gulf just at the point where the relative instability of the Northern half of the shoreline gives way to the relative stability of the Southern half, due primarily to the steeper offshore gradient in the deeper Northern half of the gulf. The presence of coarser beach deposits and offshore sandbars to the immediate North of the river testify to the dynamic potential of the river mouth (Cocco et all., 1971: 6-7).

Indeed, the toponym Lido Lago North of the mouth of the Sele recalls an extensive lagoon called the Lago Grande on early maps; similarly the area just to the South had been designated Sele Morto until fairly recently. A series of maps from the seventeenth and eighteenth centuries documents the changing nature of this area during that period. The river mouth widens into the gulf on the 1619 Hondius map (Fig. 12); this may be simply a cartographic convention, or it may represent the true configuration. Of additional interest is the tantalizingly clear depiction of an inlet of significant proportions directly seaward of Paestum. The accuracy is, of course, open to question; but, in light of the lack of volcanic tuff development in this area of the coastal barrier, bears consideration. In any case, by 1769 there is a clear representation of a delta flanked by two major distributaries (Fig. 13), and by 1791 a more or less modern configuration is depicted (Fig. 14).

Alluviating rivers such as the Sele have a tendency to carry their natural levees out into the sea, but this normal situation is affected by the general transport of offshore sediments toward the South along the Gulf of Salerno shoreline, and the tendency toward bar formation. The receding waters of the Versilian transgression of about 1500 BC, along with the continuing subsidence of the plain as a whole, would have created ideal conditions for the formation of an estuary, which may have developed a restricted opening as the Sterpina ridge began to form. Such an estuary, protected from the vagaries of the gulf waters, would have made an attractive anchorage from the late Mycenaean through the Archaic period, and the *Heraion* would indeed have been on the mouth of the Sele.

Upriver, the lower course of the Sele in ancient times is by no means established, although there are some points of reference, including the *Heraion* itself. Pliny (iii, 70) had inexplicably placed this sanctuary in Picentine territory, specifically between the Sorrento district and the Sele, but there is no evidence that the river ran on the opposite side of the shrine in his time, although the local topography would certainly not rule it out. Pliny is, however, alone in this assertion among the few ancient writers who mention the location of the sanctuary.

It is, in any case, a safe assumption that, regardless of where the river ran in later periods, it did not run South of any confirmed Greek sites during that period, since it was acknowledged as a boundary by every ancient writer who mentions it. The *Heraion*, then, delimits the maximal Southern course of the river at that point. Further upriver, a tomb and a small settlement dating from the fourth century BC on the riverbank near the Ponte Barizzo (Avagliano and Cipriani, 1987: 20-21) also provide a limiting reference point, corroborated by the Upper Pleistocene terrace which approaches to within less than 200 meters of the present bank of the river at the Ponte Barizzo. In fact, neither the Sele nor the Calore can have flowed South of the present course of the Calore inland of Ponte Barizzo during the period of interest, because of the presence of undisturbed Pleistocene deposits there (Brancaccio *et all.*, 1987: Fig. 2). The superficial topography leaves little possibility that either river has changed its course significantly since the period under study upriver of a point about three kilometers South West of Persano; downriver is, however, a different story.

From this point a band of Holocene alluvium straddling the river widens from about two kilometers to just over three kilometers wide at the Laura dune ridge; it narrows again to about 1.7 kilometers at the Sterpina ridge. Much of the alluvial plain within these limits is less than a meter above the present river, and artificial levees line the course today. There have certainly been changes in the river since the second world war, and there is no geological or topographic limit to the possible wanderings of the Sele within the limits described above, although we may assume a constriction where the river enters the gulf at approximately its present position at least since Roman times. We know of the existence there of the Portus Alburnus in the Imperial age, and its ruins are marked on at least two eighteenth century maps (Peduto 1984: 77; the maps are Delagardette, 1799, and Paoli, 1784, reproduced in Mello, 1990: Figs. 4-5). To my knowledge, there are no modern references to these remains; the question of their nature, given the imprecision of eighteenth century archaeological knowledge, is one of many that can be addressed through a systematic survey along the Sele. Of additional interest in this connection is the report of buried terraces exposed up to a width of ten meters in places along the river, bearing archaeological material relevant to the period under study (Vita-Finzi 1969: 75).

The quadrant to the East of Gromola and North of the Capodifiume remains, as has already been suggested, relatively unchanged. Much of this area is characterized by outcroppings of Pleistocene travertine, the source of which may well have been the Northernmost of the three springs which fed the Capodifiume.

The Capodifiume River itself begins at the central and most productive spring; the Southernmost has been covered over and its waters channelled away via an aqueduct. There is no question that the upper three kilometers or so of this river have not changed significantly since Classical times, with the exception of a project of the *Consorzio di Bonifica di Capaccio* which regularized its channel in the 1960s; even in this case, the changes were relatively minor, consisting of the removal of two or three minor kinks along its course. The Capodifiume survey located sites spanning the period from at least the Final Bronze Age through Roman Imperial times all along the right bank. By contrast, the left bank was nearly destitute of material until within a kilometer or so of the walls of Paestum; any variation in the river's course must have been in this direction, if anywhere, but this is extremely unlikely. The copious source springs, the minimal drainage area, and

the uniformity of grade on either side of the waterway are not typical of meandering streams.

Once again, there is a point of reference dating to Roman Imperial times in the form of the Ponte Marmoni, the remains of a bridge just to the South of the modern bridge spanning the river along the road leading East to Capaccio from Paestum (M. Mello, personal communication). It is far from clear, however, exactly how this relates to the position of the river in Archaic times. From a purely topographic point of view, the Capodifiume skirts what would appear to be its natural course at this point (Fig.15). There was a moat surrounding the ancient walls of the city from the fourth to the second centuries BC fed by running spring water, almost certainly from the Capodifiume (Schläger, 1969c; Dehm, 1969); it has long been assumed that the river was diverted to provide the water for the moat, but now it must be at least considered that these waters originally flowed into what became, with considerable modification, the moat, and were diverted later to their present course.

The area between the Capodifiume and the Solofrone has not received much geomorphological attention; what investigations have been pursued have dealt primarily with the nature of the travertine that characterizes much of the Western half of the area, bounded roughly by the city to the North, the SS 18 *autostrada* to the East, the Solofrone to the South and the waters of the gulf to the West. This travertine postdates the Greco-Roman period and thus is commonly referred to as the "medieval travertine" (Pedley, 1990: 32-33; Sevink 1985; de Wit *et all.*, 1988: 1614; and numerous others). It is over a meter thick in places, and is clearly associated with restrictions of the drainage of the Capodifiume leading to the swampy and malarial conditions for which this area became known after late antiquity. Modern toponyms testify to the nature of the area in the recent past: Acqua Sulfurea, for example, or Acqua di Ranci; on older maps (*e.g.*, Delagardette, 1799) we find "Acqua Morta detta Zozo" and "Palude detta la Paglietta." Almost without exception, maps prior to 1945 show the Capodifiume joining the Solofrone in one way or another, often with minor distributaries along the way, and springs such as the Acqua Sulfurea are intimately related to the wanderings of the former river. Today the area is controlled by artificial drainage.

The sequence of drainage restriction, swamping and travertine formation was repeated over and over throughout the geological history of this area, for we find Greco-Roman tombs, sanctuaries and roads on only one of several layers of travertine underlying the medieval *crosta*. Indeed, travertine for use as building material was already being excavated here in antiquity (Avagliano and Cipriani, 1987: 40; Greco, 1979c: 14). This reinforces the suggestion of de Wit and his colleagues that the Southern Sele Plain was naturally swampy, and that the Greco-Roman period represents an anomalous interlude.

There has been, to my knowledge, no investigation focusing on the ancient position of the shoreline South of Paestum, although such a study would contribute greatly to the understanding of the chain of events leading up to the disruption of drainage and subsequent swamping of the area. No sites are reported between the Torre di Paestum and the Solofrone within about a kilometer of the present shoreline, and systematic surveys in the area are hampered, if not prevented entirely, by the extensive removal of travertine for agricultural and other purposes, in many cases extending far into pre-Greek strata. In the absence of evidence to the contrary, however, one might expect that the shoreline between Paestum and the Solofrone has been relatively stable, if taken as a system comprising offshore sandbars as well as the shoreline itself. The offshore gradient is comparatively gentle, and, although in modern times the beach erodes and progrades from year to year by some tens of meters, there are no major changes within these limits. It is also of interest that the dune systems characteristic of the shore further North do not appear here.

To the East of this area, on the other side of the SS 18 *autostrada*, we find the largely unexplored colluvial foothills of Monte Sottane, drained by the Solofrone. We know of Lucanian tombs in the heart of this area, as well as traces of one tomb of late Archaic date (Avagliano and Cipriani, 1987: 40). Further investigation of this area would certainly be in order.

What emerges from all of the foregoing is a slightly out-of-focus picture of the Southern Sele Plain during early Archaic times, as the Greek colonists must have found it on the eve of the establishment of their city (Fig.11). The present coastal dune barrier North of the site did not, in all probability, exist, and one may assume a low, sandy beach fronting the Laura dune ridge; its extent is unclear, but cannot have been much further than the present location of the Sterpina ridge without encouraging an earlier formation of that aeolian dune. Immediately seaward of Poseidonia/Paestum the situation is more complex. It is likely, given both the geomorphological and the archaeological evidence, that the shoreline was very nearly at its present location. The lagoon was undoubtedly at least cut off from the sea, if not dry, by this time; its subsequent status is a matter for investigation, but a swamp may have formed there later. It is significant that the latest structure in this area is Hellenistic - in other words, contemporary with the probable date of the formation of the Sterpina dune ridge, which may well have played an important role in the drainage problems encountered in the plain after that period. Further North, the estuary at the mouth of the Sele must have begun filling in as the coastal barrier formed.

To the South of the city the settlers found not a swamp, but a vast, dry travertine deposit, on top of which the medieval *crosta* formed much later in response to changing drainage patterns. The rest of the plain up to the foothills, with a few minor exceptions, was the same as it is today. One of the more important matters remaining for investigation is the extent and thickness of colluvium on the sloping hillsides. Here alone is the probability for deeply buried sites high, although the existing evidence of centuriation suggests that any significant colluviation occurred before Roman times (see Max Guy's comments on the SPOT image of Paestum in Avagliano and Cipriani, 1987:54).

The cultural landscape

It has not gone without notice that a fertile deltaic plain, as yet untouched by the scourge of malaria, was not likely to be uninhabited when the Sybarites arrived in the late seventh century BC to establish a new Greek colony. Until recently, archaeological interest in the indigenous population has been, at best, sporadic, reflecting the general lack of interest in the subject displayed by ancient historians and geographers, who, for the most part, contented themselves with the recounting of myths and legends concerning the origins of Italic cultures. Not until the Lucanians of the fourth century, themselves late arrivals, did the Italic populations of the Sele Plain attract attention; even the firmly established Etruscans North of the Sele were relegated to the status of a footnote to their better known cousins in Etruria proper.

Modern scholars have duly noted ancient references to the Oenotrians, a culture of mythical Aegean origin, in their discussions of the initial colonization of the area (Sestieri, 1960; Maiuri, 1951; de la Genière, 1979; Pedley, 1990; and many others). In fact, attempts to tie down a direct reference to the Oenotrians as a people displaced by the Greeks of Poseidonia are generally unsuccessful. That the Southern Sele Plain was occupied before the arrival of the Greeks and that the occupants subsequently removed themselves inland can be inferred by reference not only to the ancient literary record, but to the archaeological record as well (see below); whether it is true remains unclear. In any case, it is doubtful, as we shall see, that at the time of these events the Oenotrians played a significant part in the local culture.

Peripheral references to the Oenotrians in the ancient literature are not hard to come by, but specific instances of their displacement by Greeks are limited to the region South of Poseidonia. Herodotos (i, 167), for example, relates that the Phocaean colony of Elea was founded on the site of an Oenotrian city on the advice of "a man of Poseidonia," but this is virtually the only instance in which the Oenotrians and Poseidonia are mentioned in the same breath, and may have more to do with literary usage than historical fact. The idea of the Oenotrians as a wide-spread cultural entity occupying most of what was to become Magna Grecia is traceable at least in part to Dionysius of Halicarnassus (i, 12-13), who, citing Antiochus of Syracuse and Pherecydes of Athens, comes to the conclusion that the Oenotrians were the ancestors of most of the indigenous Italic peoples encountered by the Greeks, having arrived in Italy from Arcadia under the leadership of Oenotros an unspecified number of generations before the Trojan war.

Other references to the Oenotrians in the ancient literature are also brief. Pliny (iii, 70) simply counts them among five peoples besides the Greeks who formerly occupied Italy South of Campania. The other four are the Pelasgi, Itali, Morgetes and Siculi; these last two are, according to Dionysius (i, 12-13), descendants of the Oenotri. Silius Italicus (i, 2; viii, 46), pushes them a step further into obscurity and uses the term as a poetic variant of "Italian;" the Romans themselves become the *Aeneadae*. This usage points to a possible source of the current ambiguity, in the early equivalence of the terms "Italy" and "Oenotria". According to Strabo (vi, 1, 4), following Antiochus, these two terms originally referred to the same area: that part of Southern Italy between the River Laos and Metaponto - in other words, Roman Bruttium. It is true that earlier (v, 1, 1) Strabo defines Oenotria as extending between the gulfs of Poseidonia and Tarentum, but clearly not in an inclusive sense, since part of at least the latter gulf fell specifically within Iapygian territory. Furthermore, the passage in question is parenthetical to a discussion of "Italy" in Strabo's time as virtually everything South of the Alps - essentially, modern Italy - so that the two gulfs are more in the nature of prominent landmarks than specific boundaries. For corroboration of this reading one need go no further than Strabo's later, more precise description of the Oenotria of Antiochus.

Some fragments from Hekataios of Miletos predating Antiochus comprise a list of Oenotrian cities, all of them described as lying "in the interior [ἐν μεσογείωι]" of Italy (Jacoby, 1923: Part 1, F 64-72). There is no sense of the Oenotrians as a coastal people, although, in another passage, the Peuceti on the Adriatic coast are called their neighbors (Jacoby, 1923: Part 1, F 89), and further on Strabo (vi, 1, 15) refers to the Metapontine war with Tarentum and the "upland Oenotrians [τοὺς ὑπερκειμένους Οἰνωτροὺς]." A cautious reading would take into account the possibility that Oenotrians were not present on the coasts at the time the Greeks were writing about them simply because they had been displaced, first by the Iapygians, then by the Italiote colonists.

We are left, then, as far as the ancient literature is concerned, with no certainty regarding the extent of Oenotrian territory. In the direction of the Sele Plain, the most specific account we have, that of Antiochus via Strabo, gives the River Laos as the Northern boundary; yet we have the specific mention by Herodotos of an Oenotrian city preceding Elea, well North of the Laos. It is worth mentioning that this river was the traditional Southern boundary of the Lucanians, who were making their presence felt at about the time Antiochus was writing.

Closely tied to the question of the extent of the Oenotrian territory is that of the identity of the Oenotrians themselves. The clearest reading of the Classical literature taken as a whole is that the Oenotrians proper were the Bronze Age ancestors of the Iron Age groups in Southern Italy, excluding the Adriatic coast, encountered by the Greeks, who sometimes called them collectively Oenotrians; however, the name has entered the modern literature denoting an Iron Age people, whatever their ultimate ancestry, centered in, but not confined to, Basilicata (e.g., de la Genière, 1970: 629-633).

In all of the ancient accounts, the Sele Plain remains marginal where Oenotrians of any stripe are concerned, and we turn hopefully to archaeology. Normally, we could expect the record to provide answers to two questions: 1) was there, in fact, a wide-spread culture in Southern Italy corresponding to the Oenotrian, and 2) if so, were they present in the Sele Plain at the time of the foundation of Poseidonia, around 600 BC?

As we have seen, Greek tradition put the arrival of Oenotros with his band of settlers in Italy well before the Trojan war, in about the seventeenth or eighteenth century BC, based on various accounts in the ancient literature (Pallottino, 1991: 41), or roughly near the beginning of the Early Bronze Age. This was a period of considerable diversity in Italian prehistory, and much remains obscure. Not only the chronology, but even the nomenclature has yet to be fully resolved. Holloway (1975 and elsewhere), for example, includes the Eneolithic in the Early Bronze Age, whereas the traditional approach separates the two periods. There are persuasive arguments for either side of what is essentially a taxonomic problem, based on technology, economy and the relative magnitude of the breaks in cultural continuity between periods. The difficulties arise largely, if not entirely, from the intractability of the three-age system, proposed in the early nineteenth century by Thomsen to account for the first fragmentary evidence for Scandinavian prehistory, and now firmly entrenched in the literature for all of Europe. The present study uses the traditional approach, without prejudice regarding other points of view, on the simple basis that if periods are to be given metallurgical names, the named metals should in some sense be characteristic of the periods, always admitting difficulties at transition points. Perhaps the difficulties could be mitigated by subsuming the Eneolithic (characterized, as the name suggests, by implements of copper and stone, but with arsenical bronze at least at some sites) and the Bronze ages under a single higher level category; I would suggest *Hapalometallic*, the age of soft metals.

In any case, the abundant lacunae in the archaeological record for this period of Italian prehistory prevent us from drawing any but the most cautious inferences. We do know that the Early Bronze Age in Southern Italy is characterized by considerable trans-Adriatic influence, so much so that Pallottino (1990: 42) has linked this period with the first wave of Indo-European immigrants, although not without controversy. Whether this influence represents the arrival of Oenotrians, in whole or in part, is unclear, and, in a sense, moot, since by the Middle Bronze Age virtually the whole of central and Southern Italy, including what may be considered Oenotrian territory, is subsumed under the Apennine culture, albeit with regional and local variations. Whether this comprised a population movement, cultural diffusion or, more likely, a combination of factors, the result was a more or less complete break in the continuity between the ancestral Early Bronze Age Oenotrians (if, indeed, they existed as such) and those of the Iron Age with whom the Greeks were acquainted. One of the more vexing problems in understanding this period is that the archaeological record for the largely homogeneous Apennine culture seems to show genetic ties to a bewildering variety of local Eneolithic cultures of quite distinct character (see Lukesh, 1984).

Two points can be made. The first is that continuous occupation at a given site, even when there appear to be intermediate forms, cannot always be construed as developmental continuity exclusive of outside influence. This is not meant to imply that local conditions are irrelevant, simply that the chosen responses to local conditions may originate externally when they represent a superior strategy.

In other words, in the absence of external influences, local development would have proceeded differently. The second relates to the pitfalls of inferences based on scanty evidence. This is especially relevant in our search for Oenotrians, since their territory purportedly lay mostly in interior Basilicata, where there are even fewer fully excavated sites than elsewhere in Southern Italy.

It is no unique insight that material remains do not always accurately reflect cultural continuity, and many archaeologists are consequently wary of dealing with the concept of culture at all. To make matters worse, there is frequent confusion of the concepts of culture and *koiné*, which refers to a widespread presence of a particular artifact style or type. This is a problem probably endemic to archaeology, although it is interesting to note that the terms *koiné* and *facies*, which refer in this context specifically to aspects of material remains, are common in Mediterranean archaeology but are rarely used in North American archaeology, which has deep roots in cultural anthropology. At least partly as a result, there is a certain amount of resistance in recent times to inferences regarding the identification of archaeological *facies* with cultural groups mentioned in the ancient literature. Lukesh (1984: 36-37), for example, has argued that such efforts are at best premature, and that we ought to be focusing instead on the broader commonalities among regional and local manifestations of Bronze Age culture in Italy. Differences can best be interpreted, she continues, once we are able to identify the larger context. This argument is persuasive in the context of the kind of particularism, on the one hand, and tenuous speculation on the other that has so often characterized the study of Italian prehistory in years past, but useful generalizations must ultimately be derived from the study of particular regions - indeed, individual sites - based on all the information available. We know that, just as today, people have always thought of themselves in terms of ethnic identity, as members of some distinguishable cultural group; is not one of the goals of archaeology the identification of such groups? Rather than regarding the identification of literary cultures as a spurious or even misleading activity, these references could be used to aid the interpretation of existing evidence and to point the way for further research. In the context of the case in point, we can say, at a minimum, that the Greeks recognized a culture in Southern Italy which they were able to distinguish from others, and which they called Oenotrian. Furthermore, they wrote about them, sometimes contradictorily, but often not; it would seem only natural to want to know whether the archaeological evidence is consistent with these reports. It is not unreasonable to look for patterns in the archaeological record with these factors in mind, nor is it inconsistent with the need for an understanding of the larger pattern, so long as the limitations of the existing evidence are acknowledged and not exceeded.

Cultural continuity in Southern Italy, such as we may find it, must begin late in the Middle Bronze Age, and it is here we must look for antecedents of the Iron Age Oenotrians. The historical record, as we have seen, is muddled; Pallottino (1990: 41) speaks of a "...complex web of identity and succession [involving Oenotrians with] ...the Chones, the Italici, the Morgetes, the Sicels and the Ausonians." To a large

extent, these differing names reflect a splintering of the literary Oenotrians under the leadership of various kings, historical or otherwise; the implication remains that there was always a branch which stayed "Oenotrian" into the Iron Age. It is this strict sense with which we are concerned, for there are references to the movements of all of the other peoples with respect to the Oenotrians in the ancient literature (see Dionysius of Halicarnassus i, 22).

Indeed, we find, archaeologically, that there is a Southern Apennine culture distinguishable from a Northern Apennine, but also that there are greater or lesser degrees of variation within these as well (Trump, 1966: 109-127, Carancini *et all.*, 1996). Two points are of interest; one is that the cultures of the Aeolian Islands and parts of Sicily during this period display strong Subapennine connections, but rather with the Northern variant than the Southern, tending to corroborate ancient accounts of the displacement of peoples from Campania. Some accounts say they were Ausonians driven out by Opicans, others by Opicans and Oenotrians. In any event, we may consider it verified that there was a movement of a North-connected culture at the end of the Apennine into the Aeolians and Sicily, presumably making way for a Southern Apennine people in Campania and, perhaps, the Sele Plain and its environs. Incidentally, the connection, direct or otherwise, between the area of this study and Sicily, rooted in the deeper past, continues right up to the moment of Roman colonization in the third century BC, as we shall see. This is undoubtedly due to the ages-long flow of culture, goods and even people from the Levant and the Aegean, through the strait of Messina and along the Tyrrhenian coast to Sardinia and Tuscany, a route recorded in various works of Greek literature as the path of Odysseus, Aeneas and Jason, among others. Questions regarding the historicity of these personages and the controversy among the ancient writers regarding their true paths miss the point in this context, which is that the Greeks were aware of the great antiquity, even in their time, of these connections.

The second point of interest concerns Apulia, where ancient sources tell us that the Oenotrians were themselves displaced by an Illyrian people called Iapygians some time around the thirteenth century BC (*e.g.*, Dionysius of Halicarnassus i, 53). Here, especially in the region of Taranto, the Apennine culture is strongly influenced by contacts with the Aegean, but there are also connections with the Terramara cultures of the more distant Italian North, and along the Apulian coast there are clear trans-Adriatic ties.

Somewhere between these two areas, presumably, were the Oenotrians. In the Iron Age, evidence of this culture is found in all of modern Basilicata and parts of Calabria, but only sporadically in Campania (de la Genière 1968, 1970 and 1979); the Bronze Age is less clear. Our general understanding of the Apennine culture in this area leaves much to the imagination, and to this extent Lukesh's argument for a focus on the culture as a whole is cogent. We still lack a basic understanding of such things as functional categories in ceramics, for example, as they relate to functional categories in site types. The long-held view of the Apennine culture as one of exclusively nomadic pastoralism (Puglisi, 1959) - one can only marvel at the notion of nomadic people trundling about the hillsides with the large and varied Apennine ceramic assemblage - has been effectively called into question in favor of a model of economic diversity including agriculture as a component equal to stock-raising (See Östenberg, 1967; Barker, 1972; Lukesh, 1984; and Bietti Sestieri, 1984; but also Peroni, 1979). Indeed, one definition of agriculture, as opposed to horticulture, involves stock-raising along with field cultivation; let it be noted that while the movement of stock between seasonal pastures need not imply nomadism, it does raise the probability of specialized sites, each with its own assemblage of artifacts associated with these activities, alongside larger, more generalized settlements.

In any event, to the extent that these matters remain unresolved, tracing the development of a culture through the Bronze and Iron Ages will be difficult. What is needed, in addition to a better understanding of Apennine ceramic typology, is a coherent pattern of cultural features by which to identify separate groups; what we have, within a context of general homogeneity, is a collection of not clearly related variations which may or may not have to do with cultural identity. House types are an example. Plans are generally either circular or oval, but a distinction between the two reveals no apparent systematic association with other cultural features. There are a few rectangular houses, but mostly these are found just outside the area of interest, where they are sometimes seen as evidence of outside influence, such as Aegean at Scoglio del Tonno, and sometimes as local idiosyncracies barely worth mentioning, as at Grotta Manaccora near Coppa Nevigata, where bronze artifacts represent a plethora of outside influences (Trump, 1966: 131, 136). Ironically, Holloway (personal communication) is extremely skeptical of any Aegean parallels at Scoglio del Tonno, and finds a more credible connection in the Ausonian II on Lipari, whereas the rectangular structures at Coppa Nevigata date to the Subapennine, precisely the period with the most Aegean connections (Manfredini et all., 1996: 31).

Burial types, which one would expect to be closely linked to cultural identity, are equally confusing. In an arc along the South East boundary of interior Basilicata we find tumulus graves, which one might fairly suspect as Aegean derivatives, but there is no corroboration in other aspects of these sites. Elsewhere there is a variety of rock-cut and trench burials rarely associated with known settlements. It is just as well at this point to reiterate the paucity of known sites of any kind in interior Basilicata for this period; accordingly it is not surprising that no pattern leaps to the eye. Nor is it clear that future surveys will add significantly to the body of evidence. Sloping mountainsides can erode away some sites entirely, and cover others with meters of colluvium, making surveys less rewarding than one would prefer.

In the Sele Plain there is evidence of occupation throughout the Bronze Age (see Holloway et all., 1978), but our understanding of protohistory here is hampered by the lack of adequate investigation of probable sites beneath later settlements. The usual practice has been to place a deep trench somewhere in an excavation to determine stratigraphy and to delve no further than the period of interest (i. e., Greco-

Roman) elsewhere; thus, prehistoric and protohistoric levels are all too often represented only in profile. In addition, many isolated sites discovered in earlier years were inadequately excavated, unpublished or simply collected without excavation, and are now represented solely or primarily in museum exhibits. This is not meant as a criticism of the investigators, many of whom have contributed incalculably to our understanding of the Sele Plain, but a simple statement of fact, reflecting the goals, priorities and technology of archaeology in the past.

As a result, however, any analysis of Bronze Age occupation in the plain must remain tenuous, although it is clear that there was continuity at least in a general sense beginning in the Eneolithic. The best known of these early sites is the Gaudo cemetery to the North of Paestum, type site of a culture widely diffused in Campania in the third millennium BC. Smaller Gaudo cemeteries in the Sele Plain are found near Eboli (Modesti, 1974) and at Pontecagnano (d'Agostino, 1974c), both North of the river, although Holloway has reported one nearby at Buccino not far inland (Holloway et all., 1975: 12). The culture is known only from burials, but lithics probably from this period recovered along the Capodifiume (see Appendix) suggest that a program of survey and subsequent excavation in the plain might prove fruitful. It is a problem, of course, that no one knows for sure exactly what Gaudo material from a habitation site might look like, but one would anticipate the presence of at least some of the types from the burials. Given the location of the original Gaudo cemetery, however, the most likely location of a significant settlement remains the shelf of travertine on which the Greeks built their city. It is noteworthy that five tombs with material assignable to the Laterza, or Protoapennine A, culture were uncovered in 1960 in the vicinity of the Temple of Athena within the city (Livadie 1986: 21); connections between Gaudo and Cellino-Laterza materials have been noted elsewhere (Lukesh, 1984). This is an encouraging suggestion of continuous occupation on the site of the city encompassing a transitional period about which little is known.

There has been a lively debate over the years regarding the origins of the Gaudo culture, whether it results from an immigration from the East (Sestieri, 1960; Voza, 1965; and Livadie, 1986) or developed indigenously (Trump, 1966). Holloway (1976) has proposed that the culture developed indigenously, but with considerable Eastern influence via expanding trade associated with this period. Although the resolution of this controversy is really outside the scope of the present study, I mention it because it may provide an instructive analogy in the search for Oenotrian origins. If modern scholars can attribute cultural origins on the basis of similarities, might not Greek historians have followed a similar line of reasoning? Which is to say, given the long contact between Italy and the Aegean, of which the Greeks were almost certainly aware, a genetic relationship may well have been the most expedient explanation of familiar cultural features among the populations they encountered during the colonization period, especially given their genealogically oriented cosmology. They certainly had no problem with altering mythology to suit their current political needs; witness the travels of Heracles along the Tyrhennian coast, unmentioned before the colonization of Italy. The possibility remains, of course, that the ancient accounts are essentially accurate, particulars notwithstanding, and herein lies the major difficulty with using ancient literature as evidence as opposed to hypothesis; only archaeology can refute or verify the accounts.

In the Sele Plain, as elsewhere, apparent continuity is obscured by the advent of the Apennine culture, traces of which are found scattered throughout the plain and the surrounding uplands (Holloway *et all.,* 1978; and Lukesh, 1984: 44). Along the Capodifiume there is a general scatter of largely undatable impasto fragments, among which are a rim of a large open vase with a finger-impressed cordon at CS-7 (Fig. 23:8) and another fragment of a less carefully finger-impressed cordon at CS-11 (Fig. 23:10). Both are types which begin late in the Middle Bronze Age, but persist to at least some extent into the Iron Age; thus their significance depends on the materials with which they are found. At CS-7 the periods represented include virtually the entire protohistory and history of the plain, but the integrity of the site may be questionable; at CS-11 the next earliest identifiable object is a rim of a Koehler Type A Corinthian transport amphora, datable to the end of the seventh century, but there is also a variety of impasto body sherds that are essentially undatable. A more thorough and extensive survey in the plain may turn up evidence of at least some occupation there. There have also been several isolated references to Apennine and Subapennine material within the walls of Paestum (Livadie, 1986; Greco and Theodorescu, 1983: 58, 150; Kilian, 1969; Schläger, 1969b; and Lukesh and Howe, 1978). It is in the Final Bronze Age, however, that things begin to differentiate sufficiently for us to draw some conclusions regarding cultural lineage *vis-à-vis* Oenotrians and others, setting aside for the moment the difficulties with identifying these groups in the Iron Age.

Although the distinctions manifest in this period do not allow the identification of a "Proto-oenotrian" *facies,* either in the Sele Plain or elsewhere, they do allow a degree of certainty regarding what is not ancestral to the Oenotrians, that is, Protovillanovan. The term was first used by Patroni over 50 years ago in reference to a Final Bronze Age cremating people (Patroni, 1937) in the interests of emphasizing the genetic relationship between these people and the later Villanovans, who in their turn would become Etruscans. While the terms "Protovillanovan" and "Final Bronze Age" are sometimes used interchangeably, the absence of a Protovillanovan component *per se* in much of Southern Italy immediately prior to the Iron Age has prompted Pallottino (1965) to distinguish between a cultural (Protovillanovan) and a chronological (Final Bronze Age) usage; these are the senses in which the terms are used in the present study. Prior to Patroni's study, the Villanovan culture was generally thought to be the result of a trans-Alpine immigration, either in an immediate sense or as a development of a previous population movement, because of several similarities in the burial rite with the Urnfield cultures of central Europe, as opposed to what appeared to be a dramatic break with the previous indigenous inhuming traditions in Italy (See Fugazzola Delpino, 1979). While the prevailing theory today eschews large migrations

in favor of cultural diffusion, this point of view is not unanimously accepted; nor are the two mechanisms mutually exclusive. Since burial rituals are the only means of ensuring a favorable disposition of the soul after death, people are not, as a rule, amenable to changing them simply as a fashion statement. In addition, a change in burial rite at this level of social complexity seldom occurs in isolation, but is often adopted as part of a complex of religious beliefs and ritual behavior, which in turn is associated with a perceived improvement in living strategy, be it agricultural, economic or otherwise.

This is not to say that this point of view on this subject is uncontroversial. Holloway (personal communication) cites the change from cremation to inhumation in Roman Imperial times among the upper classes as an instance of the culture as a whole remaining untouched in spite of this dramatic shift in funerary behavior. But in third century AD Rome we have a quantum difference from the cultures we are discussing here in both the level of social complexity and in the level and quality of communication among cultures. Morris (1992: 31-33), while dismissing appeals to the influence of oriental religions (including christianity) or other metaphysical systems as explanations for the change, acknowledges the increasing regionalism in provincial Rome alongside an increasing homogeneity at home. But the situation might be read as an example of the diffusion of the ritual into the Roman society in spite of an attempt at retrenchment; one could hardly argue against the impact of foreign influence in Rome in the third century. Indeed, one might argue that, given Hellenistic influences earlier on in Rome (*e. g.,* monumental tombs more appropriate to the Eastern practice of inhumation), the actual disposal of the remains of the dead was the most resistant element in the ritual, and only just fell into place at that moment in history. The completeness of the change and the concomitant minor adjustments in other parts of the death ritual to accommodate inhumation underscore, to my mind, the importance of the disposition of the body at death. If, as Morris suggests, we are dealing with fashion, would not the change be less thorough and, more significantly, more of a passing fancy?

In any case, in the less complex Bronze Age cultures, ritual of any kind, including burial, would have been more closely tied to subsistence skills than in the Roman Empire. Morris (1992: 48) himself stresses the point that explanations regarding changes in the disposition of the dead must be within their specific contexts, and has since come to regard this factor as extremely important in the interpretation of past cultures (personal communication); I concur wholeheartedly. While cremation versus inhumation cannot be used as a simple ethnic signature, it can certainly form an important part of the evidence for cultural coherence.

Although massive migrations involving the replacement of entire peoples are not required for these changes to take place, one must assume considerably more than casual contact such as might be expected in a long-distance trade relationship. Some combination of events, not necessarily the same everywhere, must have given rise to the Protovillanovan phenomenon.

The question of the origins of the Protovillanovan and, more crucially, its relation to subsequent cultures takes on particular significance in this study, in which the lineage of the indigenous population at the moment of Greek colonization plays an important role in their identification. The Protovillanovan was originally defined retrospectively; that is, certain features of a cremating culture at the end of the Bronze Age were related to features of the better-known Iron Age Villanovan culture in the same geographic areas. Later attempts to find genetic ties to earlier Italic cultures have met with only marginal success. A notable exception is Peroni's work in central Italy in which he has established a credible sequence from Subapennine through Protovillanovan to Villanovan at several sites, but even here we are dealing with an abrupt transition to cremation and concomitant changes in the material remains, among which can be found elements with identifiable Subapennine affinities (Fugazzola Delpino, 1979: 38-40). More common, especially in the South, is the sudden appearance of Protovillanovan with no clear link to the local past, often with evidence of burning in the previous phase. Though not conclusive, this pattern is certainly suggestive.

In the Sele Plain, there is another pattern, equally suggestive and perhaps more instructive. At the Etruscan center of Pontecagnano there appears to be no Bronze Age occupation whatsoever (d'Agostino, 1974c: 92), but we find Protovillanovan ceramics at the cave of Madonna del Granato near Capaccio Vecchia (Modesti *et all.*, 1974: 69-70), at the promontory of Agropoli South of Poseidonia, along with material assigned by the excavators to Ausonian II (Arcuri, 1985), and, to a lesser extent, near the Porta Giustizia at the Southern wall of Paestum (Kilian, 1969). This latter has been characterized by Kilian as a Subapennine assemblage with a few examples of Protovillanovan, but if Holloway *et all.* (1978: 140) are correct in reclassifying the Subapennine material as Protoapennine B, the nature of the find changes considerably, although the small quantity of the material and the absence of a clear stratigraphic context do not justify inferring a Protovillanovan site at that location.

The significance of these finds might be questionable were it not for two factors: first, all three are in areas that are likely spots for Protovillanovan sites that are virtually unexplored in this context. Madonna del Granato is on the flank of the promontory of Capaccio Vecchia overlooking the plain and guarding the pass providing access to the interior, on which the medieval town of Caputacquae was situated. All that remains today are the church of S. Maria del Granato, currently being restored, and the ruins of a castle besieged and destroyed in the 13th century AD. A reconnaissance and excavations in the area of the church have produced unspecified protohistoric materials (Mello, 1980), but no investigations further afield have taken place; the area of the castle would appear promising, not only for this period but the Greco-Roman as well. At Agropoli, excavations have been limited to a small area adjacent to the wall of the so-called "Aragonese" castle (Fiammenghi, 1985); these may be characterized as preliminary soundings, perhaps on the periphery of the site. Finally, at Paestum, although there has been intense investigation virtually since the end of the 18th century, until

very recently little attention has been paid to protohistoric levels. While this location differs from the two upland sites, its unique situation at the Southern end of an island of relatively stable travertine amid intermittent wetlands to the South and arable soil to the East must have been attractive throughout protohistory.

Second, with the coming of the Iron Age we find a firmly entrenched Villanovan horizon on both sides of the Sele. The Protovillanovan in Southern Italy has often been seen either as an anomaly or as a developmental stage between Subapennine and the succeeding Iron Age, whatever that stage may be locally, with no strong genetic link to the Villanovan. But where this stage is succeeded by Villanovan, as in the study area, the *prima facie* inference of direct continuity is sound, barring strong evidence to the contrary. What appears to be the case in the Sele Plain is an indigenous Villanovan occupation to the South of the river, augmented and eventually displaced by an immigration North of the river of Villanovans from coastal Southern Etruria; interwoven with this scenario are elements of the so-called *fossakultur*, an inhuming people dispersed along the Tyrrhenian coast from Campania to Sicily (*cf.* the Ausonian II of Agropoli).

This interpretation springs from an examination of sites in the plain with Villanovan components. At the springs of Capodifiume, a small cremation cemetery was uncovered in the late 1950s (Sestieri, 1960). Although the tomb furnishings are unquestionably Villanovan, the cinerary urns are distinguishable from the same phase elsewhere in the immediate surroundings by a lack of incised decoration and a few other stylistic points; ceramics with analogs at nearby sites are limited to types which are common throughout Southern Italy (de la Genière, 1968: 49-51). In addition, there are a few vases in apparent imitation of a geometric decoration known as Tenda, which is found distributed throughout Basilicata. D'Agostino (1974a: 22; 1974c: 106-107) regards this site as associated with an isolated farmstead, evidence of the general hegemony of the Villanovan culture in the plain centered at Pontecagnano, in spite of the differences in ceramic styles, which he attributes to an impoverished provincialism. The apparent longevity of the site, from the ninth to the seventh centuries, suggests something less ephemeral.

Another interpretation may be that this small cemetery represents an indigenous Villanovan settlement, directly descended from the Protovillanovan dispersed in and apparently confined to the Southern half of the plain, though it would be difficult to postulate a settlement of any size on the strength of six tombs. Let it be noted that large areas of the plain, including much of intramural Paestum, remain unexplored.

The hypothesis rests not only on the stylistic differences in the cinerary urns between Capodifiume and elsewhere, but in the lack of a distinct pattern there that we find at the other Villanovan centers in the area. At Pontecagnano inhuming and cremating rites co-exist from the very beginning (d'Agostino, 1974c). The inhumation tombs are analogous to the burials of the *fossakultur*. However, they differ from the cremation tombs only in this single aspect; that is, the associated material is distinctly Villanovan, with strong affinities with coastal Southern Etruria. The same general pattern is found at Sala Consilina, in the interior Vallo di Diano, although the inhumation tombs there are poorer and less numerous; *fossa* graves are common for both rites (de la Genière, 1968: 13-47). At Arenosola on the right bank of the Sele, a small cemetery comprises inhumation burials of the *fossa* type with furnishings relatable to Phase II at both Pontecagnano and Sala Consilina, a time when cremation burials had all but disappeared (de la Genière, 1968: 54-55). The common factor is the early and complete adoption of the material culture of Villanovans with strong connections in maritime Etruria, while the cremation rite, though it enjoyed a certain vogue for a time, was never completely established and ultimately disappeared. Compare this to the lack of affinity with the material at Capodifiume and the single-minded adherence to cremation there, and a distinction in cultural terms suggests itself.

Regardless of whether we are dealing with one or two cultural groups in this context, the Villanovan - and ultimately Etruscan - presence and influence in the whole of the plain remains dominant right into historic times. It must be remembered that as late as the sixth century Pontecagnano was strong enough to maintain a thriving economy in spite of the victory of the Greeks at Cumae over an invading army of Campanian Etruscans, and in 474 BC the decisive naval victory over the Etruscan fleet off Cumae appears to have had little immediate effect on relations with Pontecagnano, its ancient connections with maritime Etruria notwithstanding. As we shall see in Chapters 3 and 4, although the rise of the Etruscan site at Fratte may have been a round-about result of this altercation, the position of the Pontecagnano Etruscans in relation to nearby Greeks is inextricably bound up with the very foundation of Poseidonia. Their presence is reflected at diverse Iron Age sites in the area.

At Rovine di Palma, a small promontory overlooking the plain just South of the Sele, surface finds indicate a small settlement dating to about the seventh century (Avagliano and Cipriani, 1987: 26); the presence of *bucchero* affirms an Etruscan influence immediately prior to the arrival of the Greek colonists. Further cultural affinity is unclear, since the other material present, which remains unpublished, consists primarily of fragments of large containers of impasto. At Tempalta about eight kilometers inland of Rovine di Palma, ten *fossa* tombs dating to the second half of the seventh century were uncovered and excavated during salvage operations in 1984 (Avagliano and Cipriani, 1987: 29-30), yielding vases characteristic of types common at contemporary Pontecagnano among other types, to date unpublished. Somewhat earlier connections present themselves at Madonna del Granato, with material analogous to the first Iron Age phases at Sala Consilina and Pontecagnano (Modesti *et all.*, 1974: Plate XXVIII.2; *cf.* de la Genière, 1968: Plates 1-3). Within the walls of Paestum, material dating to the seventh century and corresponding to types found at Pontecagnano have been recovered from the area of the agora; the excavators interpret these as remnants of the furnishings of a tomb that was disturbed during the construction of the Greek street overlying it (Greco and Theodorescu, 1983: 72-74). Finally,

reports of scattered isolated finds of *bucchero* and *buccheroid* impasto throughout the plain serve to reinforce the picture of at least the strong influence of Pontecagnano just prior to the founding of Poseidonia.

But who were the people coming under this influence? As we have seen, evidence from North of the river suggests the *fossakultur*; this is true to a lesser extent to the South as well. The problem is that while we have a preponderance of burials in the Northern plain relating to this period, we have very few to the South; one is left with trying to relate settlement materials, or at least materials of unclear function, with funerary furnishings. Greco and Theodorescu (1983: 72-74) have suggested, for example, that the apparent settlement on the site of Paestum was composed of Oenotrians so assimilated into the Etruscan material culture of Pontecagnano that they are virtually indistinguishable. It is not clear whether such a position has any archaeological significance, and is, in any case, based on too literal a reading of ancient sources regarding cultural boundaries (see above).

We began this discussion with a search for the historical and archaeological antecedents of these same Oenotrians, but with little success. In the Iron Age, however, an age which is characterized throughout Italy by the emergence of identifiable *ethnoi*, the picture improves considerably. De la Genière (1970: 629-633) has identified the Oenotrians with a cultural *facies* spread through Basilicata and Northern Calabria on hillsides overlooking the upper valleys of major streams, beginning in the eighth century and continuing into Lucanian times. The earlier aspect of this culture coincides with the spread of Tenda geometric pottery in this area, probably originating in workshops in the upper Basento valley, given the increasing preponderance of impasto imitations proportional to the distance from this area (de la Genière 1979: 73-74). This was followed by the development in these same areas of distinctive bichrome geometric decorations, including examples of what has come to be known in the Sele Plain as "Oenotrian". Both Tenda and Oenotrian ceramics are present at Sala Consilina, and are reported as part of the assemblage at many sites in the plain, although in much smaller numbers than at Sala Consilina. The major difficulty is that identification of this culture is based primarily on this decorated ware; distinguishing characteristics of the far more common coarse ware remain elusive. To date, no settlements *per se* are firmly identified in the lowlands of the Sele.

There are two factors to be taken into account in the search for Oenotrian settlements in the *chora* of Poseidonia: 1) the proclivity of the Oenotrians, as testified by both the archaeological and the historical record, for relatively high places; and 2) the known inclination of the Sybarites (and hence, presumably, their descendants at Poseidonia) to deal with nearby large Italic settlements by razing them and establishing cult centers of their own on the ruins. Two locations in the immediate vicinity spring to mind: Agropoli and Capaccio Vecchia.

At the former, as we have seen, soundings which can only be considered preliminary have suggested an occupation from the Early Bronze Age through the Greek and Lucanian eras.

Furthermore, there have been persuasive suggestions that Agropoli is the site of the elusive *Poseidonion*, and perhaps even of the original *teichos* of the Sybarites (see below), propositions which, if not confirmed by the available evidence, are not entirely ruled out. One would not be surprised, therefore, to find that it was the site of a considerable indigenous settlement as well.

Against this happy thought is the lack of firm evidence for any Iron Age occupation at Agropoli predating the Greeks, and the clear association of the Bronze Age materials with Protovillanovan, *i. e.*, not "Proto-oenotrian". It must be recalled, however, that both Villanovan and Oenotrian characteristics are found side by side in the Vallo di Diano a few kilometers to the interior, and that the archaeological record at Agropoli is far from complete.

Capaccio Vecchia is equally unexplored, but one is encouraged by the presence of Tenda ceramics at Madonna del Granato nearby. Both of these sites have yielded some evidence of being important Greek sanctuaries as well (see below).

The population of the Sele Plain at the moment of Greek colonization appears to have been composed of two, and possibly three, elements, under the overall influence, if not domination, of the Etruscans at Pontecagnano. If we add a diachronic perspective we see the population in a state of fluidity, with cultures emerging and fading with some regularity: in short, a border culture. The Sele River was known as a boundary by virtually every ancient writer who mentions it; it should not surprise, then, that its deltaic plain was a meeting place for a variety of peoples throughout its history, especially considering the increasing role of trade during the period under discussion, and its position at the end of a mountain pass giving access to maritime trade routes to the East.

Ultimately, only a vigorous program of archaeological investigation, including an intensive survey of the entire plain followed by excavation within and without the walls of the ancient city will resolve the issue of the indigenous inhabitants of the Sele Plain, but some valid observations may be made. The two major components of the coastal population at the end of the seventh century BC were the Etruscans and the *fossakultur*, the latter subsumed under the former to a greater or lesser degree. There is some evidence of a movement of Oenotrians to Sala Consilina at about the time of Greek colonization (see below), but if these came from the coastal zone, it was from the highlands, and not the plain below. In this sense, there was no direct displacement of Oenotrians from the site of Poseidonia, although whether that place was occupied and, if so, what happened to the inhabitants are questions that remain open.

Chapter 3
THE FOUNDATION OF POSEIDONIA

The arrival of the Greeks

"The Sybaritae, it is true, had erected fortifications on the sea, but the settlers removed them further inland... [Συβαρῖται μὲν οὖν ἐπὶ θαλάττη τεῖχος ἔθεντο, οἱ δ᾽ οἰκισθέντες ἀνωτέρω μετέστησαν...]" (Strabo v, 4, 13). Such is the extent of Strabo's direct reference to the foundation of Poseidonia, just twelve words in the original, not even an entire sentence; but from these few seeds has sprung a veritable thicket of interpretation. The intensity of interest has been occasioned by the fact that this is the only surviving direct account in the ancient literature of the founding of Poseidonia. Much of the discussion has been philological, centering on the precise translations of various words considered central, for example *teichos*, here translated as "fortifications" and *anotero*, "further inland". At times the debate has seemed almost meretricious, but however subtle the refinements of definition may appear at first glance, the issue is nothing less than the nature and location of the original establishment that was to become Poseidonia. Indeed, interpretations of the passage in question have been offered to support virtually every location for every type of construction. *Teichos* has been read as anything from a Mycenaean trading post to an early part of the existing city wall, and *anotero* as every direction except out to sea. The only real agreement has been a loose consensus that Strabo was referring to a colonization in two phases; beyond this, everything has been open to discussion.

Most early investigators put the first fortifications of the Sybarites at the *Heraion* on the Sele or nearby at the mouth of the river. The basis of this was largely the attribution of the foundation of the sanctuary to Jason by both Strabo (vi, 1, 1) and Pliny (iii, 70), and other references to the sanctuary of the Argive Hera. This was interpreted as indicative at least of the chronological precedence of the site, if not of the identity of the first settlers. Although the rather long distance, about 7.5 kilometers as the crow flies, and Southerly direction of the eventual location of the Greek city were seen as problematic by later scholars, early on it was explained either by reading *anotero* as "to a higher elevation" or by simply assuming tautologically that since the fortifications were on the Sele, and Poseidonia was clearly where it was, then that

must be the direction to which the geographer was referring. Thus Nissen (1902: 892), in his *Italische Landeskunde,* echoes the earlier views of others (*e.g.,* Pais, 1894: 527-529) when he writes that at the mouth of the Sele was a temple of the Argive Hera alleged to have been founded by Jason, and nearby, on the beach, a fortified trading post (*eine befestigte Factorei*) built by the Sybarites. It should be noted that the location of the *Heraion* was yet undiscovered when Nissen made his observations, and so, based on his reading of the ancient literature, the beach on which he posits the Sybarite trading post was *in der Nähe*. This also explains his conclusion that the Sele ran approximately one kilometer North of its present course in ancient times; though Strabo (vi, 1, 1) clearly says that Poseidonia is within fifty stadia of the *Heraion* and not the river, Nissen measures backwards from the city to the only landmark available to him, and misreads an approximate distance for an exact one. The trading post, he continues, was later moved to the South to higher ground and subsequently subsumed by the city of Poseidonia. As we shall see, despite the misgivings of later generations of investigators, Nissen's hypothesis has held up rather well, if not completely intact.

The general interpretation of Strabo in which the first phase of the colonization is associated in some way with the sanctuary on the Sele and the river mouth has continued to be widely held, although with some significant variations. Among later scholars amenable to Nissen's point of view are Ciaceri (1927), Bérard (1957), Giannelli (1963) and Maiuri (see below), summarized admirably in Mello (1967). Dunbabin (1948: 25-26) finds the mouth of the Sele likely as the first stage of colonization, but believes the Sybarites found the Greek *Heraion* already established and flourishing. Boardman (1980: 181-184) notes only that Poseidonia "...may have been founded from Sybaris," and that the foundation of the *Heraion* was earlier, without joining in the debate concerning the initial *teichos*. Maiuri (1949: 916; 1951) assumes that the fortification was on the Sele - a location which he considers beyond doubt - and sees it as representative not of a vanguard of Sybarite colonists but of a trading post populated by Greek and Italic opportunists of various origins, which came under the sphere of influence and subsequent protection of Sybaris just at the end of the seventh century BC. The subsequent transplantation of the settlement and foundation of Poseidonia to the South is attributed to malarial conditions at the river mouth. Apart from the fact that in Strabo there is not the slightest indication of any Greeks other than Sybarites occupying fortifications South of the Sele, the model has other difficulties. There is the awkward feature of combining the idea of a commercial climate fruitful enough to attract not only the first mixed bag of entrepreneurs, but eventually of Sybaris, and an environment of sufficient hostility to require fortifications for a trading post in a malarial swamp. Setting aside the question of why a rag-tag group of itinerant merchants would have settled in such an area in the first place instead of, for example, on the outskirts of Pontecagnano, other problems remain. If the inhabitants of this early outpost were trading, as the hypothesis states, with not only the Etruscans of the right bank but with the indigenous population of the left bank as well as the interior uplands, against whom were they fortifying? Maiuri (1951: 280) suggests that the defense of the city, when finally established in its present location, was necessary against the indigenous people (*gli Enotri-Lucani*), some of whom were either absorbed or displaced when the Greeks took over the location of their existing settlement for the city; this does not explain the need to fortify the *emporion* prior to moving the settlement, the clear implication being that it was the arrival of the Sybarites with the concomitant relocation to an already occupied site that caused the change from tolerance of the Greeks to hostility. It is true that, like Nissen and Pais before him, Maiuri writes that the original *teichos* remained occupied and was transformed into the port for the city of Poseidonia, but this point begs for verification. A primary port seven or eight kilometers from a city which is itself less than a kilometer from the sea would seem, at best, unusual, and there is only the most indirect and tenuous evidence for an early port facility at the mouth of the river, in later references to the Roman Portus Alburnus (see Lucilius iii, 11, and Virgil iii, 146). Neither of these references carries much information beyond the name and approximate location of the port; no particular connection with Paestum is made. Although Pais (1894: 528) makes much of the name *Σείλαρος* (Seilaros, the Greek name for the Sele) appearing in abbreviated form on the coinage of Poseidonia through the fifth century, the existence of a port of that name is far from the only possible explanation. Indeed, the name "Portus Alburnus" suggests less an urban harbor than an outlet for timber from the upriver Alburnus Mountains, at least by Roman times. There is, of course, the possibility that timber culled from these regions was floated down the Sele for use in the city from earliest times, and that a depot of some kind was at the mouth of the river to accommodate this traffic, but in the absence of evidence this must remain speculation.

Proximity to the *Heraion*, as a sacred place, would not in itself be a sufficient reason to establish such a distant facility, especially since, as Maiuri himself argues, the antiquity of the sanctuary may have been based on the existence there of an Italic sanctuary which was transformed and dedicated to Hera by the Sybarites after the founding of the city - the kind of thing for which there is a consistent pattern at Sybaris (see de la Genière, 1970 and 1979).

In the context, then, of the philological discussion regarding Strabo's brief notice, Maiuri, like the scholars who preceded

him and many who followed, interprets *teichos* as referring to fortifications around a more or less stable trading post that predated the foundation of the city by some significant period of time. With regard to the meaning of *anotero*, Maiuri simply notes that there is no other location South of the river which would fit any definition of the word; this not only begs the question, but is not true on the face of it, since the whole of the nearby Gromola Ridge and most of the land to its East would have admirably suited the only two requirements: getting on to more stable terrain and being consistent with some possible meaning of the word in question. Where Maiuri's suggestion of the motivation for the relocation is concerned, there is not a hint of evidence that the mouth of the river would have been a swampy, malarial area at a time when the area around Poseidonia was not, unless it would have been during the much later silting in of the estuary.

There are many alternatives, of course, to these interpretations. Zancani Montuoro and Zanotti-Bianco (1951: 9-12; Zancani Montuoro, 1950), the excavators of the *Heraion* on the Sele, offer a considerably different model of the events leading up to the foundation of Poseidonia. Taking their lead from Strabo's (vi, 1, 1) passing comment that the *Heraion* was founded by Jason, they conclude that this remark alludes not only to the antiquity of the site, but to the identity of the first Greek settlers as well: "Thessalo-Minyans," perhaps from Boeotia, for whom the Thessalian Jason was a sort of national hero. The story of the Argonauts being related to the first maritime expeditions of the Thessalians and Minyans, it might also, according to the excavators of the *Heraion*, imply colonization. In corroboration they cite two passages from Diodorus Siculus (xi, 90, 3, and xii, 10, 2), who makes reference to Thessalians, presumably from Poseidonia, aiding the Sybarites in the ill-fated attempt at rebuilding their city in 453 BC, 58 years after its destruction at the hands of the Crotoniates. From these tenuous links the authors forge a chain of inference in which the first Greek settlers in the plain arrived in the mid-eighth century from Thessaly or Boeotia to establish the trading post at the mouth of the Sele. Subsequently, the authors continue, sufficient commerce flourished so that there formed a nucleus of settlers further South, at the site of the later city, possibly for the purpose of quarrying travertine for use at the sanctuary, and it was these settled (*oikisthentes*) people who moved further inland on the arrival of the Sybarites. According to Zancani Montuoro (1950: 78), the Sybarites would in any case have been constrained from arriving in the Sele Plain until 560 BC, when they defeated and destroyed Siris, which up to that time (argues the author) maintained total control of the overland routes to the valley. However, an approach from the sea, as seems to have been the case (see below), would have not only circumvented the situation, but actually mitigated it. In any case, the argument concludes that the latter settlers built a wall - the ambiguous *teichos* of Strabo - at the seaward end of the present city, and the Thessalians moved no further than to the East end, there to be forgotten to history.

This interpretation has no supporting evidence archaeologically, and very little from the ancient literature, being based almost entirely on the attribution of the *Heraion* to Jason; perhaps a simpler explanation of the Argonautic connection lies in the fact that the rulers of Miletos, which was at the Eastern end of the trade route reaching Poseidonia via Sybaris (see below), claimed descent from Minyan Argonauts from Orchomenos who had migrated there (Tripp, 1970: 382). Indeed, Strabo (xiv, 1, 3, and xiv, 1, 6) reports that although Miletos was first settled by Minoans from Crete, the contemporary Greek city was founded by Neleus, who, before ruling Pylos, was driven from his native Iolcos in Thessaly by his twin, the same Pelias against whom Jason grieved for the throne. Similarly, Athenaeus (ii, I, 43) tells us of a connection with another famous Thessalian, Achilles, son of the Argonaut Peleus. It is true that, since both the Dorians and the Ionians were said to have come ultimately from Thessaly (Herodotos i, 56, and 144-146), some connection could always be made, but the Minyan Argonauts in particular were said to have played a significant part in the foundation of various Ionian cities. Interestingly enough, Herodotos (i, 145) in a single sentence relates many of the places of significance to the history of Poseidonia: Ionia (hence Miletos); Pellene, Patrae and Aegion, the three Achaean cities with sanctuaries of Hera as at Poseidonia and Sybaris (see Presicce, 1985: 60); Helice, the home (according to Strabo vi, 1, 13) of the *oikist* of Sybaris; and Bura, where there is a spring after which Sybaris was named; and the rivers Crathis, the one at Sybaris named after the Achaean river at whose mouth we find Aegae. This passage stresses the strong historical connection between the twelve Ionian cities and the twelve Achaean cities named, as well as giving us some clues as to the origins of the colonists in Sybaris and, consequently, Poseidonia. Thus, to attribute this ancient sacred place to Jason is simply to acknowledge the primary role of Miletos in the early commercial life of the city. The allusions to Thessalians at the abortive re-establishment of Sybaris are of no apparent significance, since colonists could be drawn from a variety of regions, regardless of the mother city. Aristotle (v, 1303a, 25) notes with dismay the results of mixed origin in colonists, but then proceeds to give no fewer than eleven examples to drive home his point. It must not have been terribly unusual to have such mixtures. Furthermore, immigration to established colonies/cities was certainly not restricted by geographic origin.

Maiuri's suggestion that the source of the antiquity of the sanctuary lies in its Italic beginnings finds no support here. In spite of the presence of archaeological material of indigenous origin at the site dating from the Apennine period through the first Iron age, the excavators do not find themselves convinced that the Greek sanctuary continues an Italic one. This view is justified primarily on the basis of the utilitarian nature of the material and its paucity relative to the amount of Greek material at the site from the mid-seventh century on. Contemporaneous indigenous material that could be interpreted as votive is seen as evidence of the rude offerings of the natives to the great goddess from a distant land (Zancani Montuoro and Zanotti-Bianco, 1951: 22).

Nonetheless, the hypothesis that the first Greek colonists were eighth-century Thessalians is rather difficult to sustain. Not only is there no mention in the ancient literature of pre-Sybarite Greeks in connection with Poseidonia, but the earliest Aegean material so far recovered at the *Heraion*, with the

exception of a single Sub-Mycenaean sherd, is Late Protocorinthian (Zancani Montuoro and Zanotti-Bianco, 1951: 25-28), and therefore datable to the third quarter of the seventh century (Amyx, 1988: 428). These materials were found all over the site, but primarily near the oldest structure at the *Heraion*, the "primitive" stoa. The suggestion of sporadic contact between the Sele Plain and the Aegean since Mycenaean times is reinforced by Mycenaean III C sherds at both Paestum and in the Vallo di Diano; the greatest concentration, however, is on the island of Vivara in the Bay of Naples, where sherds spanning virtually the entire Mycenaean chronology have been recovered, but ending in III B around 1200 BC (Vagnetti, 1980: 159-160), certainly a critical time in the Aegean. Whether or not it is significant that finds on the mainland begin chronologically where the island finds end is unclear, but certainly we are not talking about anything like a settlement until much later. Interestingly, early material has been recovered at Paestum itself, namely a Middle Protocorinthian kotyle (no later than the middle of the seventh century), and even a Thapsos cup (final third of the eighth century), along with some banded cups dating to the final 20 years of the seventh century, though finds of any quantity do not begin until Middle Corinthian, five to ten years after the turn of the sixth century, and roughly contemporary with the earliest temple of Hera at the Sele sanctuary (Greco, 1981; Greco and Theodorescu, 1983: 72, and 1987: 111-114; de la Genière, 1979: 88-89). The Thapsos cup is of dubious stratigraphy, and the other material is found in association with contemporaneous indigenous material, including an aryballos of *bucchero*, in imitation of a Corinthian model. Obviously, we can entertain two interpretations of this situation: 1) that this assemblage represents the first contact between the natives and colonists in this location, or 2) that it simply reinforces our notions of the sway of the Etruscans over the Southern plain, since we find Early and Middle Protocorinthian pottery along with Italo-geometric as part of the tomb furnishings at Pontecagnano, as well as at Arenosola, in a context that suggests connections with the Greeks at Pithecusae and Cumae and the Etruscans of Tarquinia, and not traders from Sybaris, be they Milesian, Achaean or otherwise, although some Rhodian material appears (via the Euboean settlements?) (d'Agostino, 1962: 105-106; d'Agostino and Voza, 1962: 89-104). Later, however, is a different story. The relative explosion of Greek pottery in the first decade of the sixth century militates, I think, against the first interpretation; this is a crucial point to which I will return shortly.

Although the *Heraion* and its environs loom large in most hypotheses concerning the interpretation of Strabo's famous passage, by no means every savant who has given the matter consideration is of the view that the settlers first set up shop on the banks of the Sele. Sestieri (1950 and 1952), for example, separates the *Heraion* and Poseidonia as two distinct and unrelated foundations, and sees the whole Strabonian episode unfolding at the location of the present city, although, obviously, he concedes the close connection between the sites after the foundation of Poseidonia. To be sure, Strabo himself mentions the origin of the *Heraion* elsewhere than the passage we are belaboring here, at least by scholarly consensus. Meineke (1895) transposes the relevant passage to a point immediately after the first sentence of Book VI, so that the Sele sanctuary and the foundation of Poseidonia are mentioned in virtually the same breath; few, however, find merit in this view. At worst, the foundation of the colony is remarked upon at the end of Book V, and the *Heraion*, as a convenient boundary marker, is mentioned immediately at the beginning of Book VI; Strabo would simply have been avoiding redundancy, having only just commented on the history of Poseidonia in order to clarify the location of the transplanted Picentines. To pursue this idea would involve discussions of how the original scrolls were meant to be read, how they were written and how they were copied, as well as the state of common knowledge concerning his subject upon which Strabo could rely; I prefer to leave these considerations outside the scope of the present work, except to say that the very fact that there could be a disagreement about the position of the Poseidonian passage strongly supports at least the rationale behind my view.

In any case, Sestieri, focusing on the identity of the *oikisthentes* who moved further up after the initial fortifications were erected, concludes in a circumspect way that Strabo was referring to the indigenous population occupying the eventual site of Poseidonia, displaced by Sybarites. He cites a passing comment of Solinus in which reference is made to *Paestum a Doriensibus*, and a mention of Oenotrians in connection with Poseidonia by the second century BC poet Pseudo Scimnus, although the latter was almost certainly a poetic usage for "Lucanian" (Zancani Montuoro, 1950: 66-67). In light of the legendary Arcadian origin of the Oenotrians, Sestieri continues, the population that moved after the foundation of the city was the existing Oenotrian population, on the following grounds: 1) Strabo's use of the word *oikisthentes* must separate the Sybarites from the people referred to; 2) Solinus's Dorians cannot be Sybarites, who are Achaeans; and 3) Oenotrians can be Dorians, since their origin is in Arcadia. Troizenians, who are often pressed into service as Dorians in this context due to Aristotle's assertion that they participated in the settling of Sybaris and were ultimately expelled, are ruled out by Sestieri on the basis that there is no evidence whatsoever that they participated in the settling of Poseidonia, although it remains a widely held view.

I must agree with Sestieri on this point, since the expelled Troizenians of Aristotle (v, 1303a, 29-33), who caused a curse to fall on the Sybarites, must surely be the same citizens expelled under the influence of the Sybarite tyrant Telys (Diodorus Siculus xii, 9, 2-3) and who turned the Crotoniates so fatefully against their ex-compatriots. These events took place some 80-90 years after the founding of Poseidonia, so the Troizenians as a distinct group must still have been in Sybaris, since we do not hear that there were two such expulsions. Although Dunbabin (1948: 362-363) assumes that the Troizenians were expelled almost immediately upon the establishment of Sybaris, it is not clear on what grounds.

Be that as it may, there are several problems with Sestieri's interpretation. First of all, the term "Dorian" can be applied equally well to Achaean Sybarites as to Troizenian Sybarites, but only questionably to Oenotrians; Herodotos used the word

to refer to any non-Ionian Greeks (Tripp, 1970: 214), and, in any case, the supposed migration of the Oenotrians from Arcadia took place well before the spread of the Dorians into the Peloponnesos. Secondly, there is no evidence of a significant Oenotrian population in the Sele Plain, except in the generic sense of "Italians." It is true that the travertine shelf was very likely occupied by a native settlement of some kind before the establishment of Poseidonia, but, as we have shown, the primary cultural components there at that moment in history were Etruscan and *Fossakultur*, neither of which can be called Dorian by any stretch of the imagination. Thus the argument rests, ultimately, on the equivocation of terms on several levels. In any event, it seems most unlikely that Strabo, who up to this point had been at great pains not only to identify the ethnic groups in the plain, but even to discuss their origins, would leave a large, displaced indigenous group with the ambiguous and, indeed, misleading designation of the "settled".

Sestieri's interpretation has been revived in recent years by de la Genière (1970: 628), as an attractive explanation for an increase in Oenotrian material at Sala Consilina after the time of the foundation of the Greek colony. As evidence of an Oenotrian settlement at Paestum, de la Genière cites the discovery of "*plusieurs fragments*" of Oenotrian geometric pottery just South of the first temple of Hera; on reference to the cited source (Kilian, 1969: 348-349), these prove to be fragmentary indeed, especially given that older material at the same location relates to Protovillanovan. Add to this the more ubiquitous contemporary analogs with Pontecagnano, and a mixed settlement of which a small part were Oenotrians is the most that can be justified. Whether or not this is the case, and whether or not this small part of the indigenous settlement fled inland on the arrival of the Sybarites, it is hardly likely that such an event would merit Strabo's attention in this context. A portion of the original native population on the site of Poseidonia, having gone unremarked and unidentified up to this point, and having in any case played no further part in the history of the area, could hardly have been on the minds of potential readers; but a well known story about the foundation of the city by Greeks could have been. The reference to the fortifications on the sea *vis-à-vis* the movement inland (or upland, or whatever) can only be seen as an attempt to square the actual location of the city, about three quarters of a kilometer inland even then, with what must have been common knowledge: the establishment on the sea of the Sybarite fortifications. This is not to say that if Strabo didn't mean to suggest that Oenotrians were displaced to the Vallo di Diano by colonizing Greeks, that it didn't happen; it only means that his intention, and therefore the historical significance of the passage, remains unclear; this point and its implications are discussed more fully below.

The least strenuous interpretation of Strabo's *oikisthentes* is that it refers to the Sybarites themselves. This is central to Mello's (1967) reading of the passage, in an article which remains the most thorough analysis, point by point, of the subject to date. Unlike others who take this approach, however, Mello sees no compelling argument for the first phase of colonization - the Sybarite *teichos* - taking place at the mouth of the Sele. Analyzing Strabo's use of the word *anotero*, Mello concludes that in this case the only point of reference for the direction in question is the coastline, given that the fortification was said to be built on the sea. Thus, whether *anotero* is translated as "to a higher elevation" or "further inland", the final location of the city fits the definition best if the first phase was built on the beach directly seaward of it. To this end, Mello reconstructs an ancient coastline at or beyond the current one, and puts the original fortified settlement of the colonists there, citing several other instances in which Strabo recounts just such two-phased settlement. The interpretation is of an advance guard arriving and setting up a temporary outpost, and then making preparations for the arrival of the main contingent of colonists, whose numbers are needed to secure the ultimate location of the city.

Although this hypothesis is well researched and argued, there remain several unanswered objections. The philological argument suffers, in a way, from its own success: none of the cited instances in Strabo of pre-settlement at a short, convenient distance from the eventual location of the colony is ambiguous, as is the passage in question, and Mello's own review of the geographer's use of *anotero* concludes that it can have several meanings.

More unsatisfactory, however, is the fact that it fails to take into account the apparent precedence of the *Heraion* by some decades (see below), and leaves no possibility of doing so within the context of the literary analysis on which the hypothesis is based. Mello's point that more archaeological investigation on the coastline at Paestum would be rewarding is well taken, however; it is the lack of sufficient systematic archaeological research that bedevils all of the hypotheses regarding the initial settlement of Poseidonia.

There remains at least one other possibility: Greco (1975, 1979, and 1988: 475-479) has made a complete departure from tradition by suggesting Agropoli as the location of the Sybarite *teichos*. His argument on philological grounds is that the infamous *anotero* can also mean "to the North", as in cartographic convention, in which "up" refers to the top of the page, or conventional North. This is philological evidence *a posteriori*, as has been the case, if truth be told, for most of such evidence so far discussed; but it merits some attention, since it is on this point that Castagnoli (1976a and 1976b) has challenged this interpretation. The agreement that, in a general sense, Roman maps were oriented with South at the top and Greek maps with North, fails to resolve the dilemma. Strabo was a Greek, born in the town of Amasia in Pontus, on the Southern shore of the Black Sea, and it was here that he probably wrote most of his *Geography*; but he may have had a Roman father, and was certainly a Roman citizen who lived for a time in Italy and travelled to some extent the Tyrrhenian coast (Falconer, 1906). For our purposes, the fact that his sources for the sections under discussion were Greek (Artemidorus, Antiochus of Syracuse and Timaeus) is significant only in those instances where he quotes more or less directly, and we are not dealing with such an instance. Furthermore, Falconer notes that Strabo's work was intended for

> ...the information of persons in the higher departments of administration, and contains such geographical and

historical information as those engaged in political employments cannot dispense with (Falconer, 1906: viii-ix).

We may assume this means Roman administrators, so that while up may have been North from the writer's point of view, it would presumably have been South for the intended reader, a factor which the writer would probably not have failed to take into consideration. All in all, the cartographic pressures appear roughly equal; thus, as far as map orientation is concerned, Strabo may be considered either a Greek or a Roman writer, whichever best suits the point one is making.

In any case, we must bear in mind two crucial points when discussing the linguistic influences of the maps available to a geographer in Augustan times: 1) maps were not nearly as ubiquitous nor standard as those in modern times, so the influence on linguistic usage would not have been nearly as profound as in our day; and 2) as even the most cursory examination of our only remaining example of Roman cartography, the much later Peutinger Table, will reveal, a sense of direction is not rigorously maintained for any local area, the *general* orientation of the map notwithstanding. Thus, when we locate Paestum on the Peutinger Table, we find that inland, or East, is toward the top of the page.

It would therefore be more appropriate to examine the Strabonian texts internally to see if some evidence of his orientation can be found. This is precisely what Castagnoli (1976a: 63-64) does, and finds four instances (i, 3, 22; v, 1, 2; xi, 5, 8; and xv, 3, 3) which clearly indicate an orientation to the South, and comes to the conclusion that this is "up" in Strabo, barring explicit indications to the contrary. But he also finds one passage (ii, 5, 20) which favors North and another (ii, 5, 22) which favors East. There are, of course, numerous passages which provide no clear indication regarding this question, and Castagnoli's interpretations are subject to verification as well, but it is of interest that in the two passages that would contradict his Southern hypothesis, the orientation is toward the direction one would be facing when entering the restricted confines of the Ionian Sea in the one case and the Black Sea in the other. This suggests strongly that Strabo's orientation had more to do with momentum than cartography. In our case, he is clearly and unambiguously progressing Southward along the coast in the course of his narrative, both well before and well after his mention of Poseidonia. Ironically, in Greco's response to Castagnoli, he marshals yet more evidence that Strabo was oriented toward the South, in the Roman fashion, when discussing Italy in particular, but also points out that this doesn't appear to hold where coastlines and perhaps mountain ridges are concerned (Greco, 1979: 52-53). Having convincingly made this point, he nonetheless cites Strabo's Greek sources for Southern Italy as confirmation of North as the direction of orientation; but his arguments against the applicability of Castagnoli's point of view to the passage in question appear equally valid against his own position.

Greco's choice of Agropoli, apart from the obvious, and perhaps suspect, etymological suggestion, stems really from other sources, including the presence there of Greek material contemporary with, or possibly predating, the earliest Greek material from Paestum, and the suggestion by Zancani Montuoro that the sanctuary of Poseidon had been there. Excavations at Agropoli in 1982, although certainly limited, did reveal a considerable quantity of material datable to the beginning of the sixth century, including "Ionian" cups of a type common at Sybaris and also found at Poseidonia. Earlier material, however, was limited to a few cups with rims "*a filetti*" datable to the period from the end of the seventh century to the beginning of the sixth, three fragments of *bucchero* of approximately the same date, and some fragments of Koehler A Corinthian transport amphorae, also of similar age; slightly later Koehler B amphorae were also present (Fiammenghi, 1985: 57-67). In other words, the assemblage at Agropoli, while certainly early, does not predate the Paestum material, as it should under Greco's hypothesis.

While the Sybarite *teichos* is not supported by these data, there is certainly some encouragement here for the existence of an extramural sanctuary; and, in fact, Fiammenghi (1985: 65-66) suggests that the material is generally of a type more likely to be associated with a sanctuary than an *emporion*, the transport amphorae notwithstanding. The difficulty is that the votive figures so far recovered are female, including an example of the helmeted Athena type.

This is yet another setback for Greco's hypothesis, since he had associated the *teichos* with the cult of Poseidon in an involved argument that had the city of Poseidonia founded under the protection of Hera by a different set of Sybarites, contrasting the complex of *teichos*/trade/Poseidon with that of *polis*/agriculture/Hera. The city would then have taken its name from the pre-existing Poseidon cult at Agropoli, although why this would have happened under the conditions of the hypothesis remains unclear. In any event, the argument loses much of its persuasiveness if the sanctuary at Agropoli did not predate the city, and was, in any case, probably dedicated not to Poseidon, but a female deity.

We have examined all of the major interpretations of Strabo's account of the founding of Poseidonia, and if there is any common ground beyond agreement on the two-stage foundation, it is that there is insufficient archaeological evidence for certainty. Indeed, only at Agropoli was excavation at least partially motivated by a desire to test an interpretation, and in this case, tended against the hypothesis on more than one point. At the *Heraion* the opposite situation obtains; a program of excavation led to the formulation of a hypothesis, which was then, however, not sustained. In both instances, more extensive excavation is needed for unequivocal results. While it is certainly true that the *Heraion* has been thoroughly examined in those areas that have been excavated, the archaeology of the locality is by no means exhausted. Hypotheses involving the Western part of the city and the beach further West still await significant archaeological investigation; although work at the Porta Marina, or sea gate, continues sporadically, it does not appear to bear directly on this problem.

All of which brings up the question of the proper role of such theorizing, steeped in the philological roots of Classical archaeology, in our multi-lateral approach to understanding the Classical past. It would, of course, be foolish to disregard written descriptions of places and events we are trying to interpret, but a critical view of the ancient literature is crucial. Too often studies of the ancient literature seem more concerned with devising an interpretation, however tenuous and unlikely, to match a hypothesis originally formulated on other grounds, at times mere speculation. While this does not necessarily apply to the proposals examined in the present study, we do see a tendency to assume that, however ambiguous, the ancient accounts are accurate, especially with regard to Strabo, the focus of most of the discussion. The underlying premise appears to be that if we could only find out what Strabo meant to say we would know the truth about the foundation of Poseidonia; or, conversely, if we could discover the true sequence of events by other means, we would know what he meant to say.

But Strabo may have believed an inaccurate but prevalent version of the events, or he may simply not have known any more than he wrote; he was, after all, describing events which took place more than six centuries before his birth. Furthermore, our need for precision in geographic description is not always matched by the ancient writers. We know, for example, that in the sentence immediately prior to the remarks with which we are concerned, Strabo states that Poseidonia is in the center of the gulf of the same name, which it is not; that distinction lies with the Sele River, and the city is situated more than half way between the river and Agropoli. Furthermore, there may be undreamt-of errors in the generations of transcriptions that filter our reading of his work.

Or he may have known the truth and written it as concisely as possible, and the copyists may have plied their trade with perfection; in any event, the most productive use of ancient literature for archaeologists is to suggest solutions to historical problems, which can then be incorporated into programs of research. In other words, what Strabo meant to say in the passage concerning the foundation of Poseidonia is important insofar as it can provide guidance for further research.

Ironically, the most rigorous reading appears to be the least convoluted, and among the oldest: that of Nissen, who wrote just after the turn of the century. It will be recalled that he wrote that at the mouth of the Sele was a sanctuary of Hera, reputedly founded by Jason, and that on the beach nearby, a Sybarite trading post which was later moved to the South and eventually replaced by the city of Poseidonia, founded by these same Sybarites. Surely this is the most economical reading; all of the disputed vocabulary is rendered according to its *prima facie* meaning. As Mello (1967) has shown, *teichos* in unambiguous Strabonian contexts means a fortified post; *oikisthentes* must refer to the same Sybarites who built the fortifications; and all agree that *epi thalatte* can only mean directly on the sea. The remaining dispute concerns the direction of *anotero*, and here I must disagree with Mello and hold that it must mean "to the South", if not on grounds of Castagnoli's argument from Roman cartographic convention, then certainly, narrative consistency.

In this context there may or may not have been a displacement of native peoples by the Greek colonists; there may or may not have been Thessalo-Minyans, or anonymous Greeks of diverse origin, at the mouth of the Sele in the eighth century; and there may or may not have been a sanctuary of Poseidon at Agropoli. Strabo simply is silent on those subjects, although, as we have seen, much other evidence can be brought to bear in that regard.

Then why insist on the Sele location for the *teichos* of the Sybarites? Partly for extratextual reasons: the chronological precedence of the Hera sanctuary; the suitability of the Sele estuary for a first landfall; and the proximity of the Etruscans of Pontecagnano, with whom, one assumes, the early Sybarite trade was involved. But there is internal textual support for this site as well. In the context of having given the location (albeit incorrectly!) of Poseidonia, and then explaining it, Strabo's passage might best be rendered, "While it is true that the Sybarites built fortifications on the sea, those who settled moved further up," in which further up (*anotero*) means further South, along the coast, continuing the direction of the narrative. And might not this confusion concerning the site of Poseidonia and the center of the gulf be related to the location of the first outpost of the colonists?

With regard to the age of the *Heraion*, it must be borne in mind that while we do not find older Greek material *per se* at the sanctuary than we find within the city walls, the contexts differ. At Poseidonia, early (pre-600 BC) material is found along with material suggestive of the same period at Pontecagnano; at the Heraion, the oldest Greek material comprises some Transitional Corinthian (630-615 BC) oinochoai found just beneath the beaten earth floor of the oldest structure, which the excavators have termed a "primitive" *stoa* (Zancani Montuoro and Zanotti-Bianco, 1951: 25-28). The suggestion is strong that the material dates to the period of construction of this building, which is clearly Greek in type. According to the excavators, the size of the foundation stones of this structure suggests not a stone building, but one of mud-brick on a wooden frame, a notion reinforced by the signs of intense burning in the Southern part. Scattered to the South of the building is a concentration of artifacts, among them votive material contemporary with the oinochoai beneath the floor.

It has been argued that the Sele *Heraion* cannot have predated the city, because by its very nature as protector of the Northern boundary it needs the city to justify its existence. In fact, none of the most impressive architecture, including the famous metopes, dates to before 600; in other words, it is at best contemporary with what we take to be the foundation date of the city. While this does reinforce the idea that the role of the sanctuary as a boundary protector was inextricably linked with Poseidonia, something that is obvious in any case, it does not mean that it could not have had a different character as a sacred place before then. It is otherwise difficult to explain the earlier material and the apparently earlier structure, which fit well, however, with the mythical Argonautic foundation. Indeed, how else would the city and the sanctuary have come to have two entirely distinct and unrelated legends concerning origin?

By no means all of the area of the Sele sanctuary has been explored; to date, not even the limits of the *temenos* have

been defined, and there are casual reports of surface scatters of artifacts that are as yet unexamined. We do know, however, that on the opposite bank of the river, at Arenosola, is an indigenous cemetery with material comparable to the second and third phases at Pontecagnano, spanning the seventh century BC. The cemetery was unused after this period, implying abandonment of the small settlement it supported just before the foundation of Poseidonia, but after the earliest Greek material at the *Heraion*. The tombs contain a significant quantity of Protocorinthian pottery, and Tomb 14 has a Transitional oinochoe (d'Agostino, 1962: 90).

We also know that the earliest evidence at Sybaris of Etruscan material appears just after the mid-seventh century, at about the same time that Attic material (*e. g.*, SOS amphorae) begins appearing in Etruria as well as Sybaris (Guzzo, 1973: 303). The ubiquitous banded Ionian cups of the end of the seventh century are also found not only at Sybaris but at several sites in the Sele Plain.

Taken together, these events suggest a beginning of the trade through Sybaris with Etruria - and perhaps with Sardinia - that is generally considered the primary motivation for the establishment of Poseidonia. The precise nature of this trade is problematic; frequently mentioned from the Etruscan side are iron and tin, but if Miletos was to be the final destination, it would have been rather like sending coals, if not to Newcastle, then to a place very nearby, given the Anatolian sources for these same commodities. In return, the often cited Milesian textiles and other luxury goods seem insufficient in themselves to sustain a long and complex undertaking. This question is discussed more thoroughly below, but for now, let it be noted that a trade network need not involve solely, or even primarily, the movement of goods between the geographic extremes, directly or otherwise. After all, Sybaris, along with other Western Greek cities, would itself have been a logical market for the raw materials available from the Etruscans, and certainly had goods to offer in exchange. Although wine is rarely mentioned in this context, the allusions to the excellence and quantity of the Sybarite product are many. Dunbabin (1948: 77-79) recalls for us that the ancient sources tell of a complex system of pipes running directly from the cellars at the vineyards to shipping depots, and of the legendary quality of Thurian wine from the same region. He mentions also honey and beeswax, along with the imported Milesian woolens. Curiously, he insists that the city had no harbors, which seems unlikely in the midst of all this coming and going.

In any case, the portage to Laos, an earlier colony of Sybaris, was among the shortest across the Italian peninsula, and could easily have been, and probably was, serviced by Etruscan ships on the Tyrrhenian side (Dunbabin, 1948: 78-79). Whatever the reason for the subsequent foundation of Poseidonia, it must have been with the collaboration of the Etruscans, since they controlled both the Sele Plain and the trade leaving Laos. It is certainly true that there was never an Etruscan "national identity," any more than there was one for the Greeks at the time; but recall the strong material affinity between Pontecagnano and Southern coastal Etruria. Pontecagnano, quite distinctly from the Campanian Etruscans proper at Capua, Nola and elsewhere, would have a ready-made interest in the trade with Sybaris. There may, in fact, be some evidence for their participation in the founding of Poseidonia in the mysterious treaty between Sybaris and the *Serdaioi* found at Olympia (see below). It is therefore not too great a leap of imagination to envision a contingent of Sybarites setting up shop at a convenient location, while details for the new colony were worked out; the colony itself may or may not have been conceived independently of the trading post, although clearly the two would have converged after the foundation.

For the reasons given, the most likely location for the initial *entrepôt* was at the mouth of the Sele River, along the shores of a broad estuary (see Fig. 11). There remains a possibility that the location was in an as-yet unexcavated part of the *Heraion* complex, but the use of this area by indigenous people since Apennine times makes it rather dubious; a grand establishment like Poseidonia may have been important enough to displace or absorb native populations, but not the assumed small trading post. In any case, the qualification "on the sea" is better fulfilled by a location to its West, an area not well examined archaeologically, since today it lies on neither the river nor the sea. If the Arenosola cemetery serviced a small estuarial port, the events on the opposite bank would soon have made it redundant.

Little is known of the nature of the settlement at Santa Cecilia, on the right bank of the river directly opposite the *Heraion*, except that a small Bronze Age cemetery was partially excavated there in 1936 by the excavators of the *Heraion*, and a superficial survey of the immediate area was undertaken at the same time. The full results of these activities remain unpublished, but the opinion of the investigators was that they were dealing with a small settlement that extended into the first Iron Age (Zancani Montuoro and Zanotti-Bianco, 1951: 21-22; Holloway *et all.*, 1978: 141). The location certainly enhances the appeal of the site, and one can only hope for further research there. What was the extent of the site? Was the chronological range estimated by Zancani Montuoro accurate? Was there a relationship with the Arenosola cemetery, to say nothing of the *Heraion* itself? As the matter stands, our knowledge of the site serves only to fix the course of the Sele at that point between the ancient sites, and the Eastern extent of the estuary.

The foundation of Poseidonia

The establishment of a temporary settlement and the erection of fortifications could be carried out informally, as circumstances dictated; not so the foundation of a *polis*, a full-fledged city-state, for which clearly defined rules ensured success. Greco is right insofar as he separates the two events as fundamentally distinct undertakings. A Sybarite trading post could and no doubt did operate as an agency of its mother city, but once Poseidonia was born, the matter of allegiance became one of alliance between equal entities. It can be argued that such a radical step required more than just the desire for improved trade on the part of the mother city, especially since guarantees of cooperation by the new *polis* would be

weakened by the very act of its foundation. Graham (1983: 1-28) notes varying degrees of ties between colonies and their mother cities, but stresses that, failing a formal agreement, the connections remain sentimental only. One might expect some kind of formal agreement in the case of Poseidonia, if only because Strabo's wording implies that it was a state foundation of Sybaris and not a private enterprise, as some colonies apparently were. The treaty between Sybaris and the *Serdaioi* in which Poseidonia plays a role (Meiggs and Lewis, 1969: 18-19) does not necessarily involve the allegiance of that city to Sybaris (see below).

Snodgrass has defined the *polis* as "...a polity consisting of a settlement and its territory, politically united with one another, and independent of other polities" (1986: 47). In other words, while the city and its fields, vineyards, groves, woodlands and pastures could be physically separated by a wall as at Poseidonia, conceptually and legally they were indivisible. This was the case from the very inception of a new city: Homer (vi, 5-11) tells us that when Nausithous led his people to Scheria, among his first acts in addition to building a wall and houses and establishing sites for the temples was to partition the land into fields to be allotted to the colonists. We know that, in general, land in the Western Greek cities could be privately held, or could be designated as sacred land, "owned" by this or that god and administered by the state: in effect, public land that could be leased to private citizens, ideally located both near the city and at the boundaries of its territory (Métraux, 1978: 72-75). The same was true for privately held lands allocated at the foundation of the *polis*; Plato (745B-E) goes into considerable detail concerning the proper division and subdivision of property both within and without the city. Not only must each citizen and each of the twelve gods be given land, but it must consist of one parcel near the city and another distant from it; furthermore, each citizen must build a house on each of his properties. As a result, from the moment of its birth, a new *polis* had an immediate impact on an astonishingly large geographic area. For fields at the edges of a city's *chora* to be of any use, the entire territory had to be hospitable, or made so by one means or another.

It may have been the ideal for Greeks to settle in unoccupied territory, the easier to divide up the land (see Asheri, 1966: 5-6), but there is no dearth of examples to the contrary. Apart from the obvious commercial advantages of settling where there are already people, the same physiographic attributes of a site which made it attractive to the Greeks - climate, soil, anchorage etc. - would not have been lost on indigenous peoples. When prior tenants were present, there were only two ways to deal with them: by treaty or by conquest, or, perhaps less rarely than we know, by some devious combination of the two; Leontini springs to mind. We hear that the Chalcidians from Naxos, under their *oikist* Thucles, joined with Siculan natives to found the city, but that later treachery allowed a Megarian contingent to drive out and replace the Siculans despite the treaty (Métraux, 1978: 20-21; Polyaenus v, 5). We have seen that not only was some of the Southern Sele Plain occupied at the time of colonization, it was under the control of the Etruscans across the river - a force large and sophisticated enough to have made the Greek colonization against their will extremely difficult if not impossible, and perhaps pointless as well, if trade was one of the major considerations when the location was chosen. Since there is no evidence, archaeological, literary or otherwise, of conquest by the Greek colonists, we must assume there was a treaty of some sort.

Indeed, there may be evidence of one in existence, in the form of a bronze plaque from Olympia, bearing a treaty between Sybaris and a people called the *Serdaioi*:

> The Sybarites and their allies and the *Serdaioi* made an agreement for friendship faithful and without guile for ever. [Guarantors], Zeus, Apollo, and the other gods [-] and the city Poseidonia.

> ἀρμόχθεν οἱ Συβαρῖται κ' οἱ σύνμαχοι κ' οἱ Σερδαῖοι ἐπὶ φιλότατι πιστᾶι κ' ἀδόλοι ἀείδιον. πρόξενοι ὁ Ζεὺς κ' Ὀπόλον κ' ἄλλοι Θεοὶ καὶ πόλις Ποσειδανία. (Meiggs and Lewis, 1969: 18-19).

There has been much discussion regarding the purpose of the treaty, its date, and the identity of the *Serdaioi*, but perhaps the most intriguing from the point of view of the present study has been offered by VanEffenterre (1980). Based on a grammatical analysis of the original document and comparisons with similar treaties, this author argues that the role of Poseidonia is not as co-guarantor along with the gods - something which would be absolutely unique in such affairs - but as the object. In other words, the Sybarites and their allies came together with the *Serdaioi* in an agreement regarding the foundation of Poseidonia. It should be noted that, while Van Effenterre's interpretation has not been well received (and has, indeed, been widely dismissed), there has been neither a published refutation of it, beyond the simple assertion that it isn't so, nor a viable alternative offered. The prevailing point of view has been that Poseidonia was a co-guarantor of the treaty, but Meiggs and Lewis (1969: 18-19) hedge, saying only that the role of the city is "hard to determine." Giacomelli (1988: 18-20) leans toward the traditional interpretation, without reference to either VanEffenterre or Meiggs and Lewis, and this appears to remain the position among Italian scholars.

The date might be seen as problematic, given that consensus places the document in the second half of the sixth century, at the height of Sybaris's greatness, a decade or so before the disaster of 510 BC, or about 70-80 years too late. But VanEffenterre cites the foundation pacts of Cyrene and Magnesia as examples of the formalization of agreements long since consummated, and notes three features of the Olympia plaque: the use of the past tense in the description of the agreement, the mixture of an early Archaic lexicon with occasional later forms, and the probable location of the plaque at the Sybarite treasury at Olympia, a most appropriate spot for a commemorative display (VanEffenterre 1980: 171-173, especially notes). Regarding the significance of the treaty, it is suggested that this may be the actual beginning of Poseidonia as a sort of client state of Sybaris (Van Effenterre and Ruzé, 1994: 176), a point at which I must part company with Van Effenterre, for reasons discussed below.

If, then, we are dealing with a sort of commemorative reproduction of the foundation pact of Poseidonia, who were the *Serdaioi*? Clearly they were not Sardinians, as has been suggested by Zancani Montuoro (1962), among others (see Guarducci, 1962). Meiggs and Lewis, for their part, regard the *Serdaioi* as an Achaean colony somewhere in South Italy, on the basis of some coins issued contemporaneously with the plaque, but if this were the case, what purpose would be served in singling them out, since the allies of Sybaris had already been cited as a group? Apart from the astute, if cautious, suggestion by Giacomelli (1988: 19-20) that the identity of the *Serdaioi* might be sought in Ionia, if anywhere, the general consensus is that they are an unidentified Italic people, perhaps in the interior between Sybaris and Poseidonia; yet this makes little sense if the agreement is interpreted as a foundation pact. Van Effenterre himself, having attended to the meaning of the inscription, devotes little attention to the *Serdaioi*, except to note that they must have taken part in the foundation, or at least have permitted it (Van Effenterre and Ruzé, 1994: 176).

But if the inscription is correctly interpreted as a foundation document for Poseidonia, there is one native group that must, perforce, have been involved: the Etruscans of Pontecagnano. One is reminded of the legendary Lydian origin of the Etruscans as a people. Whether or not the story is true is irrelevant, since the Etruscans themselves, as well as the Greeks and even the Lydians, not only knew of the story but seem to have believed it (von Vacano, 1960: 30-31). Indeed, Herodotos (i, 94) tells us that the story originates with the Lydians, and Strabo (v, 2, 2) relates the story as the simple truth.

The major city of Lydia was Sardis, or *Sardeis*; the cognate immediately suggests itself. While it is true that we do not know of a direct instance of Etruscans calling themselves *Sardianoi*, or *Sardeioi* (let alone *Serdaioi*), either collectively or in part, we do hear from Plutarch (277 C) that after the fall of Veii the Romans taunted them with calls of "Sardians for sale!" at the Capitoline games, accompanied by crude pantomimes involving old men dressed as Veians. The Etruscans themselves are known to have developed complex genealogies linking "single families or groups of families" (Von Vacano, 1960: 31) to Eastern origins. It is entirely plausible that a connection with Sardis was a feature of either the population or the ruling family at Pontecagnano at the turn of the sixth century BC, more than a century and a half after the first Greeks arrived at nearby Pithecussae; let us recall the close affinity between the material culture of Pontecagnano and that of Veii, in contrast to Capua, Nola and elsewhere in Campania.

If so, it may well have been a feature that it was expedient to emphasize, the better to distinguish the Pontecagnano Etruscans from their Campanian cousins to the North. Those Etruscans had, in the year 524, gathered a host and marched on Cumae, only to be driven back by Aristodemos, who would later become tyrant of that city (Dunbabin, 1948: 344-345, and Dionysius of Halicarnassus vii, 3, 1-4). This crisis was occurring at precisely the same time as the estimated date of the Olympia plaque. Van Effenterre (1980:

172) speculates that the purpose of a *refondation* of Poseidonia in the form of the bronze commemorative may have been to bolster the position of the city against the Etruscan upsurge of 524, but I would suggest that, given the outcome of the battle, this misses the point. The threat, after all, was less from the defeated Etruscans than from a revitalized Cumae, a powerful Euboean settlement and commercial rival disturbingly near the Achaean outpost of Poseidonia. This was essentially the same danger that confronted Pontecagnano. Although the Etruscans there had only weak ties to the Campanian Etruscans, and therefore reprisals would presumably not have constituted a real threat (Aristodemos, in any case, later became a great friend of Etruscans), but this cannot have been immediately apparent.the battle left them isolated and rather surrounded by Greeks, all the more so because their compatriots in Etruria were at the time preoccupied with consolidating the fruits of their victory eleven years earlier, in collusion with the Carthaginians, over the Phocaeans of Alalia on the island of Corsica (Scullard, 1967: 183-185). Ironies abound; it was Phocaean refugees from Alalia who founded Elea, on the advice of none other than "a man of Poseidonia" (Herodotos i, 167). Thus the other group in the Sele Plain that needed a bolstering of legitimacy was at Pontecagnano, where a show of solidarity with Poseidonia, especially one invoking the powerful Achaean city of Sybaris, could only be beneficial to both parties; the Olympian plaque would have accomplished that, the name *Serdaioi* providing a distancing from the troublesome Campanian Etruscans, and would have made an excellent companion to whatever other accommodations were made among the parties involved. That such arrangements existed can be inferred from the continuing close relations with Poseidonia signalled by the material assemblage at Pontecagnano during this period. By the end of the century, however, Pontecagnano's role of regional *emporion* for the Greek trade was to be largely usurped by another Etruscan settlement, at Fratte, near Salerno, with strong connections with both Cumae and the Campanian Etruscan cities (d'Agostino, 1968, and G. Greco and Pontrandolfo, 1990: 310-313); this eventuality only underscores the competitiveness of the commercial climate that must have motivated the issuance of the treaty commemorative. Dunbabin (1948: 345) mentions the coming to terms between the Campanian Etruscans and Aristodemos of Cumae, something which must have seemed quite unlikely only a brief while before. Who could have foreseen later events favoring the ascendancy of Fratte and culminating in the great naval battle of 474?

Chapter 4
THE SIXTH CENTURY

Greeks and natives: the social contract

The turn of the sixth century BC, give or take a few years, begins the two-century span of the Greek city of Poseidonia, considered by most among the major settlements of Magna Grecia. One must wonder, however, what our assessment of the city's place in history would be were it not for the excellent state of preservation of its three major temples (Figs. 19-20), and the vogue it has enjoyed on this account since the end of the eighteenth century. A considerable body of work has been devoted to these temples. Already in the nineteenth century, Aurès (1868) had published a monograph on the temples of Paestum; Koldeway and Puchstein (1899) included a detailed discussion of them in their survey of the architecture of South Italy and Sicily. In more recent times they are discussed in Dinsmoor's (1950) survey; the painstakingly meticulous work of Krauss (1943 and 1959) and Hertwig (1968) stand out, and the work of Mertens (1990) on colonial architecture reflects his interest in these temples.

The ancient writers, for the most part, limit their references to this Northernmost of Achaean colonies to the parenthetical. These sidelong glances give the impression less of celebrity (except for its roses!) than of solidity: a working town whose nature reflects the pragmatic spirit of commerce, in many respects continuing the ancient border culture on which it so swiftly and thoroughly intruded. And yet the three Doric temples to which it owes much of its modern fame are more than just well-preserved examples of Western Greek architecture; they are, each in its unique way, reflections of the particular culture which made them, and as such worthy of our attention if we are to understand the dynamics of this culture. The two built during the sixth century are especially instructive in this respect.

Within forty years of the foundation of the city, the first temple was built in the Southernmost of two intramural *temenoi*: the so-called Basilica, or, more simply and accurately, Hera I. It was dedicated to Hera and, it appears likely, Zeus as well. There are several indications of this: the cella split by the central row of columns, as at the first Hera temple at Samos, and the seated male figure found in the vicinity are the two most obvious; it should be noted, however, that there is some

disagreement regarding this interpretation, even though there is precedent for the sharing of quarters by Zeus and Hera in the early temple, for example, at Argos. It was, after all, the argive Hera to whom the nearby Sele sanctuary was explicitly dedicated. In addition, votive terracottas of Zeus and Hera together and a silver plaque dedicated to Zeus have been found in association with the temple at Poseidonia, although alongside the far more numerous votive figures dedicated to Hera alone (see Berve and Gruben, 1963: 96; Pedley, 1990: 53-54; and Barletta, 1990: 69-70). It should be noted, however, that interpretation of dedication based on votive figures can be a risky business. Ammerman and Cipriani (1996) have noted a plethora of types at the Athena temple in the Northern *temenos*. Let it simply remain that the collection in association with Hera I is consistent with the dual dedication.

Architecturally, this temple has the unusual feature of narrower interaxials at the front and rear than at the sides, which has the effect of bringing the ratio of the length to the width to 2.21, near enough to the later Doric ideal of 2.26; if the interaxials were the same on all sides, however, the ratio would have been 2.07, a more characteristically Ionic proportion, although Hera I has twice the number of columns on the sides as on the front, rather than twice the number of interaxials, as in the Ionic canon (see Vitruvius iii, 3, 6 and 4, 3). With its enneastyle, almost pseudodipteral plan, its Doric columns with Ionic neck and echinus decorations, its frieze of triglyphs and metopes surmounting an architrave capped with an Ionic molding, and its ambivalent proportions, this was an eclectic structure indeed, but one need search no further than Sicily for Ionic embellishments to add to the solidly Doric Achaean tradition. Indeed, we find similar elements at Metaponto and at the mother city of Sybaris, although some caution must be exercised. The oft-cited temples C, F and G at Selinus are later than Hera I (Berve and Gruben, 1963: 421-432), as is the so-called *Chiesa di Sansone*, the temple of Apollo at Metaponto, which has very nearly the same plan as Hera I. All the same, such features as the leaf decorations of the neck and echinus, the Ionic anta capitals and other features are identified by Barletta (1990) as characteristic of an "Ionian Sea" style, broadening what had been perceived as a Western Achaean style. There are problems with this interpretation, the most striking being that although the various elements of the style are found distributed, as the name suggests, around the Ionian Sea, they are found together as a complex primarily in the Western Achaean cities and the Peloponnese; hence the origins of the influences, as I have characterized them, of Hera I are coextensive with the distribution of Barletta's Ionian Sea style with one or two additions. One is reminded as well of the long strand of commerce linking Poseidonia with Eastern Greece. Finally, and perhaps most significantly for this temple in particular, there is the influence of the great *Heraia* of the Aegean. At Argos, the first temple of Hera was so thoroughly Doric that Vitruvius (iv, 1, 3) tells us that it was Dorus himself who built it; yet it features an unusually deep pteron on three sides, an attribute echoed in Hera I at Poseidonia, but with some of the qualities of the dipteral Hera III at Samos, which was roughly contemporaneous with, though perhaps slightly earlier than, Hera I at Poseidonia.

With all the colonial exuberance and eclecticism of Hera I, then, the range of its influences was restricted to the Greek world; indeed, some aspects of its construction suggest that more than one architect was needed to finish the job (Dinsmoor, 1950: 93), all in all suggestive of a culture as yet unmelded, and certainly with little apparent local influence, unless the Ionic arrives via the Etruscans of Pontecagnano, an unlikely prospect, given the other possibilities. A tantalizing aroma of early Etruscan influence remains, however, in the large-scale terracotta figures; which may have been cult images. It was, after all, the Etruscans and not the Greeks who were masters of large-scale terracotta sculpture.

A rather different kind of eclecticism is characteristic of the temple of Athena, built at the Northern *temenos* at the opposite end of the city, just a few decades later. The Doric and Ionic elements have crystallized and are mediated, in a sense, by a new and subtle, possibly Etruscan, element. The ratio of length to width of 2.26, with thirteen columns along the sides and six at the front and rear, was to become the Doric canon, although it appears here for the first time anywhere (Symeonoglou, 1985: 56-57; Berve and Gruben, 1963; and Krauss, 1959). Taking the plan of the temple as a whole, what one sees is a structure with a Doric periphery, but once within the peristyle the building becomes almost completely Ionic. This occurs, to my knowledge, for the first time anywhere, a full 50-60 years before the Parthenon. The cella is exactly one half the width of the stylobate, typically Ionic. Like Hera I, there is no opisthodomos, although in this case the cella ends without an adytum at the rear. This is more an Ionic characteristic than a Doric one, as is the absence of antae at the ends of the cella walls. In a sense, the structure can be conceived as an Ionic prostyle temple with certain Western refinements within a Doric peristyle; even the central interaxial of the porch is enlarged, although this is not the case for the outer, Doric, row of columns.

The proportions of the front and rear elevations also reflect a Doric aesthetic, and at first glance present a Doric aspect; but there are several features which are alien to the order. The temple has a frieze of triglyphs and metopes above an architrave of Doric proportions but, in the place of the regulae and guttae at the transition between the two members is a leaf-and-dart molding, and above the frieze, the normal horizontal cornice is entirely replaced by Ionic egg-and-dart above a flatter patterned molding. Although the molding itself is an Ionic feature, the absence of the horizontal cornice, and therefore the impossibility of a pediment sculpture, may well be influenced by Etruscan neighbors.

The gables and eaves of the roof are coffered, to provide a soffit, a very unusual arrangement for a Greek temple, but a satisfactory solution to the lack of a horizontal cornice. Indeed, in light of the treatment of the pediment and the roof, the Ionic prostyle cella takes on a new character. Although the overall proportions of the cella are Ionic, the prostyle and pronaos taken together display the proportions of the Etruscan temple as described by Vitruvius (iv, 7, 1); this configuration of the inner plan is unique, and suggestive, considering the treatment of the entrance to the pronaos. As noted, there are no antae as such; instead, the transition to the porch is through engaged Ionic columns, something which is seen elsewhere only in temple D at Selinus and in two Western treasuries at Delphi, the Geloan and the (presumed) Etruscan. I hasten to point out that the prostyle plan itself is not unique; indeed, it is one of the elements of Barletta's Ionian Sea style, and as such is certainly not a rarity. However, the particular combination of elements in the realization of the porch in the Athena temple at Poseidonia is not found elsewhere. In addition, Barletta (1990: 61-62) herself considers the engaged "anta" columns a Western invention. Although she credits the architect of Temple D at Selinus with the idea some two decades before the Athena temple, there remains the hint of Etruscan influence for it in the Delphi treasury. While the temple taken as a whole is robustly Greek, even if highly innovative, there is a hint of local flavor as well.

Perhaps these structures suggest a founding community of Greeks still thoroughly identified with the homeland but, with the passage of time, rather kindly disposed toward native influences: an assimilation, in other words, not exclusively in one direction. This should not surprise; the mother city of Sybaris was known to be open to relations with Oenotrians once suitably subdued (Dunbabin, 1948: 187), and was, in fact, the subject of criticism for allegedly preferring the company of Etruscans to that of other Greeks.

To be sure, we are dealing with only the subtlest of indications regarding Greek-native relationships here; I certainly do not mean to hold up the architecture as evidence of a Greek population "gone native." Rather, the character of the architecture suggests a line of inquiry, which is pursued along different lines to the same conclusion.. The Sybarite reputation may be spurious, and the architectural *nuances* open to discussion; fortunately, we have recourse to a copious, if lacunose, archaeological record. Are these suggestions, tenuous as they are, borne out elsewhere?

A cursory examination of sixth century sites in the Sele Plain (Fig. 18) might suggest not, but a closer look is instructive. There is, indeed, a clustering of cemeteries around the city, to the extent that some have concluded that the great majority of the Greek population lived within the walls (see Greco, 1979c: 229-230). This conclusion rests on, among other things, the assumption of the virtual segregation of the Greek population from the native, on which subject, see below. Poseidonia, in this view, was an insular town, almost a citadel, standing in the center of the Southern plain, and, at least during the sixth century, surrounded by surly if not hostile natives. Agricultural fields, such as they were, were tended by day labor and a smattering of farmsteads, and relations with the indigenous population were strained; security was maintained by placing extramural sanctuaries at the frontiers. Greco (1979c and 1988) has been the strongest proponent of this scenario, as part of a general view of the city in Archaic times as much smaller and more compact than previously thought. Ironically, it is precisely this minimal Poseidonia which would have found survival extremely difficult without a cordial accommodation of the native population.

But let us examine the distribution of sites on which this hypothesis is based. Apart from the cluster of cemeteries near the city itself, there are only a few scattered in the hinterland, and it is from these that farmsteads are inferred. By implication, the spaces between are unused because sites closer to population centers are available.

There are two points to be made in this regard. The first is that the underlying assumption that archaeological discovery has been a random process - that it should have resulted in a sample with the same distribution as the actual sites - is flawed. Reference to a modern map of the area will show that it has concentrated largely in areas which have undergone land renovation, either agricultural or commercial, as one might expect. In addition, the object-oriented methodology of the first half of this century led to a focus on cemeteries, where high prestige artifacts are likely to occur. Thus, there was a system in which attention was concentrated on burial goods accidentally plowed up on developed land, i. e., near modern roads, the main ones of which happen to coincide with the travertinous belt running roughly from Gromola, through Poseidonia, to the Solofrone. There were ancient roads here, too, for much the same reason; travertine in generally swampy terrain is an excellent foundation for roads, not to mention a fine place to bury the dead. At the same time, reports of coarse-ware, everyday "pots and pans", turning up in the plowzone were either ignored or reported only in passing, often without a clear provenance. The consensus was, and to a discouraging extent, still is, that this type of artifact is essentially undatable. Naturally, this becomes a self-fulfilling prophecy, since no studies of the material are encouraged.

Unfortunately, it is exactly this kind of material that is characteristic of small extramural settlements and farmsteads, and we end by having to rely far too heavily on inferences based on cemeteries, having largely ignored the direct evidence. It may be argued that the relative ubiquity of fourth century cemeteries (see Fig. 18) vitiates this argument: if these later sites have been found, why not the earlier ones? Suffice it to say that I do not in any way challenge the idea of a population explosion in Lucanian times; I think the evidence speaks for itself, since the same limitations apply to a certain extent for this period as well. However, it will be noted that while there are certainly more fourth century sites than sixth century ones, the distribution remains roughly the same, and

the same arguments apply. Furthermore, these later tombs sometimes disturb, or, at the very least, distract from earlier sites which they superimpose. Two such instances of which we know are at Parco Ogliastro, near the better known fourth century tombs at Pagliaio della Visceglia, where an already looted tomb yielded fragments of a late sixth century lekythos, and at Tempa del Prete, where scattered sixth-fifth century material among fourth century tombs led Napoli to conclude that earlier tombs had been re-used (Avagliano and Cipriani, 1987: 40-41). How often this kind of thing went unnoticed or unnoted by earlier investigators is open to speculation. If burial goods can be passed over as insignificant, the chances of reporting early *ceramica d'uso* scattered among the environs of intact fourth century tombs are slim indeed.

The second point is that much of the "unoccupied" area is rich, arable soil, some of which is covered with thick colluvial deposits. One would not expect to find cemeteries on land which is more valuable for agriculture, and, in any event, sites under colluvium may be too deeply buried to emerge even under the chisel plow. Where this is not the case, on the other hand, if such land was utilized in antiquity, one may expect to find concentrations of varying densities of the type of material associated with small settlements and farmsteads, and a general low-density scatter associated with cultivating activities.

Thus the argument *ex absentia* for an overwhelmingly intramural settlement pattern is methodologically flawed, and furthermore, there is positive evidence to the contrary. The sample represented by the Capodifiume survey (Figs. 5-8) is strongly suggestive of just such a pattern as described above. Material firmly datable to the sixth century is scattered nearly three kilometers from the city, and much presently unidentifiable coarse ware and impasto may belong to this period as well. This is the case in CS-11, where a type A Corinthian transport amphora and a Chiote amphora, representing either end of the sixth century, are found among a variety of impasto and coarse ware fragments. Depending on the dating of these last, this may be a farmstead site; CS-12 adjacent yields a hydria handle that may also date to this period. Almost every unit on the North West side of the survey contains undated impasto; the identification of sixth century material in the study errs on the conservative side, and yet we see evidence of occupation.

On the flank of the hill toward Capaccio, CS-43 also yielded sixth century material; this is a colluvial slope, and one would expect that this material originated further up, on land most suitable for grazing. Mello (personal communication) has noted architectural material dating as early as the sixth century re-used in the terrace walls of these hillsides. Although there is confirmed occupation from this period at Capaccio Vecchia and Madonna del Granato, Mello's argument that no one would carry heavy architectural materials to use in a terrace wall over any distance, when the slopes are littered with suitable stones immediately to hand, is eminently convincing.

The most promising site uncovered in the survey is CS-15, primarily a fifth century site, but undoubtedly with roots in the sixth century, as indicated by a tile cover (*kalypter*) fragment (No. 48, figs. 26 and 53). This was a substantial establishment, either a large and wealthy household or, perhaps more likely, a sanctuary. It is situated on the opposite bank of the Capodifiume from the Spinazzo cemetery, which, while most active in the fourth-third centuries, has a small Archaic component as well (Avagliano and Cipriani, 1987: 39-40; Greco 1979a: 13).

The further significance of the Capodifiume River microcosm will be discussed later, but what can we say about the applicability of these data to the rest, that is to say the majority, of the Poseidonian *chora*? The Capodifiume survey, small and tightly focused as it is, is by no means the only one conducted in the Sele Plain. In the last five to ten years, archaeological survey has been increasingly recognized as the only way to cope with the combination of expanding interests of an anthropological nature and the rapid disappearance of the primary data as development continues apace despite laws designed to salvage and preserve antiquities. However, the lack of a standard method, or at least data that can in some way be standardized, makes the comparison of these data difficult (Skele, 1996). That is to say, whether the primary motivation for the survey is the location and identification of traditionally defined sites (*i. e.*, cemeteries and sanctuaries), in itself a wholly commendable pursuit, or the equally commendable estimation of land use and settlement pattern in antiquity, the data should be collected and reported in such a way that it will be useful regardless of which of a diversity of goals one is seeking. This uniformity of method has been lacking, but, fortunately, we can draw some conclusions on the basis of these studies, and even the reports that come down to us through decades.

The inference that cemeteries will be associated with nearby settlements is in itself a sound one; the question remains what the precise relationship between the two would be, both in a spatial and a demographic sense. Morris touches on the subject while discussing Dark Age Aegean burial sites:

The assumption here is that larger, more formal cemeteries represent areas between or beyond the groups of houses, reserved places for the dead, while smaller, less formal plots are taken as having been on the skirts of or within clusters of houses (Morris, 1987: 63).

The distinction between reserved and unreserved becomes moot by the Archaic for Morris, at least in Attica, since he concludes that by 700 BC unreserved burials have largely disappeared, except in special, isolated circumstances; but the essential principle embedded in his observation still applies: in less formal language, burials are spatially arranged for the convenience of the living, once all ritual considerations have been taken into account. If there is some idea of the place where the dead are buried as special, then in those areas where farmsteads and smaller settlements are closely situated to one another it makes sense for them to come together and dedicate a place in common as a burial ground, rather than having a dedicated burial ground for each settlement (or indeed, house). Similarly, this applies where there are larger, more centralized settlements.

On the other hand, where small settlements and farmsteads are more distantly separated, smaller cemeteries would be characteristic. To turn this around for our purposes, relatively large and formal cemeteries are indicative of either a nodal settlement pattern or a very dense population distribution, while smaller groups of burials, and especially isolated burials, would argue for a more thinly dispersed population. At the same time the location of settlements *vis-a-vis* their cemeteries must depend on whether one settlement or more than one was being serviced. A single settlement would tend to be rather nearer its cemetery than a group of settlements sharing one, since this would have to be located conveniently for all the participating settlements, after, of course, such considerations as the level of the water table, soil characteristics, drainage, etc., are taken into account.

There remains the question of optimal distance between ground dedicated to the living and the dead. A look at the distribution of the Archaic cemeteries of Athens (Fig. 22) reveals a radius of no more than two kilometers, including some intramural sites. Given the presence of intramural cemeteries, the relationship of cemetery distribution and population distribution in this case is far from obvious. Does the gradually decreasing density with distance from the city simply reflect the inconvenience of a long funeral procession, or is it instead a reflection of the density of the immediate extramural population? Kurtz and Boardman (1971: 68-72) dismiss Cicero's remarks about a religious ban on intramural burials in Athens, at least during Archaic times. These scholars feel that Archaic burials within the walls remain to be discovered. Even during Classical times, they argue, there are examples of contravention of a ban, if it existed. Morris's (1987: 66-69) point of view is that intramural burials almost entirely ceased by 700, but only because cemeteries within the city had become increasingly formalized and therefore surrounded by walls. So, the motivation for cemeteries outside the city comes down to either a simple lack of space within the walls, or the location of population centers outside. Obviously, the question is not easily resolved, although it is worth noting that if we remove the cluster of cemeteries outside the Dipylon and Sacred gates (see Fig. 22) the distribution evens out considerably. This, I think, would in itself argue strongly for the remaining cemeteries being used by extramural settlements.

In the Attic countryside, cemeteries have been discovered in a similar relationship to larger provincial settlements, but at Eleusis, for example, only children's graves have been found (Kurtz and Boardman, 1971: 68-70); yet it would be foolish to deduce that Eleusinian adults were not buried. One must tread warily when making inferences regarding settlements, especially the size and nature of these settlements, from cemeteries. Common sense, for example, would suggest that the smaller the settlement, the smaller the radius within which an associated cemetery might be expected, but the vagaries of archaeological discovery make even this a dangerous principle to apply in reverse. There are, of course, isolated graves and small groups related to single farmsteads to take into account; in this, too, the same *caveat* applies.

These objections, however, represent obstacles rather than barriers; there are some cautious conclusions that can be drawn from the data with which we are presented. From the example of Athens, suitably scaled down for our smaller city, we might make a tentative proposal that the Archaic cemeteries of Poseidonia (Fig. 22) that are beyond a radius of a kilometer are unlikely to be associated with the population of the city *per se*. This estimate is based on two closely related factors, and a third, more peripheral consideration. First is the clustering of cemeteries to the immediate North, just outside the Porta Aurea. The idea that this cluster represents the primary urban funerary "district" in the sixth century (and beyond) is reinforced by the continuing development of the pattern during succeeding centuries, independently of how the distribution changes elsewhere in the plain; it remains well defined until the third century, in Roman times. The second is the extent of unexplored intramural land to the East, which would presumably have been outside the Archaic city, that was both available and suitable for funerary use. Greco (1988: 487-488) proposes that the city did not extend East of the public area comprising the agora flanked by the two intramural *temenoi*, on the basis of the apparent absence of archaeological remains earlier than the fourth century immediately East of the agora. In addition, he has uncovered traces of tombs disturbed during the construction of the fourth century wall at the North East corner, immediately adjacent to the so-called "Corinthian necropolis" of Laghetto (Greco 1988: 488; Avagliano and Cipriani, 1987: 37-38). The indication is that this cemetery, dating from the earliest period at Poseidonia, extended into what is now the Eastern half of the city. This discovery, incidentally, illustrates the previous point about the obscuring of early sites by later occupation of archaeological interest. The construction of the city wall and the mushrooming of the Lucanian cemetery on what remained of the Archaic necropolis made the fourth century a trying one in terms of preserving the Archaic record. The sixth and fifth century components of this area are generally referred to as minor, but, all things considered, this is far from clear. Under the circumstances, there appears to be no reason why there could not have been an early intramural cemetery which we have simply not found. It is a fact that, the Laghetto cemetery notwithstanding, the vast majority of the earliest burials uncovered so far date to the middle of the sixth century, almost two generations beyond the foundation of the city.

The immediate implication of defining these nearby cemeteries as urban is that all the rest must be associated with extramural settlements. If this is indeed the case, we find a distribution that is quite consistent with a *polis* unified with its *chora* from the beginning, just as it should be, and as Mello (1980: 49-50) suggested nearly two decades ago; subsequent research has only strengthened this hypothesis.

Sanctuaries mark the boundaries of the *chora*, and nearby settlements are indicated by the presence of cemeteries, although we can by no means conclude that where there have been no burials discovered that there was no settlement. The relationship between the sanctuary at Fonte di Roccadaspide and the nearby cemetery at Boccalupo (see Fig. 17) is of particular interest, and is discussed at length below.

In general terms, the record of the sanctuaries, with the exception of the elusive *Poseidonion*, is remarkably clear, for reasons already discussed. The *Heraion* on the Sele, another *Heraion* at Fonte di Roccadaspide (Avagliano, 1986b: 65-66; Avagliano and Cipriani, 1987: 30-31) and a presently unidentified sanctuary at Agropoli are all contemporaneous with the founding of Poseidonia, the Sele *Heraion* slightly earlier; there may also have been a sanctuary at Capaccio Vecchia (Mello, 1980: 43) this early. There is a possibility of the missing sanctuary of Poseidon here; the hill not only overlooks the sea (at some distance, to be sure), but the impressive and perennial Capodifiume springs. It will be recalled that Poseidon was the god not only of the sea, but of springs as well, and there is no better vantage point from which to experience the earthquakes and natural disasters with which he is associated.

But the proximity of the christian grotto of the Madonna del Granato, a type obviously adapted from local representations of Hera, makes that goddess more likely. In point of fact, a *Heraion* here and another at Agropoli would make for a satisfyingly symmetrical arrangement; Fiammenghi (1988: 396-398) makes a distinction between the "generic" Archaic female votive figures and a Hellenistic helmeted Athena recovered at Agropoli, and notes that the presence of a late *Athenaion* need not exclude an early *Poseidonion*. For whatever reasons, there has never been any consideration of the possibility of another sanctuary of Hera, which would account for the Archaic female figures rather nicely.

In any event, the new city clearly lost no time in posting its boundaries, and soon followed up by consolidating them. By the middle of the sixth century, at Getsemani, a site that had undoubtedly had a sacred character in protohistoric times became a Greek sanctuary, dedication unknown (Avagliano, 1986a: 63-64). It is certainly intriguing, given the predominance of female deities and the character of Hera as protectress, that of all the terracotta figures recovered at Getsemane, only one can be identified as female with any certainty. Here, at last, are figures that at least could be male, in a neighborhood Poseidon might find congenial! Finally, a sanctuary of Demeter had been established at Acqua che Bolle, an echo of the sanctuary of Demeter and Kore at Lupata Torre between the city and the sea (Cipriani, 1988: 415-416).

We find evidence, too, of settlement contemporaneous with the establishment of these sanctuaries. Significantly, among the earliest tombs is an isolated one some ten kilometers to the North East of Poseidonia at Fravita, near the Catauro spring, virtually at the frontier not far from the contemporary indigenous remains at Rovine di Palma (Avagliano and Cipriani, 1987: 22-23, 26). In the same area, at Tempa San Paolo, although the earliest identifiable Greek remains are from the fifth century, there are fragments of impasto and much worn black-gloss pottery (Avagliano and Cipriani, 1987: 33-34). What we have, then, is a Greek presence, albeit small, amidst indigenous occupation, just as we see at the *Heraion* at Fonte di Roccadaspide and the nearby indigenous settlement at the aptly named Boccalupo (Avagliano and Cipriani, 1987: 30-31; Avagliano, 1986.), not to mention Tempalta and other locations in the immediate area.

The situation at Fonte is of special interest because the remains there are exactly contemporaneous with the Sele *Heraion*. If there is a single location that illuminates the relationship between the Greek colonists and the native population, this must be it. There is simply no way this sanctuary could have been maintained without a sizeable garrison unless relations were at the least cordial; an active collaboration would be better. In other words, we have just the kind of situation in the North East sector of the *chora* as we had expected, given our interpretation of the compact between Greeks and Etruscans at the founding of Poseidonia. The lesson of the sanctuary is only reinforced by the isolation of the burial at Fravita, since it is difficult to imagine a single-family settlement, to which that burial surely pertains, in the midst of a hostile population. The lack of any other indications of Greek settlement in this area in the sixth century - the result, one may tentatively conclude, of a dispersed population and the attendant small cemeteries or isolated burials, easily overlooked - could very well be proven spurious by a systematic survey. The same is true of the area between Poseidonia and the Sele *Heraion*, where there are no indications of settlement until the fourth century, in Lucanian times. Whether this reflects an actual discontinuity or only an apparent one will no doubt be made clear as research continues.

To the South East the situation is considerably more encouraging. In this direction we have undated artifact scatters covering most of the area in question, at least as far as Giungano to the East, and possibly as far as Trentinara (see below). It must be recalled that here colluvium may be a factor. There is, however, a pattern of development seaward of this area, reinforcing the probability of occupation. Here, at Linora, there was discovered a section of paved road leading from the Porta Giustizia to Agropoli, with a branch leading off in an easterly direction (Avagliano and Cipriani, 1987: 41). A quarry was also here and, by the end of the century, at least a few burials to the North at Sta. Venera (Avagliano and Cipriani, 1987: 41-42), where already by the mid sixth century there was a sanctuary of Aphrodite (Pedley and Torelli, 1993), at Spinazzo (Avagliano and Cipriani, 1987: 39-40) and to the East at Tempa del Prete, where the later, much celebrated Tomb of the Diver was discovered (Avagliano and Cipriani, 1987: 40-41) - in other words, along the road, which, while it appears to date in its improved form to the fifth century, must have existed as a well-established byway long before. Excavation in progress at this writing near the Porta Giustizia has revealed a paved *via sacra* from that gate to the altar of the Temple of Hera I (Alexandre Simon Stefan, personal communication), dating to the beginnings of the city and clearly linked, by implication, with the road to Agropoli. The importance of the area South of the city is also corroborated by the numerous rebuildings of the wall being uncovered, apparently related to the changing course of the Capodifiume. There is a profusion of sixth century material at Linora itself, and in addition to the finds at Agropoli, a kilometer or so to the East of that town, at Contrada Cupa, there are remnants of an early Archaic structure near a spring (Avagliano and Cipriani, 1987: 48-49).

The string of burials flanking the road South from the city to Agropoli, and the sparser but still undeniably present cemeteries to the North East indicate small population centers

on what was clearly agricultural land, distant but comfortably within the Poseidonian *chora*. To the South East the data are more muddled, but there are a few indications that the land between the Solofrone and the Eastern road from the city was well utilized, although from what period is unclear. At Tempa del Lepre are some looted tombs (Avagliano and Cipriani, 1987: 45), and a scatter of material all the way from there to Giungano, but the material is undated; a similar situation, but with no tombs, obtains at Maida, below modern Capaccio (Avagliano and Cipriani, 1987: 39). It will be recalled that this type of light scatter is consistent with cultivation activities. There is every reason to believe that systematic survey in these areas will clarify the situation, and certainly the question of the date.

In spite of all the difficulties, exceptions, qualifications and, above all, *lacunae*, a distinct pattern does emerge, one of dispersed farmsteads throughout the sixth century centering around a smaller version of Poseidonia than the one with which we are familiar today. We have seen evidence of this distribution from the very birth of the city, coexisting with indigenous settlements of some size in the North East section of the *chora*. Only at the end of the century do we see signs of incipient nucleation in the countryside, and this mostly in the immediate suburbs of the city; the Ponte di Ferro cemetery comes to mind, although there are some unusual features associated with this site (Avagliano and Cipriani, 1987: 35-36.). The extreme poverty of the graves there, and the slapdash arrangement surely suggest something other than an ordinary extramural settlement. Pedley (1990: 36) has suggested slaves used to unload ships, whether at a harbor, if one existed, or simply pulled up on the beach. Is it a coincidence that the cemetery was in use only from the last decade or so of the sixth century to the first decade of the fifth, just after Sybaris suffered its crushing defeat in 510 BC at the hands of Croton? The exact connection remains obscure, but the coincidence is certainly remarkable: an unusual cemetery appears as refugees from the mother city of Sybaris arrive.

In any event, the majority of evidence indicates Greeks living and working in the countryside alongside native populations under quite congenial conditions. De la Genière (1979: 86-88) would like to link the transition between the First and Second Iron Ages at Sala Consilina to a general withdrawal of native populations from the Sele Plain on the arrival of the Greek colonists, followed by a gradual overcoming of mistrust and hostility culminating by the mid sixth century in a regular, if not brisk, trade. While admitting the absorption of some of these people into the Greek community, this scholar relies on a model of occupation by conquest based largely on an analogy with the subduction of the indigenous settlement at Amendolara by Sybaris; it should be noted that all of the evidence cited for this model is from Sybaris and Locri, and not from Poseidonia. Amendolara represents a very clear case, in which a sizeable native settlement simply ceases to exist at the time of Sybarite colonization, and a Greek occupation begins. An analogy with the mother city of Sybaris would indeed seem appropriate, but our search for a similar situation at Poseidonia leads to the conclusion that there is no such unambiguous event in the Sele Plain - in fact, as we have seen, quite the opposite appears to have been the case.

At Tempalta we have a burial ground for an indigenous settlement, not a stone's throw from the Fonte *Heraion*, that was active from the mid seventh century through the fifth; in other words, spanning the critical period of contact. The early material is unquestionably local, and by the fifth, the assemblage displays "... some differences compositionally from the sober funerary collections from contemporary urban tombs" (Avagliano and Cipriani, 1987: 30). Do these "compositional differences" reflect a native population under the influence of Poseidonian Italiotes? The settlement apparently weathered the traumatic arrival of Greeks none the worse for the wear, and seemed, in fact, to harbor a distinct sympathy for Greek material culture, unless we are to attribute the unsober funerary collections of the fifth century to Greeks gone decadent under native influence. Similarly, the Archaic assemblage at Boccalupo, which includes heavy *bucchero*, is reflective as much of native cultures as Greek. Only at Rovine di Palma do we find traces of a seventh-sixth century site that may end at the moment of colonization, but, significantly, there are no signs of a Greek supersession here.

This leaves only the site of the city of Poseidonia itself, where the archaeological record to date is far too fragmentary to allow an unequivocal interpretation in this regard. However, a precedent indigenous settlement of some kind is indicated; whether this population was displaced or absorbed remains unresolved. The evidence from the countryside would be more consistent with absorption; only the population increase at Sala Consilina argues for displacement (see the discussion in Chapter 2).

Distribution of land

As we have seen, sacred (*i. e.*, public) land was customarily allocated both near the city at the heart of the *chora* and at its periphery. This was also the case for private property allocated at the foundation of the city, or so Plato (745B-E) tells us. Although Asheri (1966: 10) notes that land on the borders of the territory was considered inferior, and often remained barren, uncultivated or wooded, such land given to the gods must have had a different character, since the purpose of doing so was either to preserve a valuable resource (*e.g.*, timber, or the land itself) or to promote the cultivation of specific crops. The implication that these lands were unsuited for cultivation has, of course, a basis in fact. Poseidonia, for example, like many another Greek *polis*, was situated in a fertile deltaic plain bounded by the sea on the one horizon and the piedmont on the other; the marches of its territory tended to lie on sloping hillsides difficult to cultivate. But this was not exclusively true; the gently rolling land to the North East of Poseidonia between Capaccio Vecchia and the Sele was and is quite amenable to cultivation. It is a distinct possibility that in this area, protected by the Hera sanctuary at Fonte di Roccadaspide, were found sacred lands, improved by the state and leased to tenants in order to encourage occupation near the border (See Asheri, 1978: 69-78). It was often the case that such lands were leased to lesser citizens, to achieve two desirable ends with a single stroke: lands near the border were occupied, and potential class tensions were eased. Could the tomb at Fravita belong to an early caretaker of such a plot of land?

At least part of the other half of the ideal arrangement, sacred land near the city, may well be found along the Capodifiume River, where, in addition to the immediate surroundings of the spring, votive material - albeit quite late - was recovered at CS-4, along with sporadic isolated finds elsewhere. Local farmers and workers of the *Consorzio di Bonifica* also report seeing what they describe as "hundreds" of fragments of these figures during the canalization of the river in the 1960s; even allowing for hyperbole, there must be some basis for these assertions.

When we examine the distribution of occupation along the river through time (Figs. 5-8), we find that prehistoric and protohistoric occupation is concentrated, in the main, within about 1500 meters of the spring; during the sixth and fifth centuries, the focus shifts to the lower end of the river, and dense occupation in the vicinity of the spring is not really re-established until after the third century. This apparent avoidance of the spring is most uncharacteristic, unless the land along the river and near the spring were reserved and dedicated to a deity. Toponyms East, but not West, of the upper kilometer or so of the Capodifiume - Macchia d'Olmo, Prima Quercia - are indicative of the timber-bearing potential here.

As Métraux (1978: 59-65) has noted, one of the functions of sacred lands was to keep in reserve lots which could be awarded under lease to new colonists when needed. While the apparent lack of occupation along the left bank of the Capodifiume and near the spring continues largely unchanged until Roman times, there is an interesting pattern on the lower half of the survey, within sight of the present walls. We find there is a regular, if widely spaced, occupation of this land throughout the sixth century, but in the fifth century, the gaps begin to fill in. Such a pattern would seem unusual so near the city under private ownership, especially since this area represents some of the best agricultural land available; a more characteristic pattern would have been either a dense occupation from the beginning, or at least a gradual increase consistent with the division of inherited lands. On the other hand, the situation is just what one might expect if the land is sacred. At Heraclaea, we know that the lands of Dionysos were divided into small parcels for lease to a large number of tenants rather than fewer with larger holdings (Métraux, 1978: 59-64, and Plate III). While it is true that Heraclaea was founded almost 150 years after Poseidonia, it is one of the few instances in which we have such detailed knowledge, due to a first century BC resurvey of the sacred lands. We also know that the custom of dedicating land to deities and leasing it has a history long before Heraclaea; the assumption that Poseidonia may have had a similar disposition of these lands is not unreasonable under the circumstances. Thus, the relative density of settlement indicated by the survey in the fifth century can be related to the need to have structures - houses, stables etc. - on each of many small lots, held in reserve during the previous century and allocated to immigrants as the need arose.

Apart from this specific pattern of artifact distribution along the Capodifiume, the general ubiquity of material on the right bank as opposed to its scarcity on the left has also some interesting implications. One might expect a relatively denser scatter along a road than elsewhere, since houses would be more likely to be built with access to a road in mind. We know that such a road parallelled the river to the North West at least by the second half of the eighteenth century, since it appears quite distinctly on both Paoli's 1784 map and Delagardette's 1799 map leading, on the latter, through Capaccio Vecchia precisely to the territory which we have argued may have been the distant portion of sacred land. If, as the evidence suggests, this road already existed in earliest Greek times, it would not only have provided access to these distant parcels, but would have linked them with the nearer sacred lands as well as with the city itself.

Presumably, the road would have continued from there to the Vallo di Diano and ultimately the much discussed land route to Sybaris, although the importance of this is questionable, as is the inland connection as a whole.

The other possible location for sacred lands is in the neighborhood of Linora along the road to Agropoli, but for different reasons. It will be recalled that this area in modern times is covered with travertine of medieval origin (see Chapter 2) except where this has been stripped off in order to improve cultivation of the land. The source of the travertine was a perennial swamp fed by the many distributaries of the Capodifiume; Greek and Roman remains are found beneath the medieval *crosta* but overlying older travertines. In other words, the area was swampy before Greco-Roman times, and again after. It is rather likely that its apparent dryness during the intervening period was the result of an extensive drainage program. It is interesting to note that the Veians, whose connections with Pontecagnano we have been at some pains to demonstrate, were widely known for their considerable skills in land reclamation, especially the drainage of swamps utilizing underground aqueducts known as *cuniculi* (Hamblin, 1976: 128-129 and Scullard, 1967: 68-69, among others). Although Etruscan expertise is not an absolute necessity to explain the successful drainage of this area, it would clearly have been a big help. While it is true that we presently have no evidence of *cuniculi* in the Poseidonian *chora*, it is also true that no one has particularly looked for it; this is certainly an aspect of Poseidonian land use that would bear investigation.

Such a program would unquestionably have been beyond private means, but it would have constituted the kind of improvement to sacred land that was needed to make it desirable, partly as a quarry during the sixth century at least; the drained land would also have been suitable for livestock, if not particularly amenable to cultivation. Modern use of the land West of SS 18 and South of Sta. Venera for crops such as corn and artichokes is possible only due to the removal of enormous amounts of travertine, in places as much as three meters in depth, and the deposition of topsoil from elsewhere.

In apparent corroboration, a Gorgon antefix dating to the mid-sixth century, and votive material from the beginning of the fifth have been recovered in this area, but one must proceed with caution, here more than elsewhere, due to the presence also of a large number of ceramic wasters, indicating a kiln

(Avagliano, 1986: 61). Where the one ends and the other begins is difficult to say without further investigation.

In any event, this may seem rather a lot of sacred land, leaving little for private ownership, the allocation of which was, as we know, a principal part of the foundation of a city. But the most fertile land, the most suitable for grain, would have been from the Capodifiume South beyond the Solofrone to the Cilento foothills, reaching in an arc to the East to the colluvial slopes below Capaccio. Somewhat lesser but quite suitable land can be found North of Poseidonia to Gromola, excepting those areas with travertine outcroppings (see Fig. 11). Gasparri (1990) has found evidence from aerial photographs of centuriation in this last area, while confirming the well-documented centuriation on the slopes below Capaccio. The cadastral division of the Capaccio hillside has been noted by Guy (1987 and elsewhere). Schmiedt and Castagnoli (1955) had already noted centuriation immediately adjacent the city to the West and to the South just West of the Capodifiume. Obviously this division of land post-dates the period of interest in the present study considerably, but although the Romans were certainly as capable of reclaiming swamplands as their predecessors, none of these areas was prone to that state during the Holocene. As a point of further interest, a comparison of our geomorphological map (see Fig. 10) with Gasparri's cadastral reconstruction (our Fig. 11) shows that the gaps in the centuriation lines occur in two areas. The first is where travertines rise to the surface. Gasparri (1990: 257) interprets the majority of the lines on the aerial photographs as ancient drainage ditches along the boundaries of the lots. There is no reason why these should not have been preserved in the travertine - indeed, in better condition than elsewhere - if the travertine had been broken up and cultivated in ancient times, something that is an enormous undertaking even with today's technology. The second is within about a half a kilometer of the Capodifiume, where we have posited an ancient road. There is every indication, therefore, that this centuriated land in Roman imperial times was at least arable in Greek times, and therefore available for allocation along the lines already discussed.

Of the remaining land, the littoral zone as far back as the retro-dune area was apparently of little use agriculturally; we will return to this area shortly with regard to seafaring activities. The vast area East of SS 18 and between Capaccio Vecchia and the Sele River has already been discussed; those areas not designated as sacred lands would have been ideal to constitute the distant portions of private lands; the North-facing Capaccio Vecchia-Alburnus hillsides are today partly occupied by olive groves. There is no reason why that could not have been the case in ancient times. Topographically, geologically and climatologically - in short, all but politically - these hills constitute the Northern extreme of Cilento, justly famed today for the quality of its olives. As an alternate possibility, there is timber; the soil and palynological studies necessary to determine the character of this land (or, for that matter, other land in the plain) have yet to be carried out, so we do not know the extent of timber, although an anonymous map from 1791 (Fig. 14) shows no indication of it extending beyond the well-marked *Bosco di Persano* in the eighteenth century.

Commerce

Reference has been made throughout this study of the trade between East Greece, particularly Miletos, and the Etruscans, in which Poseidonia, through Sybaris, played a critical role. Indeed, it is a commonplace to refer the whole point of the city's existence to this trade. Although this is considerably overstating the case, there is good evidence of the importance of such trade in the city's commercial life, at least until the last decades of the sixth century.

Trade in general is a difficult thing to demonstrate archaeologically, particularly since much of what is traded is subsequently consumed. It would appear that much, if not most, of the trade in which the Greeks participated dealt with such perishable commodities; of merchants, Xenophon tells us that should they

hear that there's a vast quantity of corn somewhere: because they love it so much, they sail there to get it, which might involve crossing the Aegean or the Euxine or the Sicilian sea. Then, when they've got hold of the largest quantity they can, they transport it by sea ... [and] take the corn to where they hear corn is fetching the highest price... (20, 24)

This short but illuminating passage can tell us more than one thing of interest where trade in general is concerned. First and foremost is the impression that trade in at least perishable commodities - which would, of all commodities, be the most subject to price fluctuations - was a creature of opportunity in ancient times. One does not feel that long-term contractual arrangements characterized the grain market. At the same time, the very use of grain as an example of commercial enterprise suggests that it was a typical cargo, though, unlike the containers that carried wine, olive oil and the like, it would leave little trace once gone. A related point concerns the vast distances that these informal, opportunistic grain merchants were willing to travel: from the Euxine (Black) sea all the way to the Sicilian sea; obviously, the potential profits must have been high to justify such long journeys.

The ancient literature is not much help on specifics. Socrates, in the Xenophon passage, is holding up the grain merchants to derision for being interested only in profits, and he is only reflecting the general feeling among *aristoi* that commerce is a lowly profession, perhaps necessary, but not worthy of much discussion.

But even if Poseidonian commerce largely consisted of such unknowable trade in perishable commodities, there remains the smaller fraction, perhaps more amenable to regularized relations between buyers and sellers. Wine, for example (from where, we don't know, but why not Sybaris?) apparently arrived early on in the ubiquitous type A and B Corinthian transport amphorae; indeed, the Corinthian influence continued through most of the sixth century, longer than elsewhere in Magna Grecia, in the form of non-figured imports as well as such local "knock-offs" as Paestan Patterned ware. At the same time, pottery from East Greece was also represented; it is of interest that the decline in quantity of both these types coincides roughly with the increase in Attic

pottery in the last two decades of the sixth century. For the sixth as well as the first half of the fifth century, the material at the Santa Venera sanctuary, as documented by Menard (1990: 49-55) offers the clearest picture; also helpful are Greco (1981), Guzzo (1981) and Torelli (1981).

Corinth, one will have noticed, controls an isthmus which lies across the most direct route by far between East Greece and Italy, and its domination of commerce in the seventh century is legend; its lingering influence in Poseidonia, coterminal with East Greek material, lends some weight to the connection with Miletos, but does not explain the exact nature of the commerce. Iron, copper and tin from Etruria in exchange for Milesian textiles and other luxury items are the traditional suggestions, but although Anatolian tin sources may have been running out there would seem little benefit in importing copper and iron to the East. It is difficult to accept that these commodities could have been cheaper for the Milesians when shipped halfway across the Mediterranean than when procured next door, although the situation with the Persians must be taken into account. Even if this was the case, Sybaris itself had access to the copper mines at Temeso in inland Calabria (Dunbabin, 1948: 202), and would hardly have been interested in promoting Etruscan copper. It is true that cities in central Greece appear to have been involved in the metal trade in the eighth and seventh centuries (witness the iron industry at Pithecoussae), but this seems to have dwindled by the beginning of the sixth (see Boardman, 1980: 167-168). Curtin's (1984: 3-4) comments about trade diasporas working themselves out of business as cross-cultural differences become minimal over a period of intense contact may be relevant here. Certainly by the sixth century the Etruscan participation in the Milesian-Sybarite trade complex bespeaks a cultural parity unquestionably unlike the relationship between Pithecoussae and earlier Etruscans.

Agricultural goods might appear more promising, but given what we know about such trade, it is not the sort of thing that would forge strong ties between two distant cities; in any event, it is Metaponto, of all the Achaean colonies, rather than Poseidonia, which is known for its grain production. In fact, in the whole of Dunbabin's (1948: 211-224) thorough and concise survey of agriculture in Sicily and South Italy, the city of Poseidonia is not so much as mentioned in passing. In view of the fact that this survey was based largely on the ancient literature, it is best seen as reflective of agriculture for trade rather than domestic consumption, since fame sufficient to warrant mention could only come from export.

Another possibility is timber, since historically noted timber stands are near the Sele, especially the Persano woods, shown on an anonymous 1769 map as a vast royal timber reserve (Fig. 13). The ancient preference for the transportation of timber on water, when at all possible, is well documented (see Meiggs, 1982: 334-337), as well as appealing to common sense. However, there is no evidence in Greek times that the Sele Plain yielded any species which were not equally abundant in the rest of Greece. As with grain, Poseidonia seems to have had an ample supply for its own needs, but there is no reason to believe there was a thriving traffic in timber outside the immediate region.

This leaves us neither here nor there with regard to the nature of the trade, unless, as in the old joke about the boy smuggling baskets across the border, pottery figures much more significantly than imagined, but a connection there must have been, for the ties between Miletos and Sybaris were only slightly more famous than the ties between the Sybarites and the Etruscans. Herodotos (vi, 21) tells us that of all the cities he knew, these had the closest ties; the Milesians even went so far as to shave their heads as a sign of mourning at the fall of Sybaris in 510. Poseidonia was deftly inserted right into the flow of this traffic.

Many of the questions regarding the nature of the trade become less problematic when it is recalled that long range trade, even though it may be recognized by the presence of goods from one terminus at another, is not necessarily defined solely, or even primarily, by the direct exchange of goods between the termini. If this were the case, there would be minimal impact on the cities between; yet there is little doubt, for example, that much of Corinth's power early on (and even its artistic innovation, particularly in ceramics) derives from its favorable geography, combined, of course, with the enthusiasm of its citizens for the exploitation of its mediate position between East and West, as a participant in a series of transactions which only ultimately culminated at the geographic extremes. The same holds true for Sybaris, which had a cosmopolitan reputation as a center for far-flung enterprise in spite of the famous love of its citizens for the pleasures of the harbor. A trade network functions best and longest when each member city or culture contributes something specific; two cities and a series of rest stops do not make a lasting alliance, although the role of Sybaris seems to have been the closest to that of *entrepôt*.

The portage between Sybaris and Laos, bypassing the Sicilian straits, was already established (Scullard, 1967: 180-181; Dunbabin, 1948: 205-206), and Poseidonia gave Greek merchants a convenient *pied-à-terre*, literally and figuratively, where Etruscans could be met just short of Cumae, which must have been a factor in a political sense given its ties to Zancle and Rhegion, and thus to the situation of the Phocaean bid for control of trade in the Western Mediterranean. The linchpin of this bid, Massalia, was founded almost exactly the same time as Poseidonia, and Phocaean connections with Rhegion figure into the very reason that the land route between Sybaris and Laos could be profitable. As Dunbabin (1948: 206) points out, that portage would involve unloading ships, hauling goods over rough country by mule and then reloading ships at the other end, on the whole much more trouble and time than simply sailing directly to the straits of Messina and through. The reason for the land route, then, had to do with the tolls exacted by Rhegion and Zancle, and here is where all of the interconnectivity comes into play - Rhegion is allied with Phocaean merchants, who are currently trying to wrest control of Tyrrhenian trade from the Carthaginians and especially the Etruscans. Cumae has the advantage of the longest history of trade with Etruscans of any Greek city in Italy, but has ties with Zancle, and would, one assumes, rather not see Achaean success in the arena. Poseidonia as a commercial entity was certainly a geographical convenience as well as a political one for the Sybarites, formalizing a

mutually beneficial relationship, but in practical terms, it did not control any material or access to markets that could not easily be transferred to or, indeed, usurped by someone else.

The critical point, then, in the traditional view of Poseidonia as the agent of long range East-West trade is that it is really Sybaris which lies at the center of this commerce; therefore, the measure of the involvement of Poseidonia in the trade is its relationship to that city. Indeed, we find that it is quite strong at the beginning, with Sybaris throwing all of its considerable weight behind the establishment of the new city of Poseidonia (not without some risks) in the treaty with the *Serdaioi*, and it may be assumed that it remained cordial until at least 530-520 when that treaty was commemorated in the Olympia plaque. If, however, Poseidonia remained a sort of vassal, or even agent, of its mother city, the fall of Sybaris in 510, an event which was a watershed of sorts in Magna Grecia in general, should have had a major negative impact on it; this does not appear to be the case. Interestingly, Herodotos (vi, 21) mentions only Laos and Skydros as havens for fleeing Sybarites after its downfall; although some undoubtedly did make their way to Poseidonia (to end at the Ponte di Ferro cemetery?) the case for Sybarite influence in the city after the fall (see Chapter 5) is surely exaggerated. Changes were taking place in other cities in response to the collapse of what was, after all, an important city; one need not imagine a large contingent of Sybarites in each of them to account for this.

There is little doubt that Sybaris and the famous trade route were important for Poseidonia at the beginning, and were even an important consideration in its foundation, but undoubtedly an equally powerful motivation was simply that life around the Plain of Sybaris was getting crowded, and there was land available at the doorstep of the friendly Etruscans.

It was two to three generations after the foundation before Poseidonia began to mint its own coins, enough time to settle in and allow the lightly secured yoke of the mother city to slough off. Consider the remarkable cluster of events in the decade or so surrounding 530 BC:

1. the Phocaeans defeated at Alalia and Massalia by an alliance of Etruscans and Carthaginians are advised by "a man of Poseidonia" (Herodotos i, 167) to settle at Elea, only a few kilometers downcoast, in spite of the clash of interests between Phocaeans and Achaeans;

2. Campanian Etruscans suffer a great military defeat at the hands of Cumae, which we know to be inclined towards the support of the Phocaeans;

3. Poseidonia begins to mint its own money, but on the Campanian standard used by Cumae, although in an Achaean fabric; and

4. Sybaris issues a commemorative plaque reminding everyone of its interest in the area.

If we add to this list the fact that it is roughly during this period that we see the decline of Corinthian and East Greek pottery along with an increase of Attic pottery in the ceramic assemblages of Poseidonia, perhaps an argument could be made for a waning participation in the Milesian-Sybarite-Etruscan commercial interests, and a movement to consolidate local and regional status, the *Serdaioi* treaty serving not so much to bring Poseidonia back into the Sybarite fold as to recall its noble lineage on both the Greek and the Etruscan sides (and perhaps to reassure Sybaris of the loyalty of its erstwhile colony?).

The discussion at this point may well seem to have wandered considerably afield of the stated goal of this study - a chorography of Poseidonia - but an understanding of the city's relationship to the grand trade route is essential to an understanding of the city's chorological orientation - does Poseidonia face outward to the sea, or inward to its hinterlands? The more invested it is in its role as agent for merchants of Sybaris, or Miletos, for that matter, the more sea-bound will its interests be, and one can scarcely imagine its usefulness without at least some kind of relatively substantial port facility. The Sele-Tanagro pass has received much attention as an overland access route to Sybaris, but this makes little sense. First of all, this pass leads more naturally to Elea and Palinuro, and indeed we find connections between these places and the Vallo di Diano, quite independent of Poseidonia and not at all overshadowed by it. Secondly, even if the long and difficult trek to the Ionian sea is accomplished, one finds that the opposite pass gives onto Metaponto, and not Sybaris, surely an unnecessary complication, considering that the alternative is the far shorter and easier passage to Laos; Dunbabin (1948: 202-207) recognized this fifty years ago. The geomorphological problems associated with the discovery of the port's location are discussed at length in Chapter 2, and need not be repeated here; suffice it to say that the nature of pottery imports during at least the first half of the sixth century is suggestive of contacts with not only Corinth and East Greece, but also South Italy - just as one would expect with a seaward orientation (Menard, 1990: 49-51; Greco, 1981: 63-64). Later, as we shall see, local production indicates a turning inward.

Chapter 5
THE FIFTH CENTURY AND THE END OF GREEK POSEIDONIA

Life after Sybaris

We have already touched on this subject at the end of the last chapter and made the observation that, among other things, the destruction of Sybaris appeared to have no particular negative impact on Poseidonia, and advanced the argument that this indicated a rather loose tie by the end of the sixth century to the mother city, and therefore to the long range commerce between Etruscans and East Greeks. Indeed, there seems, if anything, to have been a positive effect.

The major urban cemeteries of the sixth century continue in use, although to differing extents; the Andriuolo and Laghetto cemeteries just to the North East of the Porta Aurea experience a slight expansion, while just to the West of these the Arcioni cemetery appears to fall from favor during the fifth century, but is revitalized later during Lucanian times. We have already discussed the strange situation at Ponte di Ferro. There does not seem, on the basis of these urban cemeteries, any significant increase in the population within the city itself. We must, of course, always bear in mind the possibility of burials gone undiscovered, both within the Archaic city and within the fourth century walls at the Laghetto necropolis. Outside the city, at the Gaudo cemetery, in the section occupied by fourth century tombs, there are not infrequent occurrences of fifth century material on the surface (Avagliano and Cipriani, 1987: 35), and Italic tombs begin to appear towards the end of the century (Cipriani, 1996), but the majority of early development lies elsewhere. The cemeteries to the South along the ancient road to Agropoli, used only slightly (so far as we know) during the sixth century, come into their own during the fifth. Even at Spinazzo, where only fifteen tombs of the 170 or so are datable to the fifth century, this represents a significant increase over the four tombs in use during the previous century.

But it is further out, at Sta. Venera, Tempa del Prete and possibly at Linora that we begin to find signs of an increased population. At Sta. Venera especially the occupation rises from a single isolated tomb in the sixth century to at least 248, at last count, in the fifth century (Avagliano and Cipriani, 1987: 42-44; Cipriani, 1986b: 105-108). The tombs date largely to

the second quarter of the century although not exclusively; the cemetery continues to be used until the middle of the third century (Pontrandolfo, 1988: 237-240; Pedley, 1990: 94-96). This rather large cemetery at some distance from the city signals a change from a dispersed extramural settlement pattern to a more nodal one, at least between Poseidonia and Agropoli. It would be difficult to interpret Sta. Venera as an urban cemetery, simply because several closer sites would have been passed over in favor of it, were that the case. Spinazzo, for example, would have been ideal, and was probably an urban burial ground in the century that followed, but was used sparingly in the fifth. Arcioni, an even closer site, does not experience heavy use until after the fifth century. The Sta. Venera *necropolis*, therefore, was undoubtedly serving extramural populations; the character of which, incidentally, has significant implications regarding the ethnic make-up of the Southern Sele Plain (see below). To the fifth century also belong the beginnings of a small cemetery to the South, at Linora, which was to continue into the fourth. It will be recalled that some votive materials dating to the beginning of the fifth century, along with a Gorgon antefix from the middle of the sixth were recovered here (Avagliano, 1986: 61; Avagliano and Cipriani, 1987: 41). This may indicate a sanctuary dedicated to an unknown female deity, although there remain some problems with the interpretation of the evidence (see above, Chapter 3).

Further afield, in the North East quadrant, near Tempa S. Paolo, are a few scattered fifth century tombs, one of which, at Pila, contained six Attic *lekythoi* and a bronze strigil (Avagliano and Cipriani, 1987: 34; Greco 1979c: 16-17); thus we find that Greeks are still living out in the countryside near the mouth of the wolf, and that among them was at least one person, perhaps an athlete, of no mean status. This assemblage, some *lekythoi* with few, if any, accompanying vases and a strigil at the side of the deceased, was to become typical of the fifth century male tombs; Pedley (1990: 96) has noted the importance of the athletic metaphor in the burial rite of this period. Its exact interpretation, however, still eludes us.

Further East, at S. Nicola di Albanella, not far from the sixth century boundary of the territory, the first years of the fifth century saw the establishment of a sanctuary of Demeter and Kore (Cipriani and Avagliano, 1987: 23-25; Cipriani, 1989). Although a modest construction, analogs are found in Sicily, but in a thesmophoric context not supported here, where the cult, according to the excavator, had to do with fertility, both in an agricultural and a matrimonial sense. There is a strong suggestion of the association of males in this cult, a most unusual occurrence for ceremonies dedicated to Demeter and Kore. Two things spring to mind in the context of this sanctuary. One is that it is indicative of a thriving, if not actually wealthy, peasant culture at the reaches of the Poseidonian *chora* - in other words, yet more corroboration, if any was needed, of the filling in of the countryside during this period. The other is that the cult has sufficiently unusual features to invite speculation regarding the blending of traditions - perhaps an Italic touch? The decidedly un-Greek muddling of sex roles, especially in a cultic context, carries a distinct Etruscan tinge.

The overall impression of the Poseidonian *chora* from the *necropoleis* and the sanctuaries of the fifth century is one of filling in, rather than territorial expansion, reflecting the same tendency seen in microcosm in the Capodifiume survey; if the site, whatever its character, at CS-15 appears to have roots in the sixth century, it comes into its own in the fifth. This is especially interesting in view of the long record of votive material at the Stazione di Paestum just outside the Porta Sirena, beginning with nude Daedalic female figures. Also recovered are enthroned female figures "..altogether similar to analogous finds at the urban sanctuaries," (Avagliano and Cipriani, 1987: 38). The fifth century Attic drinking vessels found there are also present at CS-15, where these plus the loom weights may be indicative of either a sacred context or perhaps a substantial and wealthy household. In any case, the burgeoning of an important center among so many others near the city only underlines the growth that was taking place. The population increase was quite significant, if not dramatic; some have argued that this only serves to reinforce the hypothesis that Sybarites arrived in large numbers after the fall, and had a profound influence on the affairs of the *polis* until its conquest, if conquest it was, by Lucanians.

The other evidence frequently mentioned for this eventuality is the adoption of the Achaean standard and the bull on the coinage during the fifth century, and the possible dedication of a cenotaph on the Western margin of the Poseidonian *agora* to the *oikist* of Sybaris.

With regard to the former, the adoption of the Achaean standard and the bull do not occur until about 470 BC, some forty years after the fall of Sybaris (Kraay and Hirmer, 1966: 304). Could the switch to the Achaean standard have less to do with Sybaris and all its incarnations than with the naval victory of Cumae over the Etruscan fleet just four years before? An argument may even be made that Poseidonia's previous coinage, which adhered to the Campanian standard rather than the Achaean, is indicative of the relatively greater importance of the regional economy to the city than the grand trade route, once the city was well established in its own right. The measure of Poseidonian reliance on and importance to the Milesian/Sybarite/Etruscan commercial network may very

well be the two or three generations without a sovereign mint; when money finally appears, it bears the image of Poseidon, not the bull of Sybaris. This coinage was struck right around 530 and its main expression of solidarity with Sybaris was its incuse technique, in use throughout the Achaean West - surely a symbolic gesture as compared to the weight standard, especially in light of Kraay's opinion that the technique is best exemplified not in Sybaris but in Metaponto (Kraay and Hirmer, 1966: 306). Indeed, Kraay notes that Metapontine coinage in general seems to be more important to South Italian economy than the Sybarite; this can no doubt be attributed to the rich and well-known grain production of that city. In any case, the technique is dropped in Poseidonia around 500; the monetary evidence can therefore be read either way, as an increase or a decrease in Sybarite influence after its fall, whichever best suits one's argument.

The second point, the cenotaph dedicated to the Sybarite *oikist*, is clouded by the increasing uncertainty regarding the identification of this monument, traditionally called alternatively the *sacello* or the *hypogeum*. Indeed, to argue that the monument demonstrates the involvement of Sybarite refugees begs the question, since its identification as the *heroon* of the founder of the mother city rests on its probable construction in the decade following the destruction of Sybaris. Pedley (1990: 38-39) has a lively discussion of this monument; there is, to date, no real consensus concerning its true nature. If a gift from Sybaris, as some suggest, then we must admire the Sybarites for the energy to build and dedicate such a structure in the very year of the total destruction of their city. In any case, as we shall see, independent evidence casts serious doubt that immigrant Sybarites played any significant role in the city.

As regards the population increase, the main difficulty, apart from the gradualness of it, lies in the nature of the tombs of the fifth century as contrasted with what we know of the style of living - not to say, as some ancient writers have, the arrogance and ostentation - preferred by the Sybarites. For if there is a single characteristic quality that unites the diverse graves of fifth century Poseidonia, it is modesty (Pedley, 1990: 94-96; Pontrandolfo, 1988: 235-244). Cipriani (Avagliano and Cipriani, 1987: 43) interprets the sobriety of the tomb furnishings at St. Venera, for example, as reflective not of social status but of a kind of ideology of modesty. Was it a Pythagorean modesty? It is of some interest that, according to Diodorus (xii, 9, 4,) it was Pythagoras himself who urged the Crotoniates on against Sybaris, leading to its ultimate demise. In any case, these burials are hardly what one would expect of Sybarites, or at least of the elites who would have been likely to make a significant impact in Poseidonia. Lest one think they may have arrived in the city chastened by their recent misfortune, let it be recalled that as late as the second half of the fifth century, the Athenians and other Greek settlers of Thurii, a tolerant lot if ever there was one, came so to revile the Sybarites who had filtered back into the neighborhood for their arrogance that they slew them all, or so Diodorus (xii, 11, 1-3) tells us, and Strabo (vii, 1, 13) confirms it, although in less colorful language. If there was indeed an arrival of refugees from the mother city, it was certainly not a large deputation, as evidenced by the complete lack of reference to it in the ancient literature, while such lesser towns as Laos and Skydros are mentioned by name as havens.

The assessment of the impact of the fall of Sybaris on the other cities of Magna Grecia (or, more to the point, Poseidonia specifically) is, as one might expect, inextricably bound to one's reading of the role of Sybaris before the fall. Sartori (1973: 124-125), for example, is convinced that the city had been at the center of a web of commerce that encompassed the whole of Western Greece, and, indeed, he speaks of a Magna Grecian polity that transcended the interests of the individual cities involved. Naturally, the collapse of the focal point of such a system would be momentous, and Sartori attributes, in one way or another, no less an event than the successful Lucanian conquest of these cities to this fall.

It is true that a certain amount of evidence can be marshalled to promote this point of view, but the crucial point rests on the validity of equating commercial and political dominance in Sybaris's sphere of influence, the one glaring counter example, of course, being Croton, which had sided with Sybaris in the sacking of Siris a few decades earlier but ended as the destroyer of its erstwhile ally. As Sartori himself points out, a fierce independence among the Italiote cities was not only a mechanism of defense against the dominion of any one of them, but a point of pride, a kind of badge of nobility. This was surely not an outgrowth of the fall of Sybaris - indeed, it would be more congenial to see it as the cause - nor does Sartori claim that it was; even so, his characterization of the Sybarite commercial empire leaves little alternative to that implication, or at least to the idea that Sybaris had been the last best hope in South Italy, excepting Sicily, of real cooperation among the *poleis*, and that its fall left the Italiote cities to their isolationist inclinations, easy prey to the better organized, if technologically inferior, Lucanians.

The populations of fifth century Poseidonia

One may well ask, in view of the above debate and our own assessment of the relationship between Greeks and natives in the previous century, whether the archaeological record will sustain this vision of a sort of collective siege of Greeks by Italics, brought to an end, undesired by the Italiotes, only with the internal bickering brought about by the vacuum where Sybaris was. While a detailed evaluation of the situation in the rest of South Italy is beyond the scope of the present study, a look at Poseidonia certainly merits attention.

The record of the fifth century here falls rather neatly into two halves: the first, thriving and productive, culminating in the construction of the second temple of Hera, and the second, strangely *incognito*, characterized more by a lack of news than anything else, not to say that just everything is known about the first fifty years.

We have already noted the increase in population, and saw that its distribution, judging from the cemetery evidence, favored extramural locations, particularly to the South of the city, but not excluding elsewhere. The handful of graves in the North East section represent, after all, an increase of some significance over the lonely caretaker at Fravita, and the South East slopes, it will be recalled, are characterized by a thin but consistent scatter of artifacts dating to at least the fifth century, and covering a broad arc of land. Unless the Italic peoples of the plain were either driven out or completely subjugated, then, there is every indication that cordial relations between Greeks and natives continued unabated at least until the middle of the fifth century. That the local population was by this time more or less completely hellenized may be a fair hypothesis, but the more accurate this picture is, the more difficult it must be to demonstrate, since distinctions in the archaeological remains would, under the circumstances, dwindle to a minimum. But there are some points that strongly support a continuation of the Greek/Italic alloy that was forged in the sixth century Southern Sele Plain.

The clearest is, I think, the celebrated tomb of the diver; the iconographic similarities with the Tomb of Hunting and Fishing in Tarquinia are well known and well accepted. Cerchiai, however, who suggested this analogy, makes the point that the "profound cultural solidarity" demonstrated by these iconographic similarities can be read as a lecture on the larger relationship between the Greek and Etruscan cultures (Cerchai, 1987: 123), missing the smaller, more local implication of the ethnic *mélange* in the Poseidonian territory. But even more convincing is the tomb furniture in twenty or so of the graves at Arcioni, spanning the fifth century, with strong analogs in Etruscan Campania (Pontrandolfo, 1988: 238) - direct, local evidence of non-Greeks not only participating in the affairs of the *polis*, but doing rather well.

At Sta. Venera, too, is found similar evidence: six female graves which, according to Pontrandolfo (1988: 239), are more consistent with the funeral rite of the Italic interior - Vallo di Diano and beyond - than the Greek. It is perhaps noteworthy that the author finds an affinity in the funeral rite with the high valleys of the Bradano and Basento - the first real hint of a trans-Apennine connection, apart, of course, from Sybaris, in the Greek city. Holloway (personal communication) suggests the possibility that these are graves of foreign wives, as at Cairano; this certainly merits consideration, although the distances involved seem rather large. Once again, however, the importance of systematic survey in this area, at this writing underway under the direction of Pedley in the Northern area and Greco to the South, cannot be overstated.

It is, of course, true that these examples represent a fraction of the total graves, and it may be argued that they therefore represent anomalies not to be given much weight - "the exception that proves the rule," to quote a well-known *non sequitur*. But the significance of each of these instances is that for the most part the grave goods parallel those found in the other Poseidonian tombs, at least within the limits of the diversity of the fifth century material as a whole, all of it perfectly good Greek material. In the case of the Sta. Venera graves, the furnishings are altogether typical, but the disposition of the remains offers the key to the Italic affinities. Do we not, in this state of affairs, hear the faint echo of centuries gone by? It will be recalled that there was a similar amalgam of burial rites involving Villanovan and *Fossakultur* elements long before the arrival of Sybarite colonists. In the later context of a largely hellenized population this is just what one might expect. The alternative to an ethnically diverse population would have to be that the Greeks, whose material culture, at least, dominated others to the point of eradication in some cases, included in their burial goods local ceramics, generally of an inferior quality, or altered the way the corpse was laid to rest for no particular reason.

Better, then, to say the Italic influences came packaged in Italic peoples who moved freely throughout the *chora* from the very beginning of the city. Even in the last quarter of the century, when we see the first, if only temporary, decrease in cemetery depositions, interpreted by some as a retrenchment marking the beginning of the hostilities with the Lucanians, the turning inward is exemplified by locally produced grave goods, with only a few imports present, mostly small Attic red-figured *lekythoi* (Pontrandolfo, 1988: 240-242); in other words, there is apparently no great reaching out to the Greek world in response to the advancing Lucanians. The only real sign even of hostility, in fact, comes in the sudden appearance just at the turn of the fourth century of a series of tombs, at Andriuolo, Sta. Venera and Gaudo, in which, for the first time, the male remains are accompanied by armaments. Inasmuch as these may be identified as Lucanian, for they certainly diverge dramatically from previous burials, they doubtless do represent the beginnings of Lucanian dominance of the city. But the numbers of warrior graves one would expect to find as a result of a hostile occupation of a Greek city by Lucanian interlopers are nowhere to be found. Indeed, only a handful of such tombs exist in the fifth century, not even enough to account for a small garrison. Perhaps it is as well to recall that the panhellenic victory over the Lucanians in the great Sele Plain battle around 330 BC, summarized by Pedley (1990: 108-109), only held until the death of the Greek general, Alexander of Molossos, at Pandosia a couple of years later; accounts of Alexander's contract with the Tarantines and his ultimate death can be found in Strabo (vi, 1, 5 and vi, 3, 4).

Another suggestion of the composition of the population in the Plain during this century is found in the Capodifiume Survey. A significant number of the diagnostic coarseware sherds recovered have no apparent analogs in the Greek world (see Appendix). This is not, of course, *prima facie* evidence, but while we do not know what this material is, we have a strong argument for what it is not. There always remains the possibility, not to be minimized, that material of the sort we are discussing - kitchen ware and common household vessels - has simply not been published in sufficient quantity to make identification possible. The fact remains, however, that comparison with numerous Greek and Roman sites in Italy and elsewhere, not to mention medieval sites in and around the plain itself, has left an enormous residue of unidentified material of fabrics similar to securely attributed fifth century material in the study. The most economical explanations are two: 1) that the material is Greek after all, but simply unpublished elsewhere for a lack of interest; or 2) that it is in the local Italic tradition, also unpublished for similar reasons, and continues alongside Greek material. In the face of the publication in recent years of several excellent site reports

outside the Sele Plain including coarseware, I must favor the latter interpretation, although resolution of the dilemma must await further investigation. Within the Poseidonian *chora*, too, coarseware has been included in reports, but these are of a sacred and funerary character, and not the domestic variety with which we are here concerned. One notably excellent source is Cipriani's (1989) report of excavations at the sanctuary at S. Nicola di Albanella, but here, too, the site is not a domestic one.

Commerce

The new monetary standard to which Poseidonia subscribed around 470 is certainly suggestive of a renewed interest in commercial aspects of life, and, indeed, the first half of the century thrived not only in terms of population, as we have seen, but in wealth as well. The ceramic assemblage at the Sta. Venera sanctuary reflects an interest in trade which focuses on, while by no means being limited to, Italy (Menard, 1990: 51-55). Greek trade was represented mostly by decreasing amounts of unfigured Attic black-glazed pottery. Noteworthy among Italic wares are those with Campanian Etruscan connections; it will be recalled that this area is precisely the one reflected in the Italic grave goods of the Arcioni *necropolis*. Menard notes that Paestan ware begins turning up with more regularity at Pontecagnano at about this time as well. Finally, Daunian ceramics were also noted at the sanctuary; conversely, it is interesting to note that Greek pottery only begins to appear in numbers in the Vallo di Diano and other interior centers during this century (de la Genière, 1968: 215; Greco, 1981: 64). Caution must be exercised, however, since the valley gives not only onto Poseidonia, but Elea as well.

A measure of the prosperity of the first half of the century is the construction of the second temple of Hera at just about the middle of the century. Steadfastly Doric, although not utterly shorn of Ionic influence (consider, for example, the twenty-four-fluted exterior columns, as opposed to the normal twenty in the Doric order), the temple is difficult to interpret as anything but the realization of a Greek ethnic revival. After all, just eighteen years or so before its estimated date of completion, the *stadion* at the seventy-eighth Olympiad was won by a Poseidonian named Parmenides (Diodorus xi, 65, 1); Berve and Gruben (1963: 413-415) suggest that this was an occasion for the architect to visit Olympia and examine the temple of Zeus, the plan of which is remarkably similar to that of Hera II at Poseidonia.

This is certainly an attractive idea, especially in view of the other events that were occupying the Greek mainland at the time. Diodorus (xi, 65, 2-5) recounts the destruction of Mycenae in that year by Argos; the point of contention was control over the Argive *Heraion*. Considering the dedication of the Sele *Heraion* specifically to the Argive Hera, one can easily imagine this combination of events coming together to engender a sort of genealogical fervor which culminates in the construction of an uncompromisingly Doric temple. The fact that there were, after all, a few small compromises of an Ionic nature affects this argument not at all.

But there is one glaring but often overlooked compromise: the total lack of sculptural decoration. Pedley (1990: 81-84) notes that there is no evidence, in the form of cuttings for clamps, for the attachment of sculptures to either the floor or the back of the pediment, and that there is no trace of metopal sculpture anywhere near Hera II. He concludes that the pediment and metopes were to remain undecorated.

Everything else about this temple bespeaks a kind of conservative elegance: the optical refinements of the stylobate, the angle contraction in the corners, even the neck and echinus decorations on the columns of the peristyle. But we know that the unattractive travertine of which this temple and the others was built was subsequently stuccoed and painted. It is entirely possible that the metopal and pedimental decorations were realized in fresco; further, such decoration in the context of a revival of Greek ethnic pride, on a temple designed to recall the ultimate motherland, would only have been acceptable to an architect and a people with an equally strong Etruscan tradition.

The end of the fifth century and Greek Poseidonia

Menard (1990: 52-53) notes that at the Sta. Venera sanctuary there is a marked drop in the quantity of material in general in the second half of the fifth century, and especially of imports. It will be recalled that we find a similar decline in the number of graves in the cemeteries of the period. In both cases, the decline begins in mid-century, but is most obvious in the last quarter. It was noted above that warrior graves, interpreted as Lucanian, also begin appearing at about this time.

The Lucanians were the regional manifestation of the Samnites; it is generally assumed that, being a rather warlike group, that they wrested control of Poseidonia from the Greeks by force. We have seen, however, overwhelming evidence of a policy of peaceful assimilation on the part of those Greeks.

Obviously, the apparent decline in both population and commerce at the end of the fifth century can be interpreted as the result of military conquest, but there are no other, direct, signs of this in Poseidonia, with the possible exception of the fiery devastation at the Sele *Heraion* (Tocco Sciarelli *et all.*, 1988: 387). Although the authors attribute this event to the

arrival of the Lucanians, it remains unexplained why the sanctuary would have been intentionally burned, while the city remained intact. The *Heraion* was, after all, sacred to the Lucanians, too, in subsequent years.

An alternative explanation is possible. The decline at the end of the fifth century may have been attributable to another cause, either related or unrelated to the destruction at the Sele *Heraion*. That the city was thriving in the first half of the century, when Aegean Greece was successively besieged by the Persians, underscores the argument that direct long-range commerce from the East had ceased to play an important part in Poseidonian affairs for some time. This is especially significant given the harsh punishment doled out to Miletos by the Persians in 494 following the Ionian revolt (Hammond, 1986: 207-209), which would surely have registered at Poseidonia, had this not been the case. But it was the second half of the century, and especially the last quarter, that saw the decline of Pontecagnano as a commercial node, and the rise of Fratte following the defeat of the Etruscan fleet off Cumae. Although this last event had no apparent immediate effect on Pontecagnano, it marks the beginning of its decline, in direct contrast (competition?) with the rise of Fratte. The lines of causation here are obscure, but we have continually argued for close links between Poseidonia and Pontecagnano on several levels; it is a justifiable inference that the problems of the two cities towards the end of the fifth century are related.

Whatever the case, when the Lucanians arrived in the valley, they may have been welcomed by the diminished population as a fresh source of much-needed humanity. There is certainly every sign of the survival of Greek culture after the Lucanian takeover; the ceramic workshops of the Paestan style, for example, maintained an essentially Greek identity. The best examples of this are Asteas and Python, the two great Paestan vase painters of the fourth century.

Only further intensive research in the field, with this particular problem in mind, can resolve it. Whatever the true nature of the Lucanian arrival, it signalled two things: the practical end of the Greek city, melting pot though it was, and an unprecedented explosion in not only population, but every aspect of the city and its territory. This alone strongly suggests that whatever caused declining conditions before their arrival, it was of a cultural, and not natural, origin.

Chapter 6
SUMMARY AND CONCLUSION

This study of the Greek city of Poseidonia and its *chora* begins with a definition of the physiographic and cultural environment into which the Greeks were thrust; this is true not only in a formal sense, in the way that the chapters are arranged, but in a conceptual sense as well. The emphasis throughout is on the idea of landscape, in the sense that includes the land itself, with all of its physical characteristics, and all of the people on it and their works. It is a theme of this study that the character of this place as a border area continued after the arrival of the Sybarite colonists and played a significant role in the evolution of their city. Indeed, it is not too strong a contention that it was this very aspect of the Sele Plain that drew the settlers there in the first place, although from one point of view the result was perhaps disappointing, given that Poseidonian participation in the great trade route soon waned.

In terms of the physical matrix, the Sele Plain has undergone several significant changes in the two dozen or so centuries since the period with which we are concerned. The Sele River, which roughly bisects it, is also the primary source of the materials of which it is composed and of the dynamics which shaped these materials, the other principal motivators being a series of seismically active faults and the Tyrrhenian Sea.

At roughly the turn of the sixth century BC, when the city of Poseidonia was founded, much of the plain was as it is today. A shallow arc from the city itself through a point about six kilometers upriver of the present Sele mouth and ending at the mouth of the Tusciano marks the Western boundary of this stable zone; it is of firmly Pleistocene origin. West of this line, however, there have been major changes. The area has been subject not only to the effects of nearby Vesuvius, which extended its ashfall there in AD 79, but to a long series of bradyseismic activities which caused the alternate subsidence and uplift of the plain; the effect inland was minimal, but at the shoreline it was dramatic. There remains a debate about the extent and chronology of this activity, and of the measurable effects, but a consensus is growing that the present shoreline is considerably seaward of its position in antiquity, and that the present barrier dune, the Sterpina ridge, did not form until Roman times. The Laura dune, then, very

nearly represents the shoreline in about 600 BC, and the mouth of the Sele opened into a wide estuary, possibly extending as far as the ancient sanctuary of Hera on the banks of the river. This reconstruction is relatively secure, but the situation directly seaward of the ancient city itself is less so. The evidence there is ambiguous, and there remains a possibility that a harbor of some sort was a feature in antiquity; the paved road leading towards the sea from the Porta Marina supports this notion, for there would otherwise be little reason to expend so much effort on a roadway.

South of the city, the picture is unclear, due to both ancient and recent activities, but the presence of travertines that span the entire chronology of the area strongly suggests that it was a natural floodplain for the Capodifiume and its distributaries; the relatively unstudied character of this area may well be the key to the ultimate development of malarial conditions in the plain in late antiquity. It was, however, largely dry and stable in Archaic times, for the Greeks quarried travertine for their temples there.

As far as the indigenous cultures that awaited the Greeks are concerned, we find only a minimal trace of the much-discussed Oenotrians. The cultural *mélange* in the plain at the turn of the sixth century BC was, to all intents and purposes, dominated by the Etruscans at Pontecagnano, to the North of the Sele River. These people had material affinity, at least, to the Etruscans of Veii, and appeared in the plain during Villanovan times; in time they developed considerable hegemony not only over the native *Fossakultur* of the Northern plain, but also what was perhaps an indigenously developed Villanovan settlement South of the river, represented - ambiguously, to be sure - by the burials at the Capodifiume springs. Surely the strong Protovillanovan component in the Southern plain, without counterpart in the North, is significant in this regard.

In any case, by the time we see the first sign of the Sybarites who would eventually found Poseidonia, the Pontecagnano Etruscans were firmly entrenched, having already had commerce with the Euboean cities further up the Tyrrhenian coast. To establish a large Greek city just across the river from them without their collaboration would have been extremely difficult, especially since their continued good graces would have been central to the trade which at least partially motivated the Greek settlement there.

Men of Sybaris, Strabo tells us, built a fortification on the sea and subsequently moved to a more stable location and founded the city of Poseidonia. There is no record of hostility, either in the pages of the ancient literature or in the archaeological record; there is, however, significant evidence of cooperation, both as the city developed, and at its birth. There is the sanctuary of Hera on the Sele River, attributed by ancient writers to Jason, and with some evidence of having been a sacred place to the indigenous population, which became the boundary marker for the Greek *chora*. More to the point, there is the bronze plaque from Olympia, which was inscribed in perpetual friendship between Sybaris and all its allies on the one hand and a people called the *Serdaioi* on the other, witnessed not only by Zeus and Apollo and all the other gods, but by "the city Poseidonia." Van Effenterre argues convincingly that Poseidonia is called to witness because it was the object of the treaty; in other words, that the document represents a commemorative foundation treaty. In the light of this interpretation, there can be only one group to identify as the *Serdaioi*, and that is the Pontecagnano Etruscans, cousins to the "Sardians" of Veii. Poseidonia, then, was born with at least the good will, if not the active participation, of the Etruscans who lived on the Northern Sele Plain and controlled the whole of it until the Greeks arrived.

In the ensuing century, too, we find continuing evidence of this neighborliness, in the waning reliance on Sybaris and the grand trade route, in the monetary standard, in subtle stylistic aspects of the two great sixth century temples and, most of all, in the distribution of the population in the countryside. Those who would see sixth-century Poseidonia as a citadel are perhaps dazzled by the great fortification walls that still stand today, forgetting that these date mostly to Lucanian and Roman times, the earliest attributed, and not without controversy, to no earlier than the fifth century.

The distribution of sixth century cemeteries and sanctuaries in the surrounding countryside, insofar as we know them to date, is compatible with a lightly dispersed Greek population outside the walls of the city, and this has been used as an argument in favor of a kind of siege mentality; once proper account is taken for agricultural activities, however, a different interpretation emerges. There must have been large tracts of cultivated land in ancient times, if not to generate commerce, for there is little evidence of extensive agricultural export at Poseidonia, then at least to simply feed the population. If few sites of a domestic nature have been found in the Poseidonian *chora*, it may be largely because no one has seriously looked for them. It is no great insight that the archaeology of the past was concerned with cemeteries and sanctuaries, with very little interest in domestic sites, with their coarse kitchen ware undecorated with gallant warriors in poignant moments. Only recently has there been a focus on these matters.

The Capodifiume survey has recovered a sufficient quantity of fine domestic and transport pottery to allow a tentative chronology of the use of that area, but the great majority of

the pottery recovered is the unstudied coarseware; only a small percentage of this has direct analogs in the Greek world, in spite of the fact that much of the fine pottery is identifiably Greek. This is no doubt partly due to a similar lack of interest in coarseware in the Aegean, but we have several fine sources for comparison, such as in the Athenian Agora. Another interpretation is that the distribution corroborates the close relationship between Greeks and Italics in the Sele Plain in the sixth century.

If the sixth century may be characterized as one of prosperity and harmony with native populations, then the first half of the fifth certainly continues this trend, with a mini-explosion in the overall population, dwarfed, to be sure, by the Lucanian fourth century. There are those who see the influence of Sybarite immigrants in this situation, but Sybarites are demonstrably absent from Poseidonian affairs, even, or perhaps especially, after the destruction of their city around 510 BC. The temple of Athena, sometimes attributed to their influence, bears the greatest signs of all the temples of influence from more immediate neighbors, and would in any case be an unlikely project for refugees following so hard on the heels of their tragedy at home; the underground *sacello* at the Western edge of the agora, the supposed cenotaph of the Sybarite *oikist*, is still the subject of controversy regarding its identification. The strangely impoverished cemetery at Ponte di Ferro may well be the only trace of refugees from the ravaged mother city in Poseidonia.

Other cemeteries exhibit evidence of the increasing integration, if not assimilation, of locally indigenous peoples into the population of the Greek city; all of the burials of this period are of an almost ascetic modesty, not what would be expected of the irrepressibly flamboyant Sybarites. Further afield, there is a sanctuary to the North East dedicated to Demeter, which most uncharacteristically includes men in its cult, another instance of influence from Etruscan neighbors.

The Capodifiume survey continues to reinforce the impressions gained from other sources. There is a filling in of occupation during this period; the pottery distribution is similar to that of the previous century, but there is more of it. A significant percentage of the identifiable ware dates, however, to the first half of the century, or to the very end, rather than to the second half *per se*. This signals a decline that is mirrored in the cemeteries and at the Sta. Venera sanctuary, where a similar drop in imports as well as domestic production has been noted. The reasons for the decline are unknown; perhaps environmental factors were at play, with the Sele estuary beginning to silt in, or changes in the shoreline at the city causing difficulties. Certainly, events in neighboring Campania were increasingly marginalizing Pontecagnano by this time, and this must have had an effect on its Greek neighbor. In any case, by the end of the century, some Lucanian burials appear, distinct in their military grave furnishings.

The evidence is convincing that the Lucanians, far from wresting a thriving city from the control of its Greek founders, took over and breathed life into a city that was very near to having spent its vitality. Poseidonia as a Greek city belongs to the Archaic period; by Classical times it was in decline, and was only rehabilitated, albeit in dramatic fashion, by the incursion of Lucanians, analogous in microcosm to a pattern that was seen over and over in ancient times: the barbarian revitalization of a dying culture.

Although Poseidonia retained a large measure of its Greek flavor under Lucanian rule, there was a distinct change of character. If the Poseidonian Greeks thrived in a synthesis of complementary cultures, the Lucanians, although themselves abundantly hellenized, were more completely the masters of their domain, if for no other reason than their enormous advantage in numbers.

It would, of course, be ludicrous to hold that Greeks and natives had been equal partners in the evolution of Italiote society at Poseidonia; there can be no question that the city was overwhelmingly Greek, and that, furthermore, the very natives under discussion were hellenized to a greater or lesser extent over time. The point is simply that natives participated in that development, and that they did so with the general approval and good will of the Greek colonists, and that they contributed some of the elements in the complex that came to be distinguishable as, ultimately, Paestan, subsumed rather than supervened by the Lucanians. Although this is not a startlingly new idea, neither the validity of the interpretation nor the degree to which it may have been the case have been subjected to the kind of scrutiny appropriate for the testing of a hypothesis. It is hoped that by marshalling the evidence from diverse sources which have up to now remained unsynthesized, this study has provided a secure foundation for the hypothesis.

Appendix:
CAPODIFIUME SURVEY INVENTORY

Introduction

The material in the inventory has been divided into chronological groups, then further into broad types (*e. g.*, black gloss, impasto, etc.). Each of these is assigned to a chronological category on the basis of direct, or at least very strong, analogs in the literature; probable dates for artifacts without such analogs are based on overall similarity with securely dated artifacts in terms of paste, inclusions, surface treatment and similar criteria. Diagnostics such as rims, feet and handles that cannot be dated, or can be dated only in very broad terms, are treated separately.

Ceramic pastes are described on the basis of four characteristics: color, hardness, texture and inclusions. The color is given as a Munsell color chart number; this should not be read as an absolute value, since the publishers of the charts themselves note that a perfect match is found less than one percent of the time, and individuals vary in their ability to sense color differences. It has been my own experience over the years that the greatest individual variation is in the hue readings, that is, in the selection of the right page. Therefore, in matching paste colors described by others, a variation of one page (*e. g.*, between 5YR and 7.5YR) is acceptable. The value and chroma, similarly, may vary by one increment.

Hardness, as defined in this study, was determined by scraping a fingernail on the artifact. Three levels of hardness were defined. Soft: fingernail removed material; medium: fingernail marked but did not remove material; and hard: material removed fingernail. It should be noted that hardness does not necessarily refer to the original hardness of the paste, which can be altered over time by a number of post-depositional factors; a few objects in the inventory even vary in their hardness from one spot on the piece to the next.

The remaining two characteristics, texture and inclusions, are closely related; they are necessarily more subjectively described than the first two characteristics, given the limitations of working in the field. It is assumed that such terms as fine, coarse, gritty and so on will sufficiently convey the texture. Inclusions are identified where possible (on a macroscopic level) and described where not. Although it is

clear that in some cases, where the inclusions do not occur naturally in the clay (*e. g.*, grog or tephra), they were intentionally added as temper, no attempt is made to distinguish between temper and naturally or accidentally occurring inclusions.

In all, some 750 artifacts were recovered during the survey; of these, 294 are described below comprising all of the material with diagnostic characteristics; the remainder were labelled and stored at the *Museo di Paestum* along with the diagnostics, but lacked sufficiently distinctive features to warrant inclusion in this inventory.

All items were washed and labelled with a field collection number composed of the survey unit number followed by an ordinal number. These collection numbers appear below in parentheses immediately following the inventory number. Abbreviations used in the inventory are as follows: WT = wall thickness; D = the diameter of the vessel at the point relevant to the item described (*i. e.*, at the orifice for rims, the foot for bases or the point of contact for body fragments, where such measurement is possible). Centuries BC are expressed as roman numerals; centuries AD as arabic numerals.

Part 1: DATED MATERIAL

Prehistoric and Protohistoric material

Pottery

It should be noted that in addition to the items described in this section 53 impasto body sherds with no particular distinguishing characteristics were recovered from various collection units. Although the majority of these are probably prehistoric, some impasto fabrics remained in use throughout antiquity and beyond.

1. (18-3) Figs. 23,55. **Open form**. Rim fragment. WT=1.3 cm. Coarse hard impasto with inclusions of mica, grog and crushed white lithics; black paste slipped on the exterior with 10YR 5/3 brown. Diameter not measurable, but rather large. Vertical rim notched at the top. Neolithic?

2. (9-8) Fig. 47. **Open form**. Body fragment, near rim. WT=.86 cm. D=21 cm. Coarse hard impasto with inclusions of mica and grog. Paddled exterior and half of core is 2.5YR 4/6 brownish red, interior and the rest of the core is black. Neolithic.

3. (2-21). Body fragment. WT=1.1 cm. D=24 cm. Coarse hard impasto with inclusions of mica, sand and grog. Paddled and smoothed exterior is 5YR 6/3 reddish brown, interior is 2.5YR 4/6 red; the core is 2.5YR 5/2 weak red. There is pre-depositional fire clouding on the exterior. Neolithic.

4. (38-21). Body fragment. WT=1.1 cm. D>20 cm. Coarse hard impasto with inclusions of mica and sand. Scant traces of a paddled exterior present; paste is 2.5YR 3/6 dark red. Neolithic.

5. (16-29) Figs. 23, 54. **Jug**? Rim fragment. WT=1 cm. D=4 cm. Medium coarse hard impasto with inclusions of brown and scant white lithics, undifferentiated surfaces. Paste is 10R 4/6 deep red. Rim is everted, tapering to a fine edge. The fabric is Bronze Age, but not more finely datable. Bronze Age.

6. (49-30) Figs. 23, 6. **Closed form**. Rim fragment. WT=1.1 cm. D=23 cm. Coarse hard impasto with inclusions of mica, sand, grog and scant limestone, undifferentiated surfaces. Paste is 2.5YR 6/6 light red, with a grey core. Inslanting rim with a thickened and slightly everted lip. *Cf.* Pancrazzi, 1979: Fig. 109:4. Bronze Age.

7. (7-70) Figs. 23, 46. **Plate/cover**. Rim fragment. WT=.5 cm. D=22 cm. Medium coarse hard impasto with inclusions of mica, sand and grog. Exterior and top .75 cm of interior is 5YR 4/3.5 reddish brown, remainder of interior is 5YR 4/1 dark grey; the core is black. Outslanting rim tapering slightly the last centimeter, otherwise undifferentiated. *Cf.* Pancrazzi, 1979: Fig. 116:2; identified as cover. Protoapennine.

8. (7-71) Figs. 23, 46. **Situla**. Rim fragment. WT=1 cm. D=39 cm. Coarse hard impasto with inclusions of mica, sand, grog and grey, brown and black lithics. Paste is 5YR 5/4 reddish brown, with a dark grey core. Vertical rim with a finger-impressed raised cordon 1.5 cm below slightly tapering lip. *Cf.* Pancrazzi, 1979: Fig 40.16 for the decoration. Bronze Age.

9. (7-34) Figs. 23, 46. Lug handle. Approximate D=23 cm. Very coarse hard impasto with numerous inclusions of mica, sand and grog. Paste is variable, ranging from 2.5YR 5/8 red to 2.5YR 6/4 light reddish brown. Piece is complete and unbroken, indicating poor attachment to the vessel; it consists of an approximately 1.5 cm thick cordon with finger impressions. There is a slight curvature, allowing an estimate of the outside diameter of the vessel. *Cf.* number 8, above. Bronze Age.

10. (11-15) Figs. 23, 50. Body fragment, with raised finger-impressed cordon. Medium coarse very hard impasto, with inclusions of mica and sand. *Cf.* number 8, above. Bronze Age.

11 (49-5) Figs. 23, 61. Body fragment, with raised incised cordon. WT=.8 cm. D=20 cm. Very coarse very hard impasto with inclusions of mica, sand and lithics. The raised cordon is incised with two diagonal lines. This decoration has no direct analogs; date assigned on the basis of the fabric. Bronze Age.

12. (17-16). Body fragment. WT=1.2 cm. D>15 cm. Hard coarse impasto with inclusions of mica, grog and scant sand. Paste is 5YR 3/3 dark reddish brown with a slightly darker core. Date assigned on the basis of the fabric. Bronze Age.

Lithics

13. (2-9). Chert fragment. Opaque 10R 4/6 red with a band of translucent 7.5YR 5/4 brown. Some signs of working. Prehistoric.

14. (30-13). Chert fragment. Translucent 2.5YR 3/6 dark red. Some signs of working. Prehistoric.

15. (38-5). Flint fragment. Opaque 5YR 3/1 very dark grey. No apparent signs of working. Prehistoric.

16. (40-5). Flint fragment. Opaque 2.5YR 3/0 very dark grey, cortex partially visible. No apparent signs of working. Prehistoric.

17. (40-6). Flint fragment. Opaque 2.5YR 3/4 dark reddish brown. No apparent signs of working. Prehistoric.

18. (44-2). Chert fragment. Translucent 7.5YR 4/6 brown. No apparent signs of working. Prehistoric.

19. (47-1). Chert fragment. Mottled semi-opaque 5YR 5/4 reddish brown. No apparent signs of working. Prehistoric.

20. (7-42) Fig. 24. **Flint core**. Opaque 10YR 2/2 very dark brown with traces of cortex on one surface. Prehistoric.

21. (40-7). **Flint core**. Opaque 2.5YR 3/4 dark reddish brown, with one rounded surface suggesting riverine origin. Signs of deliberate flaking. Prehistoric.

22. (48-4). **Flint core**. Opaque 5YR 3/4 dark reddish brown. Signs of deliberate flaking. Prehistoric.

23. (7-38) Fig. 24. **Flint scraper**. Opaque 10YR 2/2 very dark brown. Prehistoric.

24. (7-39) Fig. 24. **Flint blade**. Same material as number 23 above. Approximately .5 cm thick, with a clear fracture plane on each of two parallel surfaces. Edges worked. Prehistoric.

25. (7-40) Figs. 24, 46. **Chert blade**. Translucent 10YR 4/6 dark yellowish brown with slightly lighter and darker alternating bands. Edges worked. Neolithic/Eneolithic.

26. (7-41) Fig. 24. **Chert flake blade**. Translucent mottled 2.5YR 5/4 reddish brown, slightly rough texture. Edges worked. Prehistoric.

27. (16-20) Figs. 24, 54. **Chert flake blade**. Translucent 10YR 4/4 dark yellowish brown. Trapezoidal cross-section, edges worked. Neolithic/Eneolithic.

28. (30-11) Figs. 24, 57. **Chert flake blade**. Translucent 7.5YR 6/6 yellowish brown. Triangular cross-section, edges worked. Neolithic/Eneolithic.

29. (49-6) Fig. 24. **Chert flake blade**. Semi-translucent 10YR 4/6 dark yellowish brown. Triangular cross-section, edges worked. Neolithic/Eneolithic.

Other material

30. (1-16). Daub. Oxidized clay lump, 2.5YR 5/8 red with numerous inclusions. Amorphous with one long impression, as of a stick. Apparently from a burned wattle-and-daub structure. Prehistoric.

Archaic material

Much of the material included in this section dates from the cusp between Archaic and Classical, that is, the end of the VI century to the beginning of the V century; some of the span actually includes more of the Classical period than the Archaic. However, the material must be placed in one category or the other; for this purpose, the earliest date is used.

Black gloss ware

31. (15-12) Figs. 25, 53. **Skyphos**. Foot fragment. WT=.35 cm. D=8 cm. Fine hard levigated clay, 5YR 5/4 reddish brown with no inclusions. Fine lustrous black gloss on interior and tapering ring foot; lower part of body and underside of base reserved, with a slip of 10R 6/6 light red. Attic skyphos in the Corinthian style. *Cf.* Sparkes and Talcott, 1970: Fig. 259:318; Lattanza, 1992: Fig. 563:558. Late VI - early V century.

32. (49-18) Figs. 25, 61. **Cup-skyphos**. Foot fragment. WT=.46 cm. D=10 cm. Fine soft levigated clay with mica traces, 5YR 6/6 reddish yellow. Dullish black gloss on interior and exterior except on sides and bottom of the laterally flattened ring foot, which are reserved, with traces of a slip of 10R 5/8 red. The vessel is slightly deformed, with grey areas in the core, indicating poor firing. *Cf.* Menard, 1990: Fig. 30:468. Late VI - early V century.

33. (49-10) Figs. 25, 61. **Skyphos**. Foot fragment. WT=.54 cm. D=5 cm. Fine soft levigated clay with mica traces, 5YR 6/4 light reddish brown, with a slightly lighter core. Traces of diluted black gloss, ranging from 2.5YR 3/2 to 3/4 reddish brown, on the upper and lower surfaces of the ring foot. The diameter of the foot is very small (5 cm). For the shape, see number 31 above. Late VI - early V century.

34. (15-5) Figs. 25, 53. **Cup-Skyphos**. Rim fragment. WT=.5 cm. D=16 cm. Fine soft levigated clay with mica traces, 2.5YR 6/6 light red. Black gloss on exterior and interior, with a narrow reserved band just below the lip on the interior. Vertical rim slightly everted, otherwise undifferentiated. *Cf.* Cipriani, 1989: Fig. 11:D1. Mid VI - beginning V century.

35. (11-4) Figs. 25, 49. **Kylix**. Rim fragment. WT=.44 cm. D=10 cm. Fine soft levigated clay with mica traces, 5YR 6/6 reddish yellow. Black gloss on interior, somewhat streaky and diluted to 2.5YR 4/4 reddish brown just below lip. Top 1.5 cm of exterior reserved. *Cf.* Greco and Pontrandolfo, 1990: Fig. 55:7 (number 8 in text). VI - V century.

36. (15-9) Figs. 25, 53. **Ionic cup**. Rim fragment. WT=.3 cm. D=17 cm. Fine semi-soft levigated clay with mica traces, 5YR 7/6 reddish yellow. Black gloss on interior and top of lip, with a narrow reserved band on the interior at the point of inflection; exterior reserved. Everted rim with a slight thickening of the wall between lip and point of inflection. *Cf.* Lattanza, 1992: Figs. 230, 252:246-247; Menard, 1990: Fig. 49:585. Mid - late VI century.

37. (49-14) Figs. 25, 61. **Kylix**. Foot. D=7 cm. Fine soft levigated clay with mica traces and occasional finely ground grog, 5YR 6/6 reddish yellow. Traces of black gloss on exterior of the conical foot; underside reserved. Ionic kylix, form B2. *Cf.* Greco and Theodorescu, 1983, Fig. 59:1-2; Greco and Theodorescu, 1987: Fig. 88:786. 580 - 540 BC.

38. (15-10) Figs. 25, 53. **Stemmed bowl**. Rim fragment. WT=.4 cm. D=9 cm. Very fine very hard levigated clay with scant mica traces, 10R 6/6 light red, grayish core at thickest part of lip. Lustrous black gloss on all surfaces. Outslanting slightly inverted rim with the lip forming a thickened ring. Extremely fine fabric. *Cf.* Menard, 1990: Fig. 31:472. Ca. 500 BC.

Coarse ware

39. (16-21) Figs. 25, 54. **Oinochoe**. Ear. Medium coarse clay with inclusions of mica, grog and frequent sand, 5YR 4/6 reddish brown, with a black core. Gritty texture. Oinochoe "ears" are a feature of the finer Etruscan ware; no other coarse ware examples were encountered. Late VII - VI century.

40. (11-46) Figs. 25, 50. **Amphora**. Rim fragment. WT=1 cm. D=10 cm. Fine hard levigated clay with large prominent brown and black lithic inclusions, 7.5YR 7/4 pinkish buff. Vertical rim with prominent everted lip. Koehler type A Corinthian transport amphora. *Cf.* Fiammenghi, 1985: Fig. 9; d'Andria, 1977: Fig. 10. Late VII - early VI century.

41. (43-5) Fig. 25. **Amphora**. Rim fragment. D=18 cm. Coarse hard clay with inclusions of mica, grog and lithics, 5YR 7/6 reddish yellow. Strongly everted thickened rim, triangular cross-section. Koehler type B Corinthian transport amphora, but locally made. *Cf.* Koehler, 1978: Fig. 2b. End VI century.

42. (30-23) Figs. 25, 57. **Amphora**. Rim fragment. WT=.6 cm. D=13 cm. Hard coarse clay with inclusions of mica, grog and sand, 2.5YR 5/6 red with slightly darker core. Everted thickened rim, cross-section rounded triangle; slightly raised narrow cordon just below thickened section of rim. Chiote transport amphora. *Cf.* Fiammenghi, 1985: Fig. 9:56; Cipriani, 1989: Fig. 17:H58. Cipriani dates it to the first half V century, but see di Sandro, 1981: Fig. 1. Late VI - early V century.

43. (11-1) Figs. 25, 50. **Amphora**. Rim Fragment. WT=.6 cm. D=12 cm. Semi-coarse hard clay with inclusions of mica and sand, 10R 5/8 red, with post-depositional calcareous encrustations on the surfaces. Everted thickened rim, cross-section rounded triangle. Chiote transport amphora. *Cf.* number 42 above. Late VI - early V century.

44. (50-2). **Olla**. Rim fragment. WT=.7 cm. Coarse hard clay with mica and sand inclusions, 5YR 4/6 yellowish red. Outslanting rim thickened to a squarish cross-section in the upper 1 cm. Fragment too small to measure diameter. *Cf.* Pancrazzi, 1979: Fig. 40:5. VI century.

45. (44-7) Figs. 26, 60. **Mortar**? Rim fragment. WT=1 cm. D=30 cm. Coarse medium soft clay with inclusions of mica, grog and numerous lithics, 2.5YR 5/8 red with lighter core. Outslanting thickened rim, cross-section rounded triangle with a slight inversion at the lip. *Cf.* Adamesteanu, 1983: Fig. 136:387. VI century.

46. (50-13). **Olla**? Foot fragment. D=10 cm. Semi-fine soft clay with inclusions of mica, grog and crushed quartz, 5YR 6/6 reddish yellow. Flattened ring foot, trapezoidal in cross-section. *Cf.* Bagnasco, 1992: Fig. XLVI:48. Late VI - ?

47. (41-7) Figs. 26, 59. **Lamp**. Nozzle fragment. WT=.5 cm. Semi-coarse hard clay with mica traces and quartz sand inclusions, 5YR 5/6 yellowish red with traces of a slip of 5YR 4/1 dark grey. Lamp with unbridged nozzle. *Cf.* Broneer, 1977: Pl. 14.3. VI century.

48. (15-19) Figs. 26, 53. **Kalypter**. Rim fragment. WT=1.7 cm. D=22 cm. Coarse hard clay with sand, grog and lithic inclusions, 2.5YR 5/8 red, with (post-depositional?) calcareous encrustations. This is a Sicilian variant of a Laconian style tile cover. *Cf.* Orlandos, 1966: Fig. 56z. VI century.

Classical material

Black gloss ware

49. (49-13) Fig. 61. **Lekythos**. Body fragment, just above foot. WT=1.2 cm. Fine semi-hard levigated clay with scant mica traces, 5YR 7/6 beige. Traces of diluted brownish black gloss on interior and exterior. Lower portion of the expanding body; foot missing. *Cf.* Menard, 1990: Fig 20.398-399. First half VI century.

50. (38-3) Figs. 26, 58. **Skyphos**. Rim fragment with handle attachment. WT=.3 cm. D=14 cm. Fine soft levigated clay with scant mica traces, 5YR 6/4 light reddish brown. Vertical rim, slightly tapering and everted at lip; horizontal handle attached just below lip. *Cf.* Menard, 1990: Fig. 25:436. End V - beginning IV century.

51. (13-9) Figs. 26, 52. **Cup**. Rim fragment with handle attachment. WT=.44 cm. D=10 cm. Fine levigated clay, hardness varying from soft to hard, with frequent tiny mica inclusions, 5YR 5/6 yellowish red. Vertical rim, slightly thickened at lip, which is bevelled slightly inward; horizontal handle attached just below lip. *Cf.* Greco and Pontrandolfo, 1990: Fig. 34:9 and Fig. 31:4. V - IV century.

52. (13-12) Figs. 26, 52. **Cup**. Rim Fragment. WT=.44 cm. D=10 cm. Another fragment of the same vessel as number 51 above. V - IV century.

53. (31-4) Fig. 58. **Cup**. Rim fragment with handle attachment. WT=.48 cm. D=10 cm. Fine soft levigated clay with scant mica traces, 5YR 4/6 light reddish brown. Shape same as numbers 51 and 52 above. V - IV century.

54. (4-28) Figs. 26, 43. **Cup**. Body fragment, just below rim, with handle attachment. WT=.5 cm. D=10 cm. Fine levigated clay, hardness varying from soft to hard, with mica traces, 2.5YR 6/6 light red. Part of slightly outslanting wall, just below lip, with horizontal handle attached. *Cf.* numbers 51-53 above. V - IV century?

55. (11-24) Figs. 26, 49. **Skyphos**. Foot fragment. D= 6 cm. Fine soft levigated clay with mica traces, 5YR 6/6 light red. Black gloss on interior and exterior, bottom of vessel, excluding the foot, reserved, with a red slip. Part of horizontally flattened ring foot. *Cf.* Menard, 1990: Fig. 26:439-440. Mid V century.

56. (30-5) Figs. 26, 57. **Skyphos**. Foot fragment. WT=.35 cm. D=8 cm. Fine soft levigated clay with mica traces, 2.5YR 5/8 red. Black gloss on interior, traces on exterior. Horizontally flattened ring foot. *Cf.* d'Ambrosio and de Caro, 1990: Fig. 43:FC696. V - IV century.

57. (13-1) Fig. 52. **Skyphos**. Foot fragment. WT=.4 cm. D=6 cm. Fine medium-soft levigated clay with very faint mica traces, 2.5YR 5/6 red. Scant traces of black gloss on all finished surfaces. *Cf.* number 56 above. V - IV century.

58. (39-5) Fig. 26. **Cup**? Handle fragment. Fine medium-soft levigated clay with faint mica traces, 5YR 6/6 reddish yellow. Scant traces of black gloss on surfaces. Horseshoe-shaped handle with a circular cross-section, 1 cm thick. For a general discussion of the evolution of handles, see Sparkes and Talcott, 1970: 11. V century?

59. (7-60) Figs. 26, 44. **Kylix**. Foot fragment. WT=1 cm. D=11 cm. Fine soft levigated clay with mica traces, 5YR 6/6 light red. Traces of black gloss on upper surface of the inflected foot. Type C kylix. Cf. Greco and Pontrandolfo, 1990: Fig. 395:2. Early V century.

60. (11-28) Figs. 26, 49. **Kylix**. Handle fragment. Very fine hard levigated clay, no inclusions, 5YR 4/1 dark grey. Very scant traces of black gloss. Upward-turning horizontal handle with a circular cross-section, ca. .8 cm thick. See Sparkes and Talcott, 1970: 11. V century?

61. (15-11) Figs. 26, 53. **Kylix**. Handle fragment. Fine soft levigated clay with mica traces, 5YR 5/2 reddish grey. Black gloss on vessel interior and handle; inner part of handle reserved. Upward-turning horizontal handle with a circular cross-section, ca. 1.3 cm thick. V - IV century?

62. (45-10). **Kylix**. Handle fragment. Fine soft levigated clay with mica traces and occasional very finely ground grog, 2.5YR6/6 light red. Similar to number 61 above. V - IV century?

Coarse ware

63. (50-18). **Amphora**. Rim fragment. D=18 cm. Coarse hard clay with inclusions of mica, quartz sand, other sand and grog, 2.5YR 6/8 light red, with an ample core of light grey. Vertical rim, half-almond shaped in cross-section. Cf. Bagnasco, 1992: Fig. LXI:197. V - IV century.

64. (44-6) Fig. 27. **Tub**? Rim fragment. Coarse hard crumbly clay with inclusions of mica, quartz, grog and white lithics, 2.5YR 5/6 red. Vertical rim, thickened to a triangular cross-

section, bevelled outward. Piece too poorly preserved to measure diameter, but apparently large. Cf. Sparkes and Talcott, 1970: Fig. 19:1847, "pre-Persian." Early V century?

65. (18-8) Figs 27, 55. **Dolio**. Rim Fragment. D=40 cm+. Coarse soft clay with inclusions of mica, grog and white lithics, 2.5YR 4/6 red with tannish core. Exterior smoothed. Angled everted rim thickened at point of inflection. Cf. Modesti, 1980: Fig. 36:16-7, "late Archaic." Early V century?

66. (11-16) Fig. 27. **Olla**. Foot fragment. WT=.6 cm. D=11 cm. Coarse hard clay with inclusions of mica, sand grog and lithics, some limestone spalling, 2.5YR 6/6 light red. Rounded conical foot. This type of foot appears in black gloss ware in the III century (see Adamesteanu, 1983: Fig. 52:115), but coarse ware analogs are limited to the previous two centuries, interestingly, primarily at Etruscan sites. Cf. Pallottino, 1992: Figs. 212:32, 225:41. V - IV century.

67. (12-14). **Olla**. Foot fragment. WT=.6 cm. D=10 cm. Coarse soft clay with inclusions of mica, sand and fine grog. Cf. number 66 above. V - IV century.

68. (11-47) Fig. 27. **Olla**. Foot fragment. WT=.8 cm. D=11 cm. Coarse hard clay with mica, sand and grog inclusions, 5YR 6/6 reddish yellow. Cf. number 66 above. V - IV century.

69. (49-27) Fig. 27. **Olla**. Foot fragment. WT=.37 cm. D=6 cm. Coarse semi-soft clay with inclusions of mica, sand and reddish lithics, 10R 5/8 red. Cf. number 66 above. V - IV century.

70. (45-11) Fig. 27. **Olla**. Foot fragment. D=10 cm. Coarse soft clay with inclusions of mica, grog, sand and crushed travertine, 5YR 6?6 reddish yellow. Cf. number 66 above. V - IV century.

71. (49-21) Fig. 27. **Olla**. Foot fragment. D=9 cm. Coarse soft clay with inclusions of mica, sand and grog, 5YR 5/8 yellowish red. Cf. number 66 above. V - IV century.

72. (49-19) Figs. 27, 61. **Olla**. Foot fragment. WT=.7 cm. D=8 cm. Coarse soft clay with inclusions of mica, sand and grog, 2.5YR 5/8 red, with slightly lighter core. Cf. number 66 above. V- IV century.

V - III century material

Material in this category consists of items which are impossible to date securely, beyond saying that they are post-Archaic and pre-Roman, an example being the series of vertical, relatively undifferentiated black gloss rims (numbers 74-79 below), which appear on cups and skyphoi from the V century into the beginning of the III century.

Black gloss wares

73. (49-7) Fig. 27, 61. **Amphora**? Handle fragment. Fine soft levigated clay with mica traces, very fine grog and scant sand, much reduced, 7.5YR 6/0 grey except at point of attachment, 5YR 6/6 reddish yellow. Paste is black gloss

type, but none remains. Vertical handle for closed form, oblong cross-section.

74. (4-43) Fig. 27. **Kylix**? Rim fragment. WT=.6 cm. D=24 cm. Fine hard levigated clay with no inclusions, 2.5YR 6/4 light reddish brown. Black gloss on surfaces. Slightly outslanting rim, tapering slightly at lip, otherwise undifferentiated.

75. (7-2) Fig. 27. **Cup**. Rim fragment. WT=.44 cm. D=10 cm. Fine soft levigated clay with mica traces, 5YR 7/4 beige. Traces of black gloss on both surfaces. Slightly in-curving rim slightly thickened at lip, otherwise undifferentiated.

76. (7-1) Figs. 27, 44. **Cup**. Rim fragment. WT=.29 cm. D=14 cm. Fine soft levigated clay with mica traces, 5YR 6/6 reddish yellow. Black gloss on interior, lip and exterior reserved. Slightly in-curving rim slightly thickened at lip, otherwise undifferentiated.

77. (10-11) Figs. 27, 48. **Cup**. Rim fragment. WT=.42 cm. D=14 cm. Fine hard levigated clay with faint mica traces, 2.5YR 5/4 reddish brown. Black gloss on both surfaces. Slightly in-curving rim tapering at the lip.

78. (11-35) Figs. 27, 49. **Cup**. Rim fragment. WT=.44 cm. D=11 cm. Fine semi-hard levigated clay with no inclusions, 5YR 6/1 grey. Black gloss on both surfaces; visible brush strokes are horizontal on upper 2 cm of exterior, then vertical below, possibly indicating a figured vessel. Vertical slightly inverted rim, somewhat thicker just below lip.

79. (11-34) Figs. 27, 49. **Cup**. Rim fragment. WT=.38 cm. D=11 cm. Fine hard levigated clay with no inclusions, 5YR 6/6 reddish yellow. Black gloss on both surfaces. Vertical slightly inverted rim, tapering at the lip.

80. (11-53) Fig. 28. **Cup**? Handle fragment. Fine soft levigated clay with mica traces, 5YR 6/6 reddish yellow. Black gloss fabric, but none remains. Arced handle with a cross-section of a rounded triangle, ca. 1.5 cm by .8 cm thick. Arced handles are comparatively early, but usually with a circular cross-section (see Sparkes and Talcott, 1970: 11).

81. (12-15) Fig. 51. **Kylix**. Foot fragment. Fine soft levigated clay with mica traces, color varying from 10R 6/6 light red to 5YR 6/3 light reddish brown due to incomplete oxidation. Black gloss on interior and exterior, reserved on inside of foot and bottom. A small (ca. 1mm) groove runs along the upper inside of the conical foot. Piece too small to measure diameter. Similar types appear from the late V into the early II centuries; this example is most like Morel, 1965: Pl. 22:323, III century, but not sufficiently like to warrant an identification.

82. (50-7) Fig. 62. **Kylix**. Handle fragment. Fine soft levigated clay with mica traces, 2.5YR 7/6 light red. Traces of black gloss on surface; early examples have the inside surface reserved. It cannot be determined if this is the case here. Slightly upward leaning handle with a circular cross-section, ca. 1.5 cm thick.

83. (16-36). **Kylix**. Handle fragment. Fine soft levigated clay with no inclusions, 2.5YR 6/5 light brownish red. Black gloss fabric, but none remains. Horizontal handle with a circular cross-section, ca. .68 cm thick.

84. (10-6) Figs. 28, 48. **Cup**? Handle fragment. Fine hard levigated clay with very faint mica traces, 2.5YR 5/4 reddish brown. Black gloss on surfaces. Arced handle with circular cross-section, 1.2 cm thick. V century?

85. (24-2). **Cup**? Handle fragment. Fine soft levigated clay with mica traces, 7.5YR 6/4 light reddish brown. Black gloss fabric, but none remains. Arced handle with half-almond cross-section, ca. .8 cm by 1.6 cm thick.

86. (44-3) Fig. 28. **Large vessel**. Handle fragment. Semi-fine soft levigated clay with mica traces, scant inclusions of fine grog, 5YR 6/8 reddish yellow. Black gloss fabric, but none remains. The piece displays no apparent curvature, the cross-section is half-almond, ca. 1.4 cm by 2.6 cm thick.

Coarse ware

87. (11-59) Figs. 28, 50. **Olletta**. Rim fragment. WT=.37 cm. D=16 cm. Coarse hard clay with inclusions of mica and sand, 5YR 5/6 yellowish red on exterior and top .5 cm of interior, the remainder of which is black, extending ca. .5 cm into the core. Everted half-almond shaped rim.

88. (37-9) Figs. 28, 58. **Olletta**. Rim fragment. WT=.37 cm. D=15 cm. Medium-coarse hard clay with inclusions of mica and coarse grog and lithics, 2.5YR 5/6 red, self-slipped. Vertical recurved rim with half-almond cross-section. Dyson (1976, p. 26) notes that similar shapes with a slip begin at Veii in the V century, but that by the II century at Cosa the slip is no longer used.

89. (39-17) Fig. 28. **Olletta**. Rim fragment. WT=.65 cm. D=14 cm. Coarse hard clay with inclusions of mica, quartz sand, other sand and lithics, 2.5YR 4/6 brownish red, self-slipped. See number 88 above.

IV - III century material

This category represents the majority of the datable material in the Sele Plain, covering as it does the whole of the Lucanian period and the beginning of the Roman occupancy. The term "Hellenistic", frequently used for this material, was rejected because it excludes the first three quarters of the fourth century; similarly, "Lucanian" or "Lucano-Roman" would also exclude or include too much, setting aside the awkwardness of the latter term. It should be noted that this category has become something of a catch-all in the archaeology of the area; thus some of the chronological identifications are less secure than one might wish.

Black gloss ware

90. (49-23) Figs. 28, 61. **Amphoretta**. Rim fragment. WT=.43 cm. D=7 cm. Fine hard levigated clay with mica traces, 5YR 6/6 reddish yellow; of interest is the fact that the clay is hard where freshly broken and soft elsewhere. Traces of black gloss on both surfaces. Outslanting recurved rim with a horizontally flattened lip of triangular cross-section. There is a 1 cm-wide flat ridge just below the second inflection. No precise analogs were found, but similar rims are in use for lekythoi from the V century on. IV century.

91. (12-6) Fig. 51. **Guttus**? Spout fragment? WT=.5 cm. Fine soft levigated clay with mica traces, 2.5YR 6/6 light red. Traces of black gloss on interior and exterior, including the single finished edge. Hemispherical shape, with the finished edge at the point of tangency with an apparent horizontal section. IV - III century.

92. (7-31) Figs. 28, 44. **Cup**? Rim fragment with lion's head spout. WT=.52 cm. D=8 cm. Fine soft levigated clay with mica traces, 5YR 7/6 reddish yellow. Traces of black gloss on lion's head, reserved or abraded away elsewhere. Outslanting rim curved to vertical; slightly inverted lip, flattened horizontally. Immediately below the lip is a plastic lion's head with a hole through the mouth, forming a spout. No analogs of any kind have been found for this apparently unique vessel, but the rim without the lion's head is of a IV century shape. IV century.

93. (7-18) Figs. 28, 44. **Cup**. Rim fragment. WT=.44 cm. D=16 cm. Fine semi-hard clay with mica traces, 2.5YR 6/6 light red, with fire-clouded areas and a thin grayish core. Black gloss with metallic reflections on interior, exterior reserved. Outslanting rim recurved to vertical, otherwise undifferentiated. Dating is possible because of identical match with shape and paste with a stratigraphically dated cup from Paestum. Cf. Greco and Theodorescu, 1983: Fig. 60:110. End IV - beginning III century.

94. (40-12) Fig. 28. **Skyphos**. Rim fragment. WT=.45 cm. D=18 cm. Fine soft levigated clay with mica traces, 5YR 6/2 pinkish grey with some fire clouding. Traces of satiny black gloss on both surfaces. Slightly outslanting rim tapering slightly at interior of lip. Cf. Bagnasco, 1992: Fig. LIII:126. Mid IV century.

95. (4-29) Figs. 28, 43. **Skyphos**. Rim fragment. WT=.31 cm. D=10 cm. Fine hard levigated clay with mica traces, 5YR 6/2 pinkish grey. Black gloss on both surfaces. Vertical rim thickened and slightly everted at lip. Cf. Russo, 1990: Fig. 13:280, dated end IV - beginning III, but this source is frequently 50 - 100 years later than other sources. IV century.

96. (11-33) Figs. 28, 49. **Skyphos**. Rim fragment. WT=.42 cm. D=13 cm. Similar to number 95. Cf. number 95 above. IV century.

97. (7-3) Figs. 28, 44. **Cup**. Rim fragment. WT=.85 cm. Fine soft levigated clay with mica traces, 5YR 6/6 reddish yellow, with a slightly grayish core. Black gloss with metallic reflections on both surfaces. Slightly outslanting rim thickened at the exterior of the lip to a rounded form. One-handled cup. Cf. Russo, 1990: Fig. 11:106. IV century.

98. (4-45) Fig. 28. **Kylix**? Handle fragment. Fine semi-soft levigated clay with mica traces and tiny brow and black inclusions, 5YR 6/6 reddish yellow. Black gloss fabric, but none remains. Upward tending horizontal handle with a squarish cross-section, 1.5 cm thick. Dated on the basis of shape and thickness (see Sparkes and Talcott, 1970: 11). IV - III century.

99. (15-15) Figs. 28, 43. **Cup**. Base fragment with partial foot. WT=.44 cm. D=3.5 cm. Fine hard levigated clay with mica traces. Black gloss on interior and exterior, bottom

of foot and vessel reserved. The ubiquitous "carinated cup." Cf. Greco and Pontrandolfo, 1990: Fig. 34:18. End IV - beginning III century.

100. (10-5) Fig. 48. **Cup**. Foot fragment. D=3.5 cm. Fine hard levigated clay with numerous tiny mica traces, 2.5YR 6/6 light red. Traces of black gloss on interior and exterior, bottom reserved. Carinated cup. Cf. Greco and Theodorescu, 1983: Fig. 60:135. Second half IV century.

101. (7-44) Fig. 28. **Cup**. Foot fragment. D=4 cm. Fine soft levigated clay with mica traces, color varying from 2.5YR 6/4 light reddish brow to 2.5YR 6/0 grey. Diluted black gloss of 2.5YR 5/4 olive brown on all surfaces, with post-depositional calcareous encrustations. Pedestal foot with slight rounded ridge at bottom. Carinated cup. Cf. Greco and Theodorescu, 1983: Fig. 60:135. Second half IV century.

102. (41-5) Figs. 28, 59. **Kylix**? Foot fragment. WT=.5 cm. D=7 cm. Fine soft levigated clay with mica traces, with a hard core, 5YR 6/4 light reddish brown, slightly darker core. Black gloss on interior, diluted reddish brown black gloss on exterior. Conical foot with rounded edges. Cf. Bagnasco, 1992: Fig. XLVII:72. Second half of IV - beginning III century.

103. (16-12) Fig. 29. **Cup**? Foot fragment. D=4 cm. Fine soft levigated clay with mica traces, 5YR 6/5 light reddish brown. Black gloss fabric, but none remains. Ring foot with triangular cross-section. Cf. Greco and Theodorescu, 1983: Fig. 62:122, III century; Lattanza, 1992: Fig. 569:CB1702, end IV century. Late IV - early III century.

104. (11-25) Figs. 29, 49. **Cup/bowl**. Foot fragment. D=8 cm. Fine hard levigated clay with mica traces, 5YR 6/4 light reddish brown, slightly pinker core. Diluted brownish black gloss on interior of foot at bottom of vessel, abraded away (?) elsewhere. Outslanting pedestal foot, everted at bottom. Gnathian cup? Cf. Greco and Theodorescu, 1983: Fig. 60:120, Gnathian association; Pontrandolfo and Rouveret, 1992: 317, number 10. End IV - beginning III century.

105. (7-22) Figs. 29, 44. **Plate/cover**. Rim fragment. WT=.5 cm. D=23 cm. Fine very soft levigated clay with mica traces, 10YR 6/6 beige. Slightly inverted concave rim with sharp inflection 1 cm below lip. Black gloss fabric, but none remains. Similar examples are variously identified as plates or covers. Cf. Greco and Pontrandolfo, 1990: Fig. 36:37, lekane lid; Greco and Theodorescu, 1983: Fig. 60:121, plate, is similar, but less gracile, attributed to the II century. IV - III century.

106. (12-16). **Plate/cover**. Rim fragment. WT=.5 cm. D=12 cm. Fine softish levigated clay with mica traces, 2.5YR 6/6 light red. Black gloss on interior, traces on exterior. Outslanting rim curving to vertical the top 1 cm, slightly thickened at point of inflection. Cf. Morel, 1981, form 2252; Pontrandolfo and Rouveret, 1992: 314, number 4. IV century.

107. (40-11) Figs. 29, 59. **Skyphos**? Foot fragment. D=11 cm. Fine softish levigated clay with mica traces, 2.5YR 5/6 red, with grey core. Traces of black gloss at points of attachment to body. Ring foot. Cf. Greco and Theodorescu, 1983: Fig. 61:119. IV - III century.

108. (45-8) Fig. 29. **Plate**. Base with foot. WT=.43 cm. D=6 cm. Fine soft levigated clay with frequent tiny mica traces, 5YR 6/8 reddish yellow. Black gloss with metallic reflections on interior, abraded away elsewhere. Ring foot with trapezoidal cross-section, concave at center bottom. Cf. Greco and Theodorescu, 1983: Fig.61:118. III century.

109. (12-23) Fig. 51. **Bowl**. Base fragment. D=4 cm. Fine soft levigated clay with mica traces, 2.5YR 6/6 light red. Satiny black gloss on all surfaces. Partial ring foot; on the bottom of the interior is a plastic rosette. Cf. Greco and Theodorescu, 1980: 18, note 6. End IV - beginning III.

Coarse ware

110. (50-17). **Amphora**. Rim fragment. D=13 cm. Coarse semi-hard clay with inclusions of mica and grog, 5YR 6/6 reddish yellow. Everted rim with triangular cross-section. "Greco-italic" transport amphora. Cf. Bagnasco, 1992: Fig. LXII:212. III century.

111. (11-26) Figs. 29, 50. **Olletta**? Rim fragment. WT=.4 cm. D=10 cm. Fine very soft clay with inclusions of both finely and coarsely ground grog, 2.5YR 6/6 light red. Outslanting rim thickened top 1.5 cm, flattened horizontally. Cf. Lattanza, 1992: Fig. 560:296. IV century.

112. Rim fragment. (48-10) Fig. 29. **Olla**. WT=.42 cm. D=15 cm. Medium-coarse hard clay with inclusions of mica and sand, 5YR 6/8 light red. Everted vertical rim with triangular cross-section. IV century.

113. (7-13) Fig. 29. **Olla**. Rim fragment. WT=.4 cm. D=15 cm. Medium-coarse hard clay with inclusions of mica, sand and white lithics, 5YR 5/6 tannish red with a dark grey core. Post-depositional fire clouding on exterior and on fracture. Outslanting slightly inverted rim, flattened horizontally. Cf. Bagnasco, 1992: Fig. LXXVI:234. First quarter III century.

114. (7-23) Figs. 29, 45. **Olletta**. Rim fragment. WT=.53 cm. D=12 cm. Coarse hard clay with inclusions of mica, sand and white lithics, 2.5YR 5/6 red with a grayish brown core. Some fire clouding on exterior. Vertical rim with horizontally flattened everted lip. This rim treatment on relatively thin-walled coarse ware is, in a general sense, diagnostic of the IV - III century. IV century.

115. (7-32) Figs. 29, 45. **Olla**. Rim fragment. WT=.5 cm. D=14 cm. Medium-coarse hard clay with inclusions of mica, sand and black and white lithics, 2.5YR 6/8 light red. Some fire clouding on top of rim. Vertical rim with horizontally flattened everted lip thickened at center. IV century.

116. (12-3) Fig. 51. **Olla**. Rim fragment. WT=.3 cm. D=13 cm. Medium-coarse hard clay with inclusions of mica, sand and grog, some limestone spalling evident, 10R 5/8 red with a light grey core. Slightly outslanting rim with horizontally flattened everted lip, same thickness as the wall. IV century.

117. (7-43) Figs. 29, 45. **Olletta**. Rim fragment. WT=.38 cm. D=10 cm. Medium-coarse hard clay with inclusions of mica, sand and scant white lithics, 2.5YR 6/6 light red, some fire clouding. Vertical rim with horizontally flattened everted lip, same thickness as the wall. IV century.

118. (7-58) Figs. 29, 45. **Lidded pot**. Rim fragment. WT=.57 cm. D=15 cm. Medium-coarse hard clay with inclusions of mica, sand, grog and black lithics, 2.5YR 6/8 light red, some fire clouding. Slightly inslanting rim with strongly everted lip with a wide groove to accept a lid. Cf. Greco and Theodorescu, 1980: Fig. 39:18, for the rim shape only. IV - III century.

119. (11-14) Fig. 29. **Basin**. Rim fragment. WT=.99 cm. D=27 cm. Very coarse hard clay with inclusions of mica, sand, grog and lithics, 7.5YR 6/6 reddish yellow with a thick grey core. Slightly outslanting thickened at the top 2.5 cm, half-almond cross-section. Cf. de Caro, 1985: Fig. 28:78, undated but pre-III century from the context. IV century.

120. (38-20) Figs. 29, 58. **Bowl**? Rim fragment. WT=.7 cm. D=20 cm. Medium-coarse hard clay with inclusions of mica, sand and grog, 5YR 5/4 reddish brown. Thickened everted rim, triangular cross-section. Cf. Lattanza, 1992: Fig. 572:2810. Second half IV - first half III century.

121. (4-74) Figs. 29, 43. **Situla**? Rim fragment. WT=.6 cm. D=25 cm. Medium-coarse semi-hard clay with inclusions of mica, sand and brown and black lithics, 5YR 6/8 reddish yellow, with a grey core. Vertical rim with horizontally flattened everted lip, with a groove around the outside of the lip. IV - III century.

122. (10-3) Figs. 29, 48. **Bowl**. Rim fragment. WT=.5 cm. D=28 cm. Coarse soft clay with inclusions of mica, grog, sand and white lithics, 5YR 6/8 reddish yellow, with a narrow grey core. Slightly outslanting rim with a horizontally flattened everted lip, triangular in cross-section. IV - III century.

123. (37-7) Figs. 29, 58. **Bowl**. Rim fragment. WT=.5 cm. D=24 cm. Medium-coarse soft clay with inclusions of mica, grog and sand, 5YR 5/4 reddish brown. Slightly outslanting rim with horizontally flattened everted lip, triangular in cross-section. IV - III century.

124. (7-30) Figs. 29, 45. **Bowl**? Rim fragment. WT=.5 cm. D=20 cm. Coarse hard clay with inclusions of mica, sand and black lithics, 2.5YR 5/8 red, with some fire clouding on extreme edge of lip. Slightly outslanting rim with horizontally flattened everted lip, trapezoidal in cross-section. IV - III century.

125. (7-8) figs. 30, 45. **Bowl**. Rim fragment. WT=.34 cm. D=15 cm. Coarse gritty hard clay with inclusions of mica, grog, sand and occasional lithics, 5YR 6/4 light reddish brown with a slightly darker core. Outslanting rim with horizontally flattened everted lip, triangular cross-section. IV - II century.

126. (4-52) Figs. 30, 43. **Lidded pot**. Rim fragment. WT=.42 cm. D=25 cm. Medium-coarse semi-soft clay with inclusions of mica , grog and lithics, 10R 6/8 light red. Slightly outslanting rim with thickened everted lip, grooved on top to accept a cover. IV - III century.

127. (39-10) Fig. 30. **Lidded pot**. Rim fragment. WT=.32. D=18 cm. Medium-coarse hard clay with inclusions of mica and grog, 5YR 6/6 reddish yellow, with a slightly lighter core. Similar to number 126 above. IV - III century.

128. (7-36) Figs. 30, 45. **Lidded pot**. Rim fragment. D=21 cm. Medium-coarse hard clay with inclusions of mica, sand and grog, 5YR 6/4 light reddish brown. Everted horizontal lip with a wide groove on top to accept a lid. Cf. Greco and Theodorescu, 1980: Fig. 39:18; Greco and Theodorescu, 1983: Fig. 66:183-185 for widely grooved lidded vessels in general. IV - III century.

129. (7-65) Figs. 30, 45. **Lidded bowl**. Rim fragment. WT=.3 cm. D=19 cm. Medium-coarse hard clay with inclusions of mica, sand and grog, 2.5YR 6/6 light red. Outslanting rim with everted lip with a wide groove on top to accept a lid. IV - III century.

130. (7-29) Figs. 30, 45. **Lidded pot**. Rim fragment. WT=.5 cm. D=28 cm. Coarse semi-soft clay with inclusions of mica and sand, 2.5YR 6/7 light red, some fire clouding. Similar to numbers 128 and 129 above. IV - III century.

Terracotta figurines

The following artifacts are fragments of terracotta votive figurines, generally too small to date with any great precision. The single fragment of a head (number 131) can be dated by the hair style *à côtes de melon* to the IV - III century (see discussion in Mollard-Besques, 1954), although it must be noted that the style persists into the II century on occasion. The remaining fragments of drapery are consistent with this date; however, due to the circumstances, the dating in this category is perhaps less secure than in others. The advantage of listing all of the figurines together outweighs possible errors in dating, if one keeps in mind that some of the fragments may be somewhat later than the III century.

131. (4-3) Figs. 30, 41. Head fragment. Medium-coarse hard clay with inclusions of mica and sand, 5YR 5/6 reddish yellow. Only the hair remains; deep relief. Female.

132. (4-1) Figs. 30, 41. Drapery fragment. Medium-coarse hard clay with inclusions of mica, sand and grog, 2.5YR 5/6 red. From upper torso; medium relief. Female?

133. (4-4) Figs. 30, 41. Drapery fragment. Medium-coarse hard clay with inclusions of mica and lithics, 7.5YR 6/4 light brown. From upper torso; shallow relief. Female.

134. (4-5) Figs. 30, 41. Drapery fragment. Medium-coarse hard clay with inclusions of mica and sand, 2.5YR 4/6 red. From mid-torso? Shallow relief.

135. (4-6) Figs. 30, 41. Drapery fragment. Medium-coarse hard clay with inclusions of mica and sand, 5YR 5/6 yellowish red. From mid-torso? Shallow relief.

136. (4-7) Figs. 30, 41. Drapery fragment. Medium-coarse hard clay with inclusions of mica and sand, 7.5YR 5/6 brown. From near bottom of figure; medium relief. Female.

137. (4-8) Figs. 30, 41. Pedestal fragment? Medium-fine hard clay with inclusions of mica and grog, 10R 5/6 yellowish red.

138. (4-9) Figs. 30, 41. Pedestal fragment? Medium-coarse hard clay with inclusions of mica, sand and grog, 2.5YR 5/6 red.

139. (4-11) Figs. 30, 41. Drapery fragment. Medium-coarse hard clay with inclusions of mica, sand and grog, 5YR 6/4 light reddish brown, with a slightly darker area adjacent to a squarish (ca. 1.5 cm square) protrusion. Shallow relief.

140. (4-12) Figs. 30, 41. Drapery fragment? Medium-coarse hard clay with inclusions of mica and sand, 5YR 6/6 reddish yellow. Deep relief.

141. (4-13) Figs. 30, 42. Drapery fragment. Medium-coarse hard clay with inclusions of mica and sand, 5YR 5/6 yellowish red. From near bottom of figure; medium relief. Female.

142. (4-14) Figs. 31, 42. Drapery fragment. Medium-coarse hard clay with inclusions of mica and grog, 2.5YR 6/6 light red. From mid-torso; medium-deep relief.

143. (4-15) Figs. 31, 42. Drapery fragment. Medium-coarse hard clay with inclusions of mica and sand, 5YR 6/6 reddish yellow. From upper torso; shallow relief. Female.

144. (4-16) Figs. 31, 42. Drapery fragment. Medium-coarse hard clay with inclusions of mica, sand and black lithics, 5YR 5/6 yellowish red. From upper-mid torso; medium relief. Female.

145. (4-17) Figs. 31, 42. Drapery fragment. Medium-coarse hard clay with inclusions of mica, sand and black lithics, 5YR 5/6 yellowish red; same fabric as number 144 above, possibly from the same figurine. From upper torso; medium-deep relief. Female.

146. (4-18) Figs. 31, 42. Drapery fragment. Medium-coarse hard clay with inclusions of mica, sand and lithics, 2.5YR 5/6 red. From near the bottom of the figure; deep relief. Female.

147. (4-26) Figs. 31, 42. Unidentified fragment. Medium-coarse hard clay with inclusions of mica, sand and grog, 5YR 5/6 yellowish red. Smooth rounded surface; location uncertain.

148. (4-50) Figs. 31, 42. Unidentified fragment. Medium-coarse hard clay with inclusions of mica and sand, 5YR 6/6 reddish yellow. Location uncertain. Medium relief.

149. (4-70) Figs. 31, 42. Drapery fragment. medium-coarse hard clay with inclusions of mica, sand and grog, 2.5YR 6/6 light red. From just below the hips? Very shallow relief. Female.

150. (4-69) Figs. 31, 42. Drapery fragment. Medium-coarse hard clay with inclusions of mica and sand, 5YR 5/6 yellowish red. Location uncertain.

151. (7-25) Figs. 31, 46. Drapery fragment. Medium-coarse hard clay with inclusions of mica, grog and black and white lithics, 5YR 5/6 yellowish red. From foot area; medium relief. Female.

152. (7-52) Figs. 31, 46. Drapery fragment. Medium-coarse hard clay with inclusions of mica, sand and lithics, 2.5YR 5/6 brownish red. From mid-torso? Medium relief.

153. (7-64) Fig. 31. Drapery fragment. Medium-coarse hard clay with inclusions of mica and sand, 5YR 4/6 brownish red. Location uncertain. Shallow relief.

154. (24-11) Figs. 31, 56. Drapery fragment. Medium-coarse hard clay with inclusions of mica, sand and grog, 2.5YR 6/6 light red. Location uncertain. Medium-deep relief.

155. (40-13) Fig. 31. Drapery fragment. Medium-coarse hard clay with inclusions of mica, grog and small white lithics, 5YR 6/6 reddish yellow. Location uncertain. Very shallow relief.

156. (40-15) Fig. 31. Unidentified fragment. Medium-coarse soft clay with inclusions of mica, grog and lithics, 2.5YR 5/6 red. Location uncertain. Medium relief.

157. (40-17) Fig. 59. Pedestal fragment? Coarse hard clay with inclusions of mica, sand and frequent grog, 5YR 5/6 yellowish red.

158. (41-9) Fig. 59. Unidentified fragment. Coarse hard clay with inclusions of mica and sand, 5YR 6/6 reddish yellow. Location uncertain. Shallow relief, much abraded.

II - I century material

Black gloss

159. (7-5) Figs. 32, 44. **Cup**. Rim fragment. WT=.3 cm. D=13 cm. Fine very soft levigated clay with mica traces, 5YR 7/6 reddish yellow. Black gloss on interior and exterior of vertical part of rim, body below the rim is reserved. Slightly outslanting rim with a slight bulbous thickening at the lip; sharp carinated inflection at point of attachment to body. Cf. Greco and Theodorescu, 1980: Fig. 38:26-28; Greco and Theodorescu, 1983: Fig. 64:128. II - I century.

160. (7-59) Figs. 32, 44. **Bowl**. Rim fragment. WT=.5 cm. D=14 cm. Fine soft levigated clay with mica traces and some very fine grog, 5YR 6/6 reddish yellow. Black gloss with metallic reflections on interior, traces on exterior. Sloping side with everted rounded rim; the upper curve is faceted rather than smooth. Cf. Morel, 1981: Pl. 12, type 1312. II - I century.

161. (7-50) Figs. 32, 44. **Bowl**. Rim fragment. WT=.33 cm. D=13 cm. Fine soft levigated clay with mica traces, 5YR 6/6 reddish yellow. Black gloss with metallic reflections on interior, traces on exterior. Sloping side with everted rounded rim. Cf. number 160 above. II - I century.

162. (50-14) Fig. 62. **Bowl**? Foot fragment. D=5 cm. Fine hard levigated clay with mica traces, 5YR 6/6 reddish yellow. Black gloss fabric, but none remains. Vertical pedestal foot, trapezoidal in cross-section. Cf. Greco and Theodorescu, 1987: Fig. 90:583. II - I century.

163. (37-5) Fig. 32. **Bowl**. Rim fragment. WT=.55 cm. D=18 cm. Fine soft levigated clay with extremely scant mica traces, 5YR 6/8 reddish yellow. Black gloss type slip, but a dense opaque 2.5YR 4/6 brownish red, on both surfaces. Sloping side with everted rounded rim. Cf. number 160 above for the shape. Pre-sigillata. I century.

Roman thin wall

164. (7-20) Figs. 32, 44. **Beaker**. Rim fragment. WT=.25 cm. D=5 cm. Very fine soft levigated clay with mica traces, 5YR 7/4 beige. Dense opaque black matte slip. Vertical rim with slightly everted lip. Two narrow grooves directly below lip on exterior, ca. 2 cm below on interior. Cf. Marabini Moevs, 1973: Pl. 7:77. Form VII. I century.

165. (7-26) Figs. 32, 44. **Beaker**. Rim fragment. WT=.25 cm. D=5 cm. Hard fine levigated clay with no inclusions, 5YR 7/4 beige. Dense opaque black matte slip. Vertical undifferentiated rim. One narrow groove directly below lip on exterior. Cf. number 164 above. I century.

Coarse ware

166. (4-48) Figs. 32, 43. **Amphora**. Rim fragment. WT=.66 cm. D=12 cm. Medium-coarse soft clay with inclusions of mica, grog and white lithics, 10R 5/8 red. Vertical rim, thickened at lip; rounded triangle in cross-section. Cf. Peacock and Williams, 1986, Class 9 "Rhodian" amphora, but the fabric is not Rhodian. I BC - 2nd century AD.

167. (12-12) Fig. 51. **Olletta**. Rim fragment. WT=.53 cm. D=14 cm. Coarse soft clay with inclusions of mica, sand, grog and occasional large lithics, 5YR 5/8 yellowish red. Vertical rim thickened at lip, half-almond cross-section. See the discussion in Dyson 1976: 26, regarding slipping on this shape. The unslipped variety is late. II - I century.

168. (39-13) Fig. 32. **Olletta**. Rim fragment. WT=.62 cm. D=16 cm. Medium-coarse softish clay with inclusions of mica and sand, 7.5YR 4/4 dark brown, with reddish core. Vertical rim thickened at lip, half-almond in cross-section. Cf. number 167 above. II - I century.

2nd - 3rd century material

This category consists mostly of the various *sigillata* wares recovered in the survey, along with some coarse ware. The gap between the I century BC and the 2nd century AD is, I believe, only apparent.

Arretine ware

169. (30-10) Figs. 32, 57. Body fragment. WT=.56 cm. D=16 cm. Fine hard levigated clay with no inclusions, 5YR 8/4 pink. Glossy slip is 2.5YR 4/8 darkish red. Plastic decoration of bunting interspersed with florets. 2nd - 3rd century.

Terra sigillata italica

170. (30-1) Figs. 32, 57. **Bowl**. Shoulder fragment. WT=.5 cm. D=17 cm. Fine hard levigated clay with very scant mica traces, 10R 6/6 red. Glossy slip is 10R 4/8 red. Outslanting body sherd curving to vertical. Plastic decoration of two rows of raised circles with a plain raised cordon between on the vertical section, and elongated U-shaped vertical ridges interspersed with hash marks below. Cf. Oswald and Pryce, 1966: Pl. XXVI:6. 2nd - 3rd century.

Terra sigillata chiara

171. (9-1) Figs. 32, 47. **Bowl**. Rim fragment. WT=.47 cm. D=15 cm. Fine hard levigated clay with tiny white inclusions, 10R4/6 red with slightly darker core. Glossy slip is same color as paste. Vertical everted rim curving slightly downwards, with a narrow groove on the top. Cf. Lamboglia, 1958, Form 4. 2nd - 3rd century.

172. (4-39) Figs. 32, 43. **Bowl**. Rim fragment. WT=.5 cm. D=20 cm. Fine hard levigated clay with no inclusions, 10R 6/8 light red. Glossy slip is 10R 5/8 red. Shape similar to number 171 above, but without groove. Cf. Lamboglia, 1958, Form 4/36. 2nd - 3rd century.

African Red Slip ware

173. (9-5) Figs. 32, 47. **Bowl**. Rim fragment. WT=.44 cm. D=20 cm. Fine hard levigated clay with scant white inclusions, 10R 6/8 light red. Dullish slip is 10R 5/8 red. Vertical rim slightly thickened at lip in two stages. Cf. Hayes, 1972, Form 9B. 2nd century.

174. (39-14) Fig. 32. **Bowl**. Rim fragment. WT=.5 cm. D=22 cm. Fine hard levigated clay with mica traces and scant quartz sand, 2.5YR 5/8 red. Traces of slightly redder dullish slip. Everted rim with triangular protrusion on exterior just below lip, with a narrow raised ridge just below; on the interior, there is a narrow groove ca. 2 cm below the lip. Cf. Hayes, 1972, Form 8B. Second half of 2nd century.

175. (9-2) Figs. 32, 47. **Bowl**. Rim fragment. WT=.4 cm. D=16 cm. Fine hard levigated clay with mica traces, 10R 6/4 pale red. Dullish slip is 10R 5/8 red. Similar to number 174 above, with alternating diagonal incisions ca. 1.5 cm below lip. Cf. number 174 above. Second half of 2nd century.

176. (39-1). **Bowl**. Rim fragment. Semi-fine hard levigated clay with mica traces, 2.5YR 6/8 light red. Traces of dullish red slip. Only the lip remains; diameter and thickness not measurable. Cf. number 174 above. Second half of 2nd century.

177. (9-6) Figs. 33, 47. **Bowl**. Rim fragment. WT=.45 cm. D=19 cm. Fine hard levigated clay with scant mica traces, occasional tiny white inclusions, 10R 6/8 light red. Dullish slip is 10R 5/8. Vertical rim with strongly everted lip, curved horizontally. Date assigned on the basis of the fabric. 2nd - 3rd century.

178. (4-58). Body fragment. WT=.33 cm. Fine hard levigated clay with mica traces, 10R 6/8 light red. Dullish slip is slightly redder. Three concentric grooves. Date assigned on the basis of the fabric. 2nd - 3rd century.

179. (38-10). Body fragment. WT=.44 cm. Fine hard levigated clay with mica traces and occasional fine sand, 10R 5/8 red. Dullish slip of the same color. Six closely spaced concentric grooves with triangular cross-section. Date assigned on the basis of the fabric. 2nd - 3rd century.

180. (39-11). **Bowl**. Body fragment. WT=.64 cm. D=15 cm. Fine hard levigated clay with mica traces, 10R 6/8 light red. Dullish slip is slightly darker. Outslanting wall curving

to vertical, with a row of dentate incisions at the point of inflection. Cf. Hayes, 1972, Form 9. 2nd century.

181. (30-15) Figs. 33, 57. **Bowl**. Body fragment. WT=.46 cm. D=17 cm. Fine hard levigated clay with mica traces and occasional fine grog, 10R 5/8 red. Dullish slip of the same color. Shape similar to number 180 above, but with two rows of dentate incisions. Cf. number 180 above. 2nd century.

182. (9-4) Figs. 33, 47. **Bowl**. Body fragment. WT=.54 cm. D=18 cm. Fine hard levigated clay with very faint mica traces, 10R 5/6 red. Dullish slip is 10R 5/8 red. Shape and decoration same as number 180 above. 2nd century.

183. (4-51) Figs. 33, 43. Body fragment. WT=.44 cm. D=19 cm. Fine hard levigated clay with mica traces, 10R 6/6 light red. Dullish slip is 10R 6/8 light red. Wall sherd with a double row of dentate incisions. 2nd - 3rd century.

Coarse ware

184. (39-21) Fig. 33. **Amphora**. Rim fragment. WT=.8 cm. D=12 cm. Medium-coarse softish clay with mica traces and inclusions of grog, 5YR 6/6 reddish yellow, with slightly darker core. Vertical rim thickened at top 5 cm, slightly everted with a concave exterior. Cf. Panella and Carandini, 1973: Figs. 15-17, Tripolitana I. 2nd century.

185. (1-20) Fig. 33. **Amphora**. Spike fragment. Coarse hard clay with inclusions of mica and sand, 2.5YR 6/6 light red, some fire clouding. Rather thick amorphous solid tapering spike. The shape is consistent with a number of late transport amphorae, including Peacock and Williams type Africana II; the fabric is identical to that identified as Tunisian. Cf. Peacock and Williams, 1986: 154-155. Late 2nd - late 4th centuries.

186. (11-41) Fig. 33. **Closed form**. Rim fragment. WT=.75 cm. D=20 cm. Coarse hard clay with inclusions of mica, sand and grog, 5YR 4/6 brown, with a grey core. Thick slightly everted rim, tapering somewhat to the lip. Cf. Dyson, 1976: Fig. 66:21. 3rd - 4th century.

187. (41-6) Figs. 33, 59. **Lidded pot**. Rim fragment. WT=.48 cm. D=18 cm. Medium-coarse hard clay with inclusions of mica and scant sand and lithics, 5YR 6/6 yellowish red, with a redder core. Vertical rim with a thickened rounded lip, horizontally flattened and grooved to accept a lid. Cf. Panella and Carandini, 1973: Fig. XXXVII:267-268. 2nd - 4th century.

188. (2-4). **Plate/cover**. Rim fragment. WT=.45 cm. D=21 cm. Medium-coarse hard clay with inclusions of mica, sand and fine grog, 2.5YR 6/8 light red; exterior of lip is 5YR 7/6 reddish yellow, but does not appear to be slipped. Outslanting rim with thickened lip *ad orlo annerito*. Cf. Panella and Carandini, 1973: Fig. XXXVII: 332-333. 2nd century.

189. (4-66) Fig. 43. **Plate/cover**. Rim fragment. WT=.5 cm. D=31 cm. Same as number 188 above. 2nd century.

190. (30-3) Fig. 57. **Plate/cover**. Rim fragment. WT=.56 cm. Same as number 188 above. 2nd century

191. (1-12). **Plate/cover**. Rim fragment. WT=.46 cm. Same as number 188 above. 2nd century.

Medieval material

Only two items recovered during the survey could be placed in this category with any confidence; however, the impression remains that some of the unidentified items also date from medieval times, although the malarial character of the bottom lands in this period may well have served to keep evidence of occupation low. This is a comparatively new field in Italian archaeology, and the literature is sparse.

192. (15-14) Fig. 33. **Open form**? Foot fragment. WT=.56 cm. D=11 cm. Coarse hard but crumbly clay with inclusions of mica, grog and travertine, 2.5YR 5/8 red, with calcareous encrustations. Thickened ring foot. Cf. Peduto, 1984: Fig. XXXVII:14. 11th - 12th century.

193. (44-10) Fig. 33. **Open form**? Foot fragment. WT=.5 cm. D=9 cm. Coarse soft clay with inclusions of mica, grog and white lithics, 2.5YR 6/8 light red. Shape similar to number 192 above, but with foot faceted rather than rounded. Cf. Peduto, 1984: Fig. XXXVII:15. 11th - 12th century.

PART 2: UNDATED MATERIAL

Greco-Lucanian material

This category includes material of which it can only be said that it is historic and pre-Roman. Occasionally, a date will be suggested on the basis of associated materials in the same collection unit.

Black gloss

194. (49-1) Figs. 33, 61. **Closed form**. Rim fragment. WT=.23 cm. D=20 cm. Fine semi-soft levigated clay with mica traces, 2.5YR 6/8 light red. Black gloss fabric, but none remains. Inslanting rim curving to vertical, thickened at the point of inflection.

195. (30-6) Fig. 57. **Closed form**. Neck fragment. WT=.4 cm. Fine soft levigated clay with mica traces, 5YR 7/4 beige. Traces of black gloss on interior. Inslanting shoulder curving to slight eversion, thickened at point of inflection.

196. (40-3) Figs. 33, 59. **Open form**. Rim fragment. WT=.43 cm. D=26 cm. Fine soft levigated clay with mica traces, 5YR 6/3 light reddish brown with red core. Traces of black gloss on both surfaces. Outslanting rim with thickened everted lip.

197. (4-54) Figs. 33, 43. **Open form**. Rim fragment. WT=.43 cm. D=18 cm. Fine very soft levigated clay with mica traces, 5YR 6/4 light reddish brown. Traces of black gloss on both surfaces. Shape similar to number 196 above.

198. (13-10) Figs 33, 52. **Cup**. Rim fragment. WT=.34 cm. D=10 cm. Fine soft levigated clay with mica traces, 5YR

5/2.5 brown. Black gloss on both sides, top 1.5 cm of exterior possibly reserved, probably abraded away. Outslanting rim slightly thickened at lip. This shape is very similar to ones categorized above as V - III century, but some Archaic examples exist.

199. (39-3) Fig. 33. **Skyphos**. Rim fragment. WT=.38 cm. D=14 cm. Fine soft levigated clay with very faint mica traces, 5YR 6/6 reddish yellow. Black gloss on both sides. Vertical rim slightly everted at the lip. The black gloss is lustrous, with a narrow band of matte black ca. 1 cm below the lip on the interior, possibly indicating overpainting. The fineness of the piece suggests it is early, but the overpainting suggests late.

200. (11-27) Fig. 49. Base fragment. D=5 cm. Fine hard levigated clay with mica traces, 5YR 6/4 light reddish brown. Traces of black gloss on all surfaces. Concave on interior and exterior, foot not present. The fabric is consistent with VI - V century material, but the shape has no direct analogs; not enough remains for confident dating. Early?

201. (39-2) Fig. 33. Body fragment. WT=.5 cm. Fine hard levigated clay with mica traces, 5YR 6/6 reddish yellow. Black gloss on exterior, with a pattern in matte black, suggesting overpainting, as shown in Fig. 33.

Loomweights

The following loomweights have no incised markings on the surfaces; these would help immensely in dating them. As it is, they appear to be Archaic or early Classical on the basis of associated material, but the fabrics and shapes continue in use throughout the pre-Roman period.

202. (30-16) Figs. 34, 57. **Loomweight**. Almost entire, with a ca. 1 cm thick section broken off of one side. Medium-coarse semi-soft clay with inclusions of mica and various lithics, 10R 5/8 red. Slightly trapezoidal with rounded corners in one cross-section, curved rectangular in the other; base is rectangular. There is a ca. 1 cm hole ca. 2 cm below the top through the widest dimension.

203. (15-21) Figs. 34, 53. **Loomweight**. Almost entire, with the portion above the cord holes broken off. Coarse hard clay with inclusions of mica, travertine, sand and scant tephra, 5YR 5/6 yellowish red. Pyramidal in shape with a rectangular base. There are two adjacent holes through the narrowest dimension near the top. A similar shape is published in Pancrazzi, 1979: Fig. 73:10, but other similar shapes have varying dates.

204. (15-20) Figs. 34, 53. **Loomweight**. Entire. Medium-coarse softish clay with inclusions of mica and unidentified material, 5YR 6/6 reddish yellow. Pyramidal in shape with a square base. Ubiquitous shape throughout the period in question.

205. (50-19) Fig. 62. **Loomweight**. Almost entire, top broken off. Coarse very hard clay with inclusions of mica, grog and sand, 5YR 4/6 brown. Slightly pyramidal in shape with a square base; no holes are evident.

Large basins, tubs and pithoi

206. (39-22) Fig. 34. **Basin/tub**. Rim fragment. WT=2.5 cm. D>45 cm. Very coarse hard clay with inclusions of mica, grog and frequent sand, 2.5YR 5/6 reddish brown. Vertical everted rim, triangular in cross-section.

Greco-Roman material

This category slightly expands the previous one to include material from the Roman period, Republican through Imperial.

207. (30-27) Figs. 34, 57. **Basin/tub**. Rim fragment. WT=1.15 cm. D=45 cm. Medium-coarse hard clay with inclusions of mica and grog, 5YR 5/6 yellowish red with grey core. Outslanting everted rim, trapezoidal in cross-section.

208. (41-10) Figs. 34, 59. **Pithos**? Rim fragment. WT>2.5 cm. D=28 cm. Coarse hard clay with inclusions of mica, sand, grog and lithics, 5YR 5/6 yellowish red. Slightly outslanting everted rim with a triangular cross-section, with a flat ridge just below the lip.

Coarse ware

209. (15-18) Figs. 35, 58. **Olla**? Rim fragment. WT=.69 cm. D=16 cm. Medium-fine soft clay with inclusions of mica, fine travertine and grog, 2.5YR 5/6 red. Slightly everted thickened rim, oval in cross-section with a flattened lower edge. Possibly an amphora, although no direct analog was found.

210. (44-9) Figs. 35, 60. **Olla**? Rim fragment. WT=.8 cm. D=13 cm. Coarse hard clay with inclusions of mica and sand, 2.5YR 6/6 light red. Outcurving everted rim with thickened lip, oval in cross-section. There is a plastic attachment just below the lip, presumably part of a handle.

211. (20-2) Fig. 56. **Open form**. Rim fragment. WT=.57 cm. D=24 cm. Coarse soft clay with inclusions of mica and frequent sand, 5YR 6/6 reddish yellow. Everted rim, slightly thickened at lip. This shape is ubiquitous throughout the pre-Roman chronology.

212. (20-5) Figs. 35, 56. **Open form**. Rim fragment. WT=.66 cm. Very coarse hard clay with inclusions of mica, grog, sand and large lithics, 5YR 4/6 yellowish red with grey core. Shape similar to number 211 above.

213. (20-6) Figs 35, 56. **Open form**. Rim fragment. WT=.6. Shape and fabric identical with number 212 above. Part of the same vessel?

214. (17-13) Fig 35. **Closed form**. Rim fragment. WT=.6 cm. D=14 cm. Coarse softish clay with inclusions of mica, grog and tiny white inclusions, 5YR 5/6 yellowish red. Outslanting rim with everted thickened lip, trapezoidal in cross-section.

215. (39-6) Fig. 35. **Closed form**. Rim fragment. WT=.45 cm. D=12 cm. Medium-coarse hard clay with inclusions of mica, sand and grog, 5YR 6/6 reddish yellow with a

grey core. Inslanting rim with everted thickened lip, horizontally flattened oval in cross-section.

216. (1-18). **Closed form**. Rim fragment. WT=.46 cm. D=7 cm. Medium-coarse soft clay with inclusions of white and grey lithics, 5YR 7/5 beige, self-slipped, with a red core. Shape similar to number 215 above.

217. (13-16) Figs. 35, 52. **Closed form**. Rim fragment. WT=.68 cm. D=10 cm. Medium-coarse softish clay with inclusions of mica, grog and white lithics, 5YR 5/4 reddish brown, with a pale red core. Inslanting rim with apparently everted thickened lip; the outer part of the lip is missing. Cross-section is semi-circular as is.

218. (4-76) Fig 35. **Closed form**. Shoulder fragment. WT=.6 cm. D=20 cm. Medium-coarse soft clay with inclusions of mica, grog and lithics; exterior is 5YR 6/4 light reddish brown, interior is 2.5YR 5/8 red, core is grey; no apparent slip. Sharply inslanting shoulder broken off just before the point of upward inflection. Thickened at point of inflection.

219. (35-5) Fig. 58. **Closed form**. Shoulder fragment. WT=.3 cm. D=15 cm. Medium-coarse hard clay with inclusions of mica and tephra, 2.5YR 5/6 red exterior, deeply fire clouded, with a 5YR 6/3 light reddish brown interior and core, no apparent slip. Part of a small apparently spherical vessel with very thin walls.

220. (39-8) Fig. 35. **Bowl**. Rim fragment. WT=.34 cm. D=18 cm. Medium-coarse soft clay with inclusions of mica and sand, 10R 6/8 light red. Slightly outslanting rim with thickened very slightly inverted lip.

221. (2-16). **Open form**. Rim fragment. WT=.75 cm. D=24 cm. Medium-coarse hard clay with inclusions of mica and sand, 5YR 5/4 reddish brown. Strongly everted curved rim, slightly thickened at extremity.

222. (4-75) Fig. 35. **Open form**. Rim fragment. WT=.7 cm. D=28 cm. Very coarse hard clay with inclusions of mica, grog and sand, 2.5YR 5/8 red. Very battered rim, vertical, thickened at the lip to a horizontal triangular cross-section. The fabric is similar to one of the types of so-called "Greco-Italic" amphorae, but the orifice is much too wide.

223. (13-14) Figs. 35, 52. **Pyxis**? Base fragment. WT=.3 cm. D=3 cm. Medium-fine softish clay with mica inclusions, 2.5YR 5/8 red with a grey core. Very thin walled small vessel with undifferentiated base.

224. (49-9) Figs. 35, 61. Foot fragment. D=18 cm. Medium-fine soft clay with inclusions of mica, sand and grog, 10R 6/4 light red, with a slip of 2.5YR 6/8 light red. Disc foot slightly thickened at outer edge.

225. (43-6) Fig. 60. **Cover**. Cover fragment. WT=2.5 cm. D=33 cm. Coarse hard clay with inclusions of mica, grog and sand, 2.5YR 6/6 light red. Flat disc cover, undifferentiated.

Indeterminate materials

This last category contains items which cannot be confidently placed in even the previous broad categories. It may seem strange that impasto fabrics are included here, and indeed many of them are probably prehistoric; but impastos continued in use even into medieval times, obscuring the chronology where diagnostic shapes, surface treatments and so on are not present. Similarly, the wide variety of coarse wares can probably mostly be attributed to antiquity, but not with any assurance in any given case. The fact that no analogs in the Greek world were found suggests the possibility that many of them are local Italic wares, possibly contemporaneous with the Greek tenure at Poseidonia, strengthening the hypothesis that Greeks and natives lived side by side in friendship.

Impasto

226. (9-7) Figs. 36, 47. **Closed form**. Rim fragment. WT=.9 cm. D=5 cm. Coarse hard impasto with inclusions of mica, grog and white lithics, 10R 4/6 rusty red. Traces of an exterior slip of 10R 4/8 red, interior fire clouded. Undifferentiated vertical rim.

227. (43-1) Fig. 60. **Closed form**. Rim fragment. Wt=.7 cm. D=Var. Coarse hard impasto with inclusions of mica, grog and tephra? 2.5YR 5/6 red with grey core. Vertical rim everted at lip ca. 1.2 cm from top, shallow groove on horizontally flattened lip.

228. (11-52) Fig. 36. **Open form**. Rim fragment. WT=Var. D=27 cm? Coarse hard impasto with inclusions of mica and sand, 2.5YR 5/6 red, with a dark grey core. Slightly everted curved rim.

229. (49-26) Fig. 61. **Open form**? Rim fragment. WT=1.24 cm. D=Var. Coarse hard impasto with inclusions of mica, sand and organic material, 5YR 4/6 brown with a dark grey core. Vertical rim, similar in shape to number 227 above, but ungrooved.

230. (16-17) Fig. 54. Body fragment. WT=.73 cm. D>40 cm. Coarse hard impasto with inclusions of mica and small to medium grey and white lithics, 2.5YR 4/6 brick red, with a dark grey core. The only distinguishing feature is an angled ridge near one edge, possibly a point of inflection?

231. (17-18) Fig. 36. Unidentified fragment. WT=1.3 cm. D=34 cm. Very coarse hard impasto with inclusions of mica and large grog and lithics, 7.5YR 4/2 dark brown. Vertical sherd with two raised rounded cordons at right angles.

232. (46-1). Body fragment. WT=1.1 cm. D=Var. Coarse hard impasto with inclusions of mica and sand, 5YR 4/3 reddish brown with black core. Only distinguishing feature is a 1 cm by .3 cm protrusion on the exterior.

233. (7-48) Figs. 36, 46. Body fragment. WT=Var. D=Var. Medium-coarse hard impasto with inclusions of mica, sand and grog, 5YR 5/4 reddish brown with a core of 5YR 4/2 dark brownish grey. Only distinguishing feature is a raised portion with a ca. 1.2 cm long incised groove.

Coarse ware, closed forms

234. (7-54) Figs. 36, 46. Rim fragment. WT=.98 cm. D=14 cm. Coarse hard clay with inclusions of mica and sand,

with one large chunk of travertine, exterior is 10YR 3/1 very dark grey, interior is 10R 5/6 red with some fire clouding. Slightly inslanting rim curving to everted rim ca. 1 cm from top, slightly thickened at point of inflection.

235. (7-35) Figs. 36, 45. Rim fragment. WT=.77 cm. D=12 cm. Medium coarse hard clay with inclusions of abundant mica and some sand, 2.5YR 6/4 light reddish brown, with some post-depositional fire clouding. Vertical rim curving outward and narrowing slightly.

236. (17-9) Fig. 36. Rim fragment. WT=.7 cm. D=22 cm. Medium-coarse softish clay with inclusions of mica and sand, 2.5YR 5/8 red, with some fire clouding on interior. Shape similar to number 235 above.

237. (2-3) Fig. 36. Rim fragment. WT=.64 cm. D=17 cm. Medium-coarse softish clay with inclusions of mica, sand and grog, 2.5YR 5/8 red. Shape similar to number 235 above.

238. (48-9) Fig. 36. Shoulder fragment. WT=1.04 cm. D=16 cm. Very coarse hard clay with inclusions of mica, sands and large black lithics, 2.5YR 5/8 red, interior fire clouded, core is black. Inslanting shoulder, recurved to outslanting, apparently just below rim.

239. (18-6) Figs. 36, 55. Shoulder fragment. WT>1 cm. D=38 cm. Medium-coarse hard clay with inclusions of mica, grog and sand, 2.5YR4/6 red, partially fire clouded in the kiln. Incurving shoulder, recurved to vertical, slightly thickened at point of inflection, carinated on interior.

240. (18-9) Figs. 36, 55. Rim fragment. WT=1.3 cm. D=24 cm. Medium-coarse soft clay with inclusions of mica, grog, quartz sand and white flecks. Vertical rim strongly everted at lip, thickened slightly at point of inflection, tapering to extremity.

Coarse ware, open forms

241. (38-8) Figs. 37, 58. **Cup**? Rim fragment. WT=.8 cm. D=15 cm. Medium-fine hard clay with inclusions of mica, fine sand and grog, 2.5YR 5/6 red, with a grey core. Slightly outslanting rim, bevelled to the interior at the lip.

242. (17-8) Fig. 37. **Cup**? Rim fragment with partial handle. WT=.5 cm. D=13 cm. Medium-fine hard clay with inclusions of mica and quartz sand, 5YR 6/6 reddish yellow. Slightly outcurving rim with handle attached just below rounded lip.

243. (4-32) Figs. 37, 43. **Cup**? Rim fragment. WT=.9 cm. D=12 cm. Medium-fine hard clay with inclusions of mica and tiny brown lithics, 10YR 7/3 pale brown. Outslanting rim expanding to the inward bevelled lip.

244. (13-8) Fig. 52. **Cup**? Rim fragment. WT=.6 cm. D=13 cm. Coarse softish clay with inclusions of mica, grog and limestone. Outslanting rim thickened at everted rim, roughly triangular in cross-section.

245. (40-4) Figs. 37, 59. Rim fragment. WT=.5 cm. D=18 cm. Coarse hard clay with inclusions of mica, fine sand and grog, 2.5YR 5/6 red, with a darker core. Outslanting rim thickened at the lip with a vertical external face, roughly triangular in cross-section.

246. (12-2) Fig. 51. **Bowl**? Rim fragment. WT=.5 cm. D=16 cm. Coarse soft clay with inclusions of mica and scant sand, 5YR 5/8 yellowish red. Outslanting rim thickened to a triangular cross-section at the lip.

247. (16-23) Fig. 54. **Bowl**? Rim fragment. WT=.4 cm. D=23 cm. Medium-coarse hard clay with inclusions of mica and tiny grey and black lithics. Outslanting rim thickened to a roughly circular cross-section at the lip.

248. (40-2) Figs. 37, 59. Rim fragment. WT=.8 cm. D=15 cm. Coarse hard clay with inclusions of mica and grog, 7.5YR 5/6 yellowish red. Outslanting rim bevelled to the vertical externally.

249. (49-4) Figs. 37, 61. **Bowl**? Rim fragment. WT=.65 cm. D=22 cm. Medium-coarse hard clay with inclusions of mica, sand and fine grog, 5YR 5/4 reddish brown, with a grey core. Outslanting rim with everted lip.

250. (18-1) Figs 37, 55. Rim fragment. WT=.57 cm. D=14 cm. Medium-fine soft clay with inclusions of mica nd sand, 5YR 5/6 yellowish red. Everted rim with flattened horizontal surface.

251. (35-3) Fig. 58. **Cup**? Rim fragment. WT=.54 cm. D=11 cm. Medium-coarse hard clay with inclusions of mica, grog and sand. Outslanting rim with everted lip.

252. (39-15) Fig. 37. **Bowl**? Rim fragment. WT=.82 cm. D=30 cm. Coarse softish clay with abundant inclusions of mica and sand, 5YR 5/4 reddish brown, fire clouded on exterior. Outslanting rim thickened at the lip, which has a flattened horizontal surface.

253. (17-12) Fig. 37. **Bowl**? Rim fragment. WT=.8 cm. D=23 cm. Coarse hard clay with inclusions of mica and grog, 2.5YR 5/6 red. Shape similar to number 252 above.

254. (42-7) Figs. 37, 60. Rim fragment. WT=.62 cm. D=32 cm. Medium-coarse softish clay with inclusions of mica, grog, sand and tiny white flecks, 2.5YR 5/8 red with a brownish core. Vertical rim with an everted lip with triangular cross-section.

255. (18-5) Figs. 37, 55. Rim fragment. WT=.9 cm. D=20 cm. Medium-coarse softish clay with inclusions of mica, grog and tiny white flecks, 5YR 5/4 reddish brown, some fire clouding, with a black core. Shape similar to number 254 above.

256. (13-2) Fig. 52. Rim fragment. WT=1.06 cm. D=16 cm. Coarse soft clay with inclusions of mica and occasional grog and white flecks, 5YR 5/6 yellowish red. Outslanting rim recurved to vertical, with an interior groove of triangular cross-section at the point of inflection.

257. (16-25) Fig. 54. Rim fragment. WT=.9 cm. D=24 cm. Medium-coarse hard clay with inclusions of mica, sand and grog, 2.5YR 6/6 brownish red. Everted rim slightly thickened at the vertical edge.

258. (17-26) Fig. 37. Rim fragment. WT=1.25 cm. D=38 cm. Coarse hard clay with inclusions of mica, grog and crushed white lithics, 5YR 5/6 yellowish red with a grey core. Vertical rim, undifferentiated.

Bases

259. (49-17) Fig. 38. Base fragment. WT=.9 cm. D=10 cm. Medium-coarse hard clay with inclusions of mica, grog and lithics, 5YR 6/4 light reddish brown on exterior and half of core, 2.5YR 6/5 light red on interior and half of core. Undifferentiated flat base with prominent rilling on interior.

260. (38-17)Fig. 38. Base fragment. WT=.6 cm. D=10 cm. Medium-coarse hard clay with inclusions of mica and grog, 2.5YR 6/6 light red. Undifferentiated flat base with prominent rilling on interior.

261. (1-8) Fig. 38. Base fragment. WT=.6 cm. D=7 cm. Medium-fine hard clay with inclusions of mica, grog and scant lithics. Shape same as number 260 above.

Handles

262. (10-2) Figs. 38, 48. **Hydria**? Handle fragment. Coarse soft clay with inclusions of mica, grog and white flecks, 10R 6/8 light red, with a slightly redder core. Slight curvature, circular cross-section, 2.6 cm thick.

263. (11-43) Figs. 38, 50. **Hydria**? Handle fragment. Coarse hard clay with inclusions of mica, sand, grog and one large piece of sandstone, 2.5YR 6/6 light red with a grey core. Slight curvature, flattened attachment present; cross-section is circular, 3 cm thick.

264. (12-19) Fig. 51. Handle fragment. Coarse softish clay with inclusions of mica, sand and grog, 2.5YR 6/8 light red. Slight curvature, flattened attachment present; circular cross-section, 3 cm thick. This might possibly be another piece of number 263 above; they were recovered at adjacent survey units.

265. (50-16) Fig. 62. Handle fragment. Medium-coarse hard clay with inclusions of mica, grog and shell? !0r 5/6 red with a light grey core. Slight inflected curvature, circular cross-section, 2.2 cm thick.

266. (49-24) Fig. 61. Handle fragment. Medium-coarse soft clay with inclusions of mica and black and white lithics, 7.5YR 6/6 reddish yellow, with a brown core. Curved to the expanding attachment, oval in cross-section, 1.2 cm by 2.7 cm.

267. (7-62) Fig. 38. Handle fragment. Medium-coarse hard clay with inclusions of mica, sand and grog, 5YR 6/6 reddish yellow with a dark grey core. No curvature, oval in cross-section, 2 cm by 3.04 cm.

268. (1-6) Fig. 38. Handle fragment. Medium-coarse soft friable clay with inclusions of mica, sand and grog, 5YR 6/7 reddish yellow. Expanding attachment and small portion of body, oval cross-section, 1.2 cm by 2.3 cm.

269. (2-27). Handle fragment. Medium-coarse semi-hard clay with inclusions of mica, sand and grog, 2.5YR 6/7 light red, with a grey core. No apparent curvature, expanding slightly near attachment, oval in cross-section, 2.8 cm by 3.6 cm.

270. (10-1) Figs. 38, 48. Handle fragment. Coarse softish clay with inclusions of mica, grog and white flecks, 2.5YR 6/8 light red with a grey core. Slight curvature, almond-shaped in cross-section, 2.5 cm by 4.8 cm.

271. (7-61) Fig. 38. Handle fragment. Coarse hard clay with inclusions of mica, sand and grog, 2.5YR 6/8 light red with a grey core. No apparent curvature, expanding slightly near attachment. Half-almond in cross-section, 1.8 cm by 4.5 cm.

272. (15-16) Fig. 38. Handle fragment. Medium fine hard clay with inclusions of mica and fine grog, 5YR 5/6 yellowish red, with a grey core. Slight curvature near absent attachment, peanut-shaped in cross-section, 1.3 cm by 2.5 cm.

273. (42-2) Fig. 38. Handle fragment. D=13 cm (vessel diameter at point of attachment). Coarse hard clay with inclusions of mica, grog and sand, 2.5YR 5/8 red with some fire clouding; core is reddish grey. Abrupt curvature, expanding at point of attachment. Handle is half-almond shaped in cross-section, 1.7 cm by 4.4 cm.

274. (11-23) Fig. 39. Handle fragment, attachment and small part of body. D=11 cm. Medium-coarse hard clay with inclusions of mica, sand and grog, with some limestone spalling. 10R 6/8 light red with a grey core. Handle is half-almond shaped in cross-section, 1.1 cm by 3.3 cm.

275. (7-49) Fig. 39. Handle fragment. Very coarse hard clay with inclusions of mica, sand and grog, 10YR 5/3 brown, with a grey core. Severe curvature, oval cross-section, 1.2 cm by 3.2 cm.

276. (7-27) Fig. 39. Handle fragment. Medium-fine very soft clay with inclusions of mica, grog and occasional brown lithics, 7.5YR 7/4 light yellowish red. Strap handle with prominent curvature, very elongated oval in cross-section, .3 cm by 1.3 cm.

277. (7-53) Fig. 39. Handle fragment. D=20 cm (vessel diameter measured at attachment). Medium-coarse soft clay with inclusions of mica, grog and lithics, 5YR 6/6 reddish yellow. Strap handle with severe angled curvature, expanding to attachment. Cross-section is crescent shaped, .7 cm by 3 cm.

278. (13-19) Figs. 39, 52. Handle fragment. Medium-fine hard clay with inclusions of mica, grog and white flecks, 2.5YR 6/6 light red, with a slip of 7.5YR 7/4 beige. Inflected curvature near one end; cross-section is a grooved oval, ca. 2.3 cm by 4.2 cm.

279. (4-55) Figs. 39, 43. Handle fragment. Medium-coarse semi-hard clay with inclusions of mica and sand, 2.5YR 6/8 light red. No curvature, Irregular crescent shaped cross-section, ca. 1.5 cm by 2.2 cm.

280. (42-6) Fig. 39. Handle fragment. D=10 cm (vessel diameter measured at attachment). Coarse hard clay with inclusions of mica, grog and occasional sand, 2.5YR 6/8 light red with a grey core. Strap handle expanding slightly to attachment. Cross-section is elongated oval, 1.7 cm by 6.1 cm.

281. (38-25) Figs. 39, 58. Handle fragment. D=7 cm (vessel diameter measured at attachment). Medium-coarse hard clay with inclusions of mica and lithics, 2.5YR 6/6 light

red with a grey core. Ridged strap handle with attachment. Cross-section is irregular elongated oval, ca. 1.5 cm by 7.6 cm.

282. (30-14) Fig. 39. Handle fragment. D=22 cm (vessel diameter measured at attachment). Medium-coarse semi-soft clay with inclusions of mica, sand, grog and lithics, 2.5YR 6/6 light red with a grey core. Inflected curvature to expanding attachment. Cross-section is elongated oval, 1.4 cm by 4.6 cm.

283. (49-29) Fig. 61. Handle fragment. Coarse hard clay with inclusions of mica, sand and grog, 5YR 4/6 yellowish red with a grey core. Slight inflected curvature, expanding towards attachment; cross-section is rectangular, 1.7 cm by 2.5 cm.

284. (16-34) Fig. 39. Handle fragment. Coarse hard clay with inclusions of mica, grog and brown and white lithics, 2.5YR 6/6 light red with a grey core; a portion of the vessel interior is attached, too small to measure curvature, 5YR 5/4 reddish brown. Twisted rope handle with slight curvature, rectangular in cross-section, 1.53 cm by 1.34 cm.

Lid knobs

285. (46-5). WT=.6 cm. Coarse hard clay with inclusions of mica, grog and sand, 2.5YR 5/6 red exterior; core and interior are 5YR 5/3 reddish brown. Circular, 3 cm in diameter, with a solid profile.

286. (24-13) Fig. 56. Partial lid knob. Coarse hard clay with inclusions of mica, sand and grog, black. Circular, 4 cm in diameter with a concave top. Solid profile.

287. (7-37) Fig. 40. WT=.55 cm. Coarse hard clay with inclusions of mica, sand and grog, with much limestone spalling; 2.5YR 5/6 red. Circular, 3 cm in diameter, with a horizontal ridge on top. Semi-hollow profile.

288. (7-11) Fig. 40. WT=.44 cm. Coarse hard clay with inclusions of mica and sand, 2.5YR 5.5/8 light red with much grayish efflorescence. Irregular rectangle, 1.2 cm by 1.7 cm. Semi-hollow profile.

289. (50-10) Fig. 62. WT=.4 cm. Medium-fine very soft clay with inclusions of mica and grog, 5YR 6/6 reddish yellow. Rectangular, 1.5 cm by 2.4 cm. Hollow profile.

Miscellaneous material

290. (11-42) Figs. 40, 50. **Ring stand**? Fragment. WT=.67 cm. D=23 cm. Coarse very hard clay with inclusions of mica, sand, grog and white flecks, 2.5YR 6/6 light red. Double flanged vertical ring, possibly for holding round-bottomed pots; no fire clouding, no analogs.

291. (11-22) Figs. 40, 50. Body fragment. Medium coarse hard clay with inclusions of mica, sand, grog and lithics, 5YR 6/6 reddish yellow, with a grey core. Irregular shape, all edges but one finished.

292. (16-30) Fig. 54. Body fragment. Medium-coarse hard clay with inclusions of mica, sand and brown lithics, 5YR 4/4 reddish brown with a dark grey core. Irregular shape, but apparently part of a vessel.

293. (50-11) Fig. 62. Fragment. Coarse hard clay with inclusions of mica, sand and grog, 2.5YR 5/6 red with a light grey core. Irregular "shoe" shape, possibly part of a terracotta figurine?

294. (42-3) Figs. 40, 60. Unknown, apparently entire. 5YR 4/4 reddish brown soft gritty sandstone. Three-dimensional triangle with rounded top. Loomweight or fishing net weight?

References

ADAMESTEANU, Dinu, 1990: "Greeks and natives in Basilicata", in Jean-P. Descoedres (ed.) *Greek Colonists and Native Populations* (Oxford) 143-150.

ADAMESTEANU, Dinu, (ed.), 1983: *Metaponto II. NSc* XXXI, Supplemento, (Rome).

ADAMESTEANU, Dinu, MERTENS, Dieter, & D'ANDRIA, F, 1980: *Metaponto I. NSc* XXIX, Supplemento, (Rome).

ADAMS, Robert McCormick, & NISSEN, Hans J., 1972: *The Uruk Countryside* (Chicago).

AMMERMAN, Rebecca Miller, & CIPRIANI, Marina, 1996: "Votive Offerings at Paestum: Continuity and Change in Cult Practice at the Temple of Ceres" (paper presented at the Annual Meeting of the AIA, New York).

AMYX, Darrell A., 1988: *Corinthian Vase-Painting of the Archaic Period* (Berkeley).

ANGER, Gerd, 1969: "Mineralogische Untersuchungen an Einigen Proben aus Paestum", *RM* LXXVI: 383-387.

ARCURI, Flaminia, 1985: "I materiali protostorici", *AION* VII: 69-76.

ARCURI, Flaminia, 1989: "Preistoria e protostoria", in P. Cantalupo, & A. La Greca (edd.) *Storia delle Terre del Cilento Antico* (Acciaroli) 53-68.

ASHERI, David, 1966: *Distribuzioni di Terre nell'antica Grecia* (Torino).

AURÈS, A., 1868: *Études des dimensions du grand temple de Paestum au double point de vue de l'architecture et de la métrologie* (Nimes).

AVAGLIANO, Giovanni, 1986a: "Santuario del Getsemani", in *Il Museo di Paestum* (Capaccio) 63-64.

AVAGLIANO, Giovanni, 1986b: "Santuario di Fonte", in *Il Museo di Paestum* (Capaccio) 65-66.

AVAGLIANO, Giovanni, & CIPRIANI, Marina, 1987: *Paestum. Città e territorio nelle colonie greche d'occidente* I (Taranto).

AVERSANO, Enzo, 1989: "Aspetti geografici del terrotorio", in P. Cantalupo, & A. La Greca (edd.) *Storia delle terre del Cilento antico* (Acciaroli) 27-44.

BAGGIONI-LIPPMANN, Mireille, 1982: "Néotectonique et géomorphologie dans l'Apennin campanien (Italie méridionale)" *Revue de géologie dynamique et de géographie physique* 23: 41-54.

BAGNASCO, M. Barra (ed.), 1992: *Locri Epizefiri IV* (Firenze).

BARKER, Graeme, 1972: "The conditions of cultural and economic growth in theBronze Age of central Italy", *PPS* 38: 170-208.

BARKER, Graeme, 1981: *Landscape and Society: Prehistoric Central Italy* (NewYork).

BARLETTA, Barbara A., 1990: "An 'Ionian Sea' style in archaic Doric architecture", *AJA* 94: 45-72.

BÉRARD, Jean, 1955: "A l'Héraion du Silaris, près de Paestum: II. Le petit temple archaique", *RA* XLV: 121-140.

BERGONZI, Giovanni, & CATENI, Gabriele, 1979: "L'Età del Bronzo Finale nella Toscana marittima", *Atti della riunione scientifica dell'Istituto Italiano di Preistoria e Protostoria* XXI: 249-265.

BERVE, Helmut, & GRUBEN, Gottfried, 1963: *Greek Temples, Theatres and Shrines* (London).

BIETTI SESTIERI, Anna Maria, 1981: "Economy and society in Italy between the Late Bronze Age and Early Iron Age", in G. Barker, & R. Hodges (edd.) *Archaeology and Italian Society. BAR* 102 (Oxford) 133-155.

BIETTI SESTIERI, Anna Maria, 1984: "Central and southern Italy in the Late Bronze Age", in T. Hackens, N. D. Holloway & R. R. Holloway (edd.) *Crossroads of the Mediterranean, Archaeologia Transatlantica* II (Louvain-la-neuve and Providence) 55-122.

BINTLIFF, John, 1985: "The Boeotia survey", in S. Macready, & F. H. Thompson (edd.) *Archaeological Field Survey in Britain and Abroad* (London) 196-216.

BINTLIFF, John, & SNODGRASS, Anthony, 1988a: "Mediterranean survey and the city", *Antiquity* 62: 57-71.

BINTLIFF, John, & SNODGRASS, Anthony, 1988b: "Off-site pottery distributions: A regional and interregional perspective", *CA* 29: 506-513.

BISOGNO, Giuseppina, 1984: "Tegole e mattoni", in P. Peduto (ed.) *Villaggi fluviali nella pianura Pestana del secolo VII* (Altavilla Silentina) 149-156.

BISOGNO, Giuseppina, & GUARINO, Vittoria, 1984: "La ceramica", in P. Peduto (ed.) *Villaggi fluviali nella pianura Pestana del secolo VII* (Altavilla Silentina) 103-124.

BOARDMAN, John, 1980: *The Greeks Overseas* (New York).

BRADFORD, John, 1957: *Ancient Landscapes* (London).

BRANCACCIO, L., *et all.*, 1986: "Isoleucine epimerization dating and tectonic significance of Upper Pleistocene sea-level features of the Sele Plain (Southern Italy)", *Zeitschrift für Geomorphologie* 62: 159-166.

BRANCACCIO, Ludovico, *et all.*, 1987: "Evoluzione tettonica e geomorfologica della Piana del Sele (Campania, Appennino Meridionale)", *Geografia fisica e dinamica del quaternario* 10: 47-55.

BRONEER, Oscar, 1977: *Terracotta Lamps. Isthmia III* (Princeton).

BROWN, Frank E., 1980: *Cosa: The Making of a Roman Town* (Ann Arbor).

BUTI, Gianna G., & DEVOTO, Giacomo, 1974: *Preistoria e storia delle regioni d'Italia* (Firenze).

CANTALUPO, Piero, & LA GRECA, Amadeo, (edd.) 1989: *Storia delle terre del Cilento antico* (Acciaroli).

CAPANO, Antonio, 1989: "Periodo greco e lucano", in P. Cantalupo, & A. La Greca (edd.) *Storia delle terre del Cilento antico* (Acciaroli) 69-82.

CARRATELLI, Giovanni Pugliese, 1962: "Santuari extramurani in Magna Grecia", *ParPass* 17: 241-246.

CARANCINI, Gian Luigi, *et all.*, 1996: "L'Italia", in Clarissa Belardelli, *et all.* (edd.) *The Bronze Age in Europe and the Mediterranean. XIII International Congress of Prehistoric and Protohostoric Sciences: Colloquia* 11 (Forlì) 75-86.

CARDARELLI, Andrea, & DI GENNARO, Francesco, 1996: "L'Italia", in Clarissa Belardelli, *et all.* (edd.) *The Bronze Age in Europe and the Mediterranean. XIII International Congress of Prehistoric and Protohostoric Sciences: Colloquia* 11 (Forlì) 259-266.

CARTER, Joseph Coleman, 1983: "Preliminary report on the excavation at Pizzica Pantanello (1974-1976)", *NSc* XXXI: 407-499.

CARTER, Joseph Coleman, 1990: "Metapontum - land, wealth, and population", in Jean-P. Descoedres (ed.) *Greek Colonists and Native Populations* (Oxford) 405-441.

CARTER, Joseph Coleman, & D'ANNIBALE, Cesare, 1985: "Metaponto and Croton", in S. Macready, & F. H. Thompson (edd.) *Archaeological Field Survey in Britain and Abroad* (London) 146-157.

CASTAGNOLI, Ferdinando, 1976a: "L'orientamento nella cartografia greca e romana", *Rendiconti della Pontificia Accademia Romana di Archeologia* 48: 59-69.

CASTAGNOLI, Ferdinando, 1976b: "Le origini di Poseidonia in Strabone", *Rendiconti della Pontificia Accademia Romana di Archeologia* 48: 71-74.

CIARANFI, N., *et all.*, 1981: "Proposta di zonazione sismotettonica dell'Italia meridionale", *Rendiconti della Società Geologica Italiana* 4: 493-496.

CINQUE, Aldo, *et all.*, 1987: "Osservazioni preliminari sull'evoluzionegeomorfologica della Piana del Sarno (Campania, Appennino meridionale)", *Geografia e fìsica dinamica del quaternario* 10: 161-174.

CIPRIANI, Marina, 1986a: "I santuari che circondano l'area urbana", in *Il museo di Paestum* (Agropoli) 57-60.

CIPRIANI, Marina, 1986b: "Le necropoli di V sec. a.C.", in *Il museo di Paestum* (Agropoli) 103-108.

CIPRIANI, Marina, 1986c: "La tomba del tuffatore", in *Il museo di Paestum* (Agropoli) 109-110.

CIPRIANI, Marina, 1988: "Acqua o fontana che bolle", in *Poseidonia-Paestum. Atti del Convegno di Studi sulla Magna Grecia* 27: 415-416.

CIPRIANI, Marina, 1989: *S. Nicola di Albanella. Scavo di un santuario campestre nel territorio di Poseidonia-Paestum* (Rome).

CIPRIANI, Marina, 1996: "Prime presenze italiche organizzate alle porte di Poseidonia", in Marina Cipriani & Fausto Longo (edd.) *I Greci in Occidente: Poseidonia e i Lucani* (Napoli) 119-158.

COCCO, E., *et all.*, 1971: "Erosione e trasporto dei sedimenti lungo il litorale di Paestum (Campania)", *Atti del convegno nazionale di studi sui problemi della geologia applicata* 2: 1-20.

COULSON, W. D. E., 1976: "Paestum", *PECS* 663-665.

COULSON, W. D. E., 1984: *Cross-cultural Trade in World History* (Cambridge).

D'AGOSTINO, Bruno, 1974a: "La civiltà del ferro nell'Italia meridionale e nella Sicilia", in M. Pallotino, & G. Mansuelli (edd.) *Popoli e civiltà dell'Italia antica* (Rome) 11-91.

D'AGOSTINO, Bruno, 1974b: "Il mondo periferico della Magna Grecia", in M. Pallotino, & G. Mansuelli (edd.) *Popoli e civiltà dell'Italia antica* (Rome) 179-271.

D'AGOSTINO, Bruno, 1974c: "Pontecagnano", in G. B. Modesti, B. d'Agostino, & P. Gastaldi (edd.) *Seconda mostra della preistoria e della protostoria nel Salernitano* (Salerno) 87-108.

D'AGOSTINO, Bruno, 1990: "Relations between Campania, southern Etruria, and the Aegean in the eighth century BC", in Jean-P. Descoedres (ed.) *Greek Colonists and Native Populations* (Oxford) 73-86.

D'AGOSTINO, Bruno, & VOZA, Giuseppe, 1962: "Necropoli dell'Arenosola", in M. Napoli, B. d'Agostino, & G. Voza (edd.) *Mostra della preistoriae della protostoria nel Salernitano* (Salerno) 89-104.

D'AMBROSIO, A., & DE CARO, S., 1990: "Un contributo all'architettura e all'urbanistica di Pompei in età ellenistica. I saggi nella Casa VII, 4, 62", *AION* XII: 173-215.

D'ARGENIO, B., *et all.*, 1983: "I travertini di Pontecagnano (Campania):geomorfologia, sedimentologia, geochimica", *Bolletino della Società Geologica Italiana* 102: 123-136.

DE CARO, Stefano, 1985: "Nuove indagini sulle fortificazioni di Pompei", *AION* VII: 75-124.

DEHM, Richard, 1969: "Die Mollusken aus dem antiken Wallgraben von Paestum", *RM* LXXVI: 355-370.

DELAGARDETTE, C. M., 1799: *Les Ruines de Paestum ou Posidonia, Ancienne Ville de la Grande Gréce, a Vingt-deux Liettes de Naples, dans le Golfe de Salerne* (Paris).

DE LA GENIÈRE, Juliette, 1968: *Recherches sur l'âge du fer en Italie méridionale: Sala Consilina* (Naples).

DE LA GENIÈRE, Juliette, 1970: "Contribution à l'étude des relations entre Grecs et indigènes sur la Mer Ionienne", *MEFR* 82: 621-636.

DE LA GENIÈRE, Juliette, 1979: "The Iron Age in southern Italy", in D. Ridgway, & F. R. Ridgway (edd.) *Italy before the Romans: the Iron Age, Orientalizing and Etruscan Periods* (New York) 59-94.

DE LA GENIÈRE, Juliette, 1984: "Contributions to a typology of ancient settlements in southern Italy (IXth to IVth century BC)", in T. Hackens, N. D. Holloway, & R. R. Holloway (edd.) *Crossroads of the Mediterranean. Archaeologia Transatlantica* II (Louvain-la-neuve and Providence) 163-186.

DELEZIR, Jean, & GUY, Max, 1988: "Les conditions géomorphiques du site et du terroir de Paestum étudiees d'après des images de satellites (Landsat TM et Spot)", in *Poseidonia-Paestum. Atti del Convegno di Studi sulla Magna Grecia* 27:463-470.

DE WIT, H. E., *et all.*, 1988: "Geological answers to archaeological questions: an example", in Marinos, Koukis (ed.) *Engineering Geology of Ancient Works, Monuments and Historical Sites* (Rotterdam) 1613-1622.

DI GENNARO, Francesco, 1979: "Contributo alla conoscenza del territorio etrusco meridionale alla fine dell'Età del Bronzo", *Atti della riunione scientifica dell'Istituto Italiano di Preistoria e Protostoria* XXI: 267-274.

DINSMOOR, William Bell, 1950: *The Architecture of Ancient Greece* (New York).

DI SANDRO, Norma, 1981: "Le anfore 'Massaliote' in Campania", *AION* III: 49-53.

DI VITA, A., 1990: "Town planning in the Greek colonies of Sicily from the time of their foundations to the Punic wars", in Jean-P. Descoedres (ed.) *Greek Colonists and Native Populations* (Oxford) 343-364.

DRAGO, Ciro, 1953: "Lo scavo di Torre Castelluccia (Pulsano)", *Bollettinodi paletnologia Italiana* 8: 155-161.

DUNBABIN, T. J., 1948: *The Western Greeks* (Oxford).

DYSON, Stephen L., 1976: *Cosa: The Utilitarian Pottery. MAAR* XXXIII (Rome).

FIAMMENGHI, Carla Antonella, 1985: "Agropoli: primi saggi di scavo nell'area del castello", *AION* VII: 53-76.

FIAMMENGHI, Carla Antonella, 1988: "Agropoli", in *Poseidonia-Paestum. Atti del Convegno di Studi sulla Magna Grecia* 27:396-398.

FINLEY, M. I., 1977: "Paestum", in M. I. Finley (ed.) *Atlas of Classical Archaeology* (London) 128-130.

FLANNERY, Kent V., *et all.*, 1971: "Farming systems and political growth in ancient Oaxaca", in S. Struever (ed.) *Prehistoric Agriculture* (Garden City) 157-180.

FLEMMING, N. C., 1969: "Archaeological evidence for eustatic change of sea level and earth movements in the western Mediterranean during the last 2,000 years", *Special Papers of the Geological Society of America* 109: 3-98.

FOTI, Giuseppe, 1962: "La tarda età del bronzo e la prima età del ferro in Calabria", *Klearchos* 4: 32-37.

FRACCHIA, Helena, 1986: "An ancient route in southeastern Lucania", *AJA* 90: 441-445.

FUGAZZOLA DELPINO, M. A., 1979: "The Proto-Villanovan: a survey", in D. Ridgway, & F. R. Ridgway (edd.) *Italy before the Romans: the Iron Age, Orientalizing and Etruscan Periods* (New York) 31-54.

GASPARRI, Domenico, 1990: "La fotointerpretazione archeologica nella ricerca storico-topografica sui territori di Pontecagnano, Paestum e Velia", *AION* XII: 253-265.

GAUTHIER, Philippe, 1972: *Symbola: les étrangers et la justice dans les cités grecques* (Nancy).

GIACOMELLI, Roberto, 1988: *Achaea Magno-Graeca. Le iscrizioni arcaiche in alfabeto acheo di Magna Grecia* (Brescia).

GIANGIULIO, M., 1992: "La öëëüôçò tra Sibariti e Serdaioi (Meiggs-Lewis, 10)", *ZPE* 93: 31-44.

GIGANTE, Marcello, 1970: "Senofane e 'la colonizzazione di Elea'", *ParPass* XXV: 236-240.

GRAHAM, A. J., 1971: "Patterns in early Greek colonization", *JHS* 91: 35-47.

GRAHAM, A. J., 1983: *Colony and Mother City in Ancient Greece* (Chicago).

GRECO, Emanuele, 1979a: "Poseidonia entre le VI et le IV siècle avant Jésus-Christ", *RA* 74: 219-234.

GRECO, Emanuele, 1979b: "Qualche riflessione ancora sulle origini de Poseidonia", *Dialoghi di archeologia* 2: 51-56.

GRECO, Emanuele, 1979c: "Ricerche sulla *chora* poseidoniate: il 'paesaggio agrario' dalla fondazione della città alla fine del sec. IV a. C.", *Dialoghi di archeologia* 2: 7-25.

GRECO, Emanuele, 1981: "La ceramica arcaica a Poseidonia", in M. Mello (ed.) *Il Commercio greco nel Tirreno in età arcaica* (Salerno) 57-66.

GRECO, Emanuele, 1982: "Considerazioni su alcuni modelli di organizzazione dello spazio agrario nelle città greche dell'Italia meridionale", *Archeologia* XXXIII: 47-58.

GRECO, Emanuele, 1988: "La città e il territorio: i problemi di storia topografica", in *Poseidonia-Paestum. Atti del Convegno di Studi sulla Magna Grecia* 27: 471-500.

GRECO, Emanuele, & THEODORESCU, Dinu, 1980: *Poseidonia-Paestum I: la curia* (Rome).

GRECO, Emanuele, & THEODORESCU, Dinu, 1983: *Poseidonia-Paestum II: l'agora* (Rome).

GRECO, Emanuele, & THEODORESCU, Dinu, 1987: *Poseidonia-Paestum III: forum nord* (Rome).

GRECO, Giovanna, & PONTRANDOLFO, Angela, 1990: *Fratte: un insediamento etrusco- campano* (Modena).

GUALTIERI, Maurizio, *et all.*, 1990: *Roccagloriosa I* (Naples).

GUARDUCCI, Margherita, 1962: "Osservazioni sul trattato fra Sibari e i Serdaioi", *Atti dell'Accademia Nazionale dei Lincei: rendiconti* XVII: 199-201.

GÜNTHER, A. E., 1964a: "Re-drawing the coast line of southern Italy: a survey of shifting sea-levels from Gaeta to Malta, with reference to Paestum", *Illustrated London News*, January 18:. 86-89.

GÜNTHER, A. E., 1964b: "Historical marine levels in South Italy", *Nature* 201: 909-910.

GÜNTHER, Robert T., 1903: "The submerged Greek and Roman foreshore near Naples", *Archeologia* LVIII: 1-62.

GÜNTHER, Robert T., 1904: "Earth-movements in the Bay of Naples", *Nature* 69: 274-275.

GUZZO, Pier Giovanni, 1973: "Scavi a Sibari", *ParPass* XXVIII: 278-314.

GUZZO, Pier Giovanni, 1981a: "Scalea (Cosenza). Loc. Petrosa. - Scavo di una stratificazione di epoca alto-arcaica", *NSc* XXIV: 393-440.

GUZZO, Pier Giovanni, 1981b: "Vie istmiche della Sibaritide e commercio tirrenico", in M. Mello (ed.) *Il Commercio greco nel Tirreno in età arcaica* (Salerno) 35-56.

GUZZO, Pier Giovanni, 1990: "Myths and archaeology in south Italy", in Jean-P. Descoedres (ed.) *Greek Colonists and Native Populations* (Oxford) 131-142.

HAMBLIN, Dora Jane, 1976: *The Etruscans* (New York).

HAMMOND, N. G. L., 1986: *A History of Greece to 322 B. C.* (Oxford).

HAYES, J. W., 1972: *Late Roman Pottery* (London).

HEMANS, Frederick P., 1992: "New discoveries in the temple of Poseidon at Isthmia", *AIA Newsletter* 7: 1-3.

HERTWIG, Otto, 1968: *Über geometrische Gestaltunggrundlagen von Kultbauten des VI. Jahrhunderts v. Chr. zu Paestum* (München).

HOLE, Frank, *et all.*, 1969: *Prehistory and Human Ecology of the Deh Luran Plain* (Ann Arbor).

HOLLOWAY, R. Ross, 1970: *Satrianum* (Providence).

HOLLOWAY, R. Ross, 1971: "Archaeological news from south Italy and Sicily", *AJA* 75: 75-81.

HOLLOWAY, R. Ross, 1976: "Gaudo and the east", *JFA* 3:2: 143-158.

HOLLOWAY, R. Ross, 1990: "The geography of the southern Sicels", in Jean-P. Descoeudres (ed.) ΕΥΜΟΥΣΙΑ: *Ceramic and Iconographic Studies in Honour of Alexander Cambitoglou* (Sydney) 147-153.

HOLLOWAY, R. Ross, *et all.*, 1975: "Buccino: the Early Bronze Age village of Tufariello", *JFA* 2:1: 11-81.

HOLLOWAY, R. Ross, *et all.*, 1978: "The development of the Italian Bronze Age: evidence from Trentinara and the Sele valley", *JFA* 5:2: 133-144.

HORSNAES, Helle, 1991: "The Ager Picentinus", *Acta Hyperborea* 3: 219-234.

HORSNAES, Helle, 1992: "The Etruscan Necropolis at Arenosola", *Apollo* 8: 9-16.

HORSNAES, Helle, 1994: "En etruskisk forpost", *Piranesi* 8: 49-69.

INGOLD, Tim, 1993: "The temporality of the landscape", *WorldArch* 25: 152-174.

JACOBY, Felix, 1923: *Die Fragmente der Griechischen Historiker* (Berlin).

JAMESON, Michael H., *et all.*, 1995: *A Greek Countryside: The Southern Argolid from Prehistory to the Present Day* (Stanford).

JOHANNOWSKI, Werner, *et all.*, 1983: "Excavations at Paestum 1982", *AJA* 87: 293-303.

KELLER, Donald R., & RUPP, David W., 1983: *Archaeological Survey in the Mediterranean Area. BAR* 155 (Oxford).

KILIAN, Klaus, 1969: "Neue Funde zur Vorgeschichte Paestums", *RM* LXXVI: 335-349.

KOEHLER, Carolyn G., 1978: "Evidence around the Mediterranean for Corinthian export of wine and oil", in J.

B. Arnold (ed.) *Beneath the Waters of Time* (Austin) 231-239.

KOLDEWAY, R., & PUCHSTEIN, O., 1899: *Die griechischen Tempel in Unteritalien und Sizilien* (Berlin).

KRAAY, Colin M., & HIRMER, Max, 1966: *Greek Coins* (New York).

KRAUSS, Friedrich, 1941: *Paestum: die Griechischen Tempel* (Berlin).

KRAUSS, Friedrich, 1959: *Die Tempel von Paestum: Der Athenatempel* (Berlin).

KURTZ, Donna C., & BOARDMAN, John, 1971: *Greek Burial Customs* (Ithaca).

LAMBOGLIA, Nino, 1958: "Nuove osservazioni sulla 'terra sigillata chiara' (tipi A e B)", *RStLig* 24: 257-330.

LANE, Arthur, 1948: *Greek Pottery* (London).

LATTANZI, Elena, (ed.), 1992: *Sibari V. NSc* XLII-XLIII, III Supplemento (Rome).

LAUTER, Hans, 1984: "Ein archäischer Hallenbau in Poseidonia/Paestum", *RM* XCI: 23-45.

LAWRENCE, A. W., 1983: *Greek Architecture* (New York).

LIVADIE, Claude Albore, 1986: "Cenni sulla frequentazione preistorica e protostorica dell'agro pestano", in *Il Museo di Paestum* (Capaccio) 19-22.

LO PORTO, Felice Gino, 1964: "Satyrion: scavi e ricerche nel luogo del piu antico insediamento laconico in Puglia", *NSc* XVII: 177-279.

LO PORTO, Felice Gino, 1973: *Civiltà indigena e penetrazione greca nella Lucania orientale. MontAnt* 1-3 (Rome).

LO PORTO, Felice Gino, 1979: "Il Bronzo Finale nella Puglia centro-meridionale", *Atti della riunione scientifica dell'Istituto Italiano di Preistoria e Protostoria* XXI: 531-535.

LO SCHIAVO, Fulvia, & PERONI, Renato, 1979: "Il Bronzo Finale in Calabria", *Atti della riunione scientifica dell'Istituto Italiano di Preistoria e Protostoria* XXI: 551-569.

LUKESH, Susan Snow, 1984: "Italy and the Apennine culture", in T. Hackens, N. D. Holloway, & R. R. Holloway (edd.) *Crossroads of the Mediterranean. Archaeologia Transatlantica* II (Louvain-la-neuve and Providence) 13-54.

LUKESH, Susan Snow, & HOWE, Sally, 1978: "Protoapennine vs. Subapennine: mathematical distinction between two ceramic phases", *JFA* 5:3: 339-347.

MAIURI, Amedeo, 1949: "Paestum", in *Enciclopedia Italiana* (Rome) 916-919.

MAIURI, Amedeo, 1951: "Origine e decadenza di Paestum", *ParPass* VI: 274-286.

MALONE, Caroline, & STODDART, Simon (edd.), 1992: "The neolithic site of San Marco, Gubbio (Perugia), Umbria: survey and excavation 1985-7", *BSR* LX: 1-70.

MANFREDINI, Alessandra, *et all.*, 1996: "Coppa Nevigata", in R. G. Cremonesi, and F. Radina (edd.) *Puglia e Basilicata. Guide Archeologiche: Preistoria e Protostoria in Italia* 11 (Forlì) 27-37.

MARABINI MOEVS, Maria Teresa, 1973: *The Roman Thin Walled Pottery from Cosa (1948-1954). MAAR* XXXII (Rome).

MAYANI, Zacharie, 1962: *The Etruscans Begin to Speak* (New York).

MEIGGS, Russel, 1982: *Trees and Timber in the Ancient Mediterranean World* (Oxford).

MEIGGS, Russell, & LEWIS, David, 1969: *A Selection of Greek Historical Inscriptions to the End of the Fifth Century B.C.* (Oxford).

MELILLO, Luigia, 1984: "I materiali premedievali", in P. Peduto (ed.) *Villaggi Fluviali nella Pianura Pestana del Secolo VII* (Altavilla Silentina) 163-170.

MELLO, Mario, 1967: "Strabone V 4.13 e le origine di Poseidonia", *ParPass* XXII: 401-428.

MELLO, Mario, 1980: "Note sul territorio di Poseidonia", in *Settima miscellanea greca e romana* (Rome) 287-304.

MELLO, Mario, 1981: *Il Commercio greco nel Tirreno in età arcaica* (Salerno).

MELLO, Mario, 1983: *Ricerche sul territorio di Paestum nell'antichità* (Salerno).

MELLO, Mario, 1984: "Archeologia classica e archeologia cristiana nel territorio di Paestum", *Rendiconti della Pontificia Accademia Romana di Archeologia* LV-LVI: 313-327.

MELLO, Mario, 1989: "Periodo romano", in P. Cantalupo, & A. La Greca (edd.) *Storia delle terre del Cilento antico* (Acciaroli) 83-114.

MELLO, Mario, 1990: *Visitare Paestum: aspetti e problemi dalla riscoperta ad oggi* (Napoli).

MENARD, Theresa D. M., 1990: *The Archaic and Classical Pottery from the Sanctuary at Località Santa Venera in Paestum, Italy.* (diss., University of Michigan).

MERTENS, Dieter, 1990: "Some principal features of west Greek colonial architecture", in Jean-P. Descoedres (ed.) *Greek Colonists and Native Populations* (Oxford) 373-384.

MÉTRAUX, Guy P. R., 1978: *Western Greek Land-use and City-planning in the Archaic Period* (New York and London).

MIZOGUCHI, Koji, 1993: "Time in the reproduction of mortuary practices", *WorldArch* 25: 223-235.

MODESTI, Gianni Bailo, 1974: "Eboli, necropoli eneolitica", in G. B. Modesti, B. d'Agostino, & P. Gastaldi (edd.) *Seconda mostra della preistoria e della protostoria nel salernitano* (Salerno) 25-42.

MODESTI, Gianni Bailo, 1980: *Cairano nell'età arcaica* (Napoli).

MOLLARD-BESQUES, Simone, 1954: *Catalogue raisonné des figurines et reliefs en terre-cuite grecs et romains* (Paris).

MOREL, Jean-Paul, 1965: *Céramique à vernis noir du Forum Romain et du Palatin* (Paris).

MOREL, Jean-Paul, 1981: *Céramique campanienne: les formes* (Rome).

MOREL, Jean-Paul, 1984: "Greek colonization in Italy and the west (problems of evidence and interpretation)", in T.

Hackens, N. D. Holloway, & R. R. Holloway (edd.) *Crossroads of the Mediterranean. Archaeologia Transatlantica* II (Louvain-la-neuve and Providence) 123-162.

MORRIS, Ian, 1987: *Burial and Ancient Society* (Cambridge).

MORRIS, Ian, 1992: *Death-ritual and Social Structure in Classical Antiquity* (Cambridge).

MUHLY, James David, 1973: "Copper and tin: the distribution of mineral resources and the nature of the metals trade in the Bronze Age", *Transactions of the Connecticut Academy of Arts and Sciences* XLIII: 155-535.

NAPOLI, Mario, *et all.*, 1962: *Mostra della preistoria e della protostoria nel salernitano* (Salerno).

NATELLA, Pasquale, 1984: "San Lorenzo di Altavilla Silentina e la piana del Sele tra tardo antico e medioevo", in P. Peduto (ed.) *Villaggi fluviali nella pianura Pestana del secolo VII* (Altavilla Silentina) 9-28.

NISSEN, Heinrich, 1902: *Italische Landeskunde* (Berlin).

ORLANDOS, A., 1966: *Les matériaux de construction et la technique architecturale des anciens grecs* (Paris).

ÖSTENBERG, C. E., 1967: "Luni sul Mignone e problemi della preistoria d'Italia", *Acta instituti romani regni sueciae* 25: 1-306.

OSWALD, Felix, & PRYCE, Thomas Davies, 1966: *An Introduction to the Study of Terra Sigillata* (Farnborough).

PAIS, Ettore, 1894: *Storia della Sicilia a della Magna Grecia* (Torino).

PALLOTTINO, Massimo, 1965: "Proposto di una classificazione e di una terminologia delle fasi culturali del bronzo e del ferro in Italia", *Atti del congresso internazionale delle scienze preistoriche e protostoriche* VI:II: 396-402.

PALLOTTINO, Massimo, 1979: "Storia critica dei concetti di 'Protovillanoviano' e di 'Bronzo Finale'", *Atti della riunione scientifica dell'Istituto Italiano di Preistoria e Protostoria* XXI: 19-26.

PALLOTTINO, Massimo, 1991: *A History of Earliest Italy. Jerome Lectures* 17 (Ann Arbor).

PALLOTTINO, Massimo (ed.), 1992: *Pyrgi. NSc* XLII-XLIII, II Supplemento (Rome).

PANCRAZZI, Orlanda, 1979: *Cavallino I: scavi e ricerche 1964-1967* (Galatina).

PANEBIANCO, Venturino, 1970: "L'indicazione di Poseidonia e di Elea nel periplo di Ps.-Scilace", *ParPass* XXV: 241-243.

PANEBIANCO, Venturino, 1971: "Laos, Lavinion, Mercurion e l'origine anatolico-ausonia dei bretti e dei lucani", *ParPass* XXVI: 313-322.

PANELLA, C., & CARANDINI, A. (edd.), 1973: *Ostia III* (Roma).

PAOLI, P. A., 1784: *Rovine della città di Pesto detta ancora Posidonia* (Napoli).

PATRONI, G., 1937: *La preistoria. Storia politica d'Italia* (Milano).

PEACOCK, D. P. S., & WILLIAMS, D. F., 1986: *Amphorae and the Roman Economy* (New York).

PEARSON, Lionel, 1987: *The Greek Historians of the West: Timaeus and his Predecessors. Philological Monographs of the American Philological Association* XXXV (Atlanta).

PEDLEY, John Griffiths, 1972: *Ancient Literary Sources on Sardis. Archaeological Exploration of Sardis* 2 (Cambridge).

PEDLEY, John Griffiths, 1985: "Excavations at Paestum 1984", *AJA* 89: 53-60.

PEDLEY, John Griffiths, 1990: *Paestum* (London).

PEDLEY, John Griffiths, & TORELLI, Mario, 1984: "Excavations at Paestum 1983", *AJA* 88: 367-376.

PEDLEY, John Griffiths, & TORELLI, Mario, 1993: *The Sanctuary of Santa Venera at Paestum I* (Rome).

PEDUTO, Paolo (ed.), 1984: *Villagi fluviale nella Pianura Pestana del secolo VII* (Altavilla Silentina).

PERONI, Renato, 1967: *Archeologia della Puglia Preistorica* (Rome).

PERONI, Renato, 1979: "From Bronze Age to Iron Age: economic, historical and social considerations", in D. Ridgway, & F. R. Ridgway (edd.) *Italy before the Romans: the Iron Age, Orientalizing and Etruscan Periods* (New York) 7-30.

PONTRANDOLFO, Angela, 1979: "Segni di trasformazioni sociali a Poseidonia tra la fine del V e gli inizi del III sec. a. C.", *Dialoghi di archeologia* 2: 27-50.

PONTRANDOLFO, Angela, 1988: "Le necropoli dalla città greca alla colonia latina', in *Poseidonia-Paestum. Atti del Convegno di Studi sulla Magna Grecia* 27: 225-265.

PONTRANDOLFO, Angela, & ROUVERET, Agnès, 1992: *Le tombe dipinte di Paestum* (Modena).

PRESICCE, Claudio Parisi, 1985: "L'importanza di Hera nelle spedizioni coloniali e nell'insediamento primitivo delle colonie greche", *ArchCl* XXXVII: 44-83.

PUGLISI, S. M., 1959: *La civiltà appenninica: origine della communità pastorali in Italia* (Firenze).

RANDALL-MACIVER, David, 1927a: *The Etruscans* (Oxford).

RANDALL-MACIVER, David, 1927b: *The Iron Age in Italy* (Oxford).

RAPP, George Jr, & GIFFORD, John A., 1985: *Archaeological Geology* (New Haven).

RIDGWAY, David, 1989: "Archaeology in Sardinia and south Italy, 1983-88", *Archaeological Reports* 35: 130-147.

RIDGWAY, David, 1990: "The first western Greeks and their neighbors 1935-1985", in Jean-P. Descoedres (ed.) *Greek Colonists and Native Populations* (Oxford) 61-72.

RIEMANN, H., 1965: "Zur Grundrissinterpretation des Enneastylos von Poseidonia", *RM* LXII: 198-208.

ROTROFF, Susan I., & OAKLEY, John H., 1992: *Debris from a Public Dining Place in the Athenian Agora* (Princeton).

RUSSO, Mario, 1990: *Punta della Campanella: epigrafe rupestre osca e reperti vari dall'Athenaion* (Roma).

SARTORI, Franco, 1973: "Riflessioni sui regimi politici in Magna Grecia dopo la caduta di Sibari", *ParPass* XXVIII: 117-156.

SAUER, Carl O., 1941: "Forward to historical geography", *Annals of the Association of American Geographers* 31: 1-24.

SCHLÄGER, Helmut, 1969a: "Zu den Bauperioden der Stadtmauer von Paestum", *RM* LXXVI: 22-26.

SCHLÄGER, Helmut, 1969b: "Vorbemerkungen zu den Tierknochenfunden in Paestum", *RM* LXXVI: 371-381.

SCHLÄGER, Helmut, 1969c: "Weiteres zum Wallgraben von Paestum", *RM* LXXVI: 350-354.

SCHMIEDT, Giullio, 1970: "Contributo alla ricostruzione della situazione geotopografica di Velia nell'antichita", *ParPass* 25: 65-92.

SCHMIEDT, Giulio, & CASTAGNOLI, Ferdinando, 1955: "Fotografia aerea e ricerche archeologiche: il complesso urbanistico di Paestum", *L'Universo* 35: 117-144.

SCULLARD, Howard H., 1967: *The Etruscan Cities and Rome* (Ithaca).

SCULLY, Vincent, 1969: *The Earth, the Temple and the Gods* (New York).

SESTIERI, Pellegrino Claudio, 1950: "Le origini di Posidonia alla luce delle recenti scoperte di Palinuro", *ArchCl* II: 180-186.

SESTIERI, Pellegrino Claudio, 1952: "Ancora sulle origini di Posidonia", *ArchCl* IV: 77-80.

SESTIERI, Pellegrino Claudio, 1960: *Paestum, the City, the Prehistoric Necropolis in Contrada Gaudo, and the Heraion at the Mouth of the Sele* (Rome).

SEVINK, Jan, 1985: "Some observations on the superficial geology of the excavation site and their implications", *AJA* 89: 59-60.

SKELE, Mikels, 1996: "Archaeological survey in the Iron Age Mediterranean" (paper presented at the Annual Meeting of the SAA, New Orleans).

SMITH, James Reuel, 1922: *Springs and Wells in Greek and Roman Literature* (New York).

SMITH, Neil, 1989: "Geography as museum: private history and conservative idealism in The Nature of Geography", in J. N. Entrikin, & S. D. Brunn (edd.) *Reflections on Richard Hartshorne's The Nature of Geography* (Washington) 89-120.

SNODGRASS, Anthony, 1986: "Interaction by design: the Greek city state", in C. Renfrew, & J. F. Cherry (edd.) *Peer Polity Interaction and Socio-political Change* (Cambridge) 47-58.

SORDI, Marta, 1991: "C. Mario e una colonia etrusca in Tunisia", *ArchCl* XLIII: 363-366.

SPARKES, Brian A., & TALCOTT, Lucy, 1970: *Black and Plain Pottery of the 6th, 5th and 4th Centuries B.C. Agora* XII (Princeton).

STROM, Ingrid, 1990: "Relations between Etruria and Campania around 700 BC", in Jean-P. Descoedres (ed.) *Greek Colonists and Native Populations* (Oxford) 87-98.

SYMEONOGLOU, Sarantis, 1985: "The doric temples of Paestum", *Journal of Aesthetic Education* 19: 49-66.

TAYLOUR, William, 1958: *Mycenaean Pottery in Italy and Adjacent Areas* (Cambridge).

TOCCO SCIARELLI, Giuliana, 1988: "I Santuari", in *Poseidonia-Paestum. Atti del Convegno di Studi sulla Magna Grecia* 27: 361-452.

TOCCO SCIARELLI, Giuliana, *et all.*, 1988: "Heraion alla Foce del Sele. In *Poseidonia-Paestum. Atti del Convegno di Studi sulla Magna Grecia* 27: 385-396.

TORELLI, Mario, 1971: "Il santuario di Hera a Gravisca", *ParPass* 26: 44-67.

TORELLI, Mario, 1990: "Il commercio greco in Etruria tra l'VIII ed il VI secolo a.C.", in M. Mello (ed.) *Il commercio greco nel Tirreno in età arcaica* (Salerno) 67-82.

TRILLMICH, Clara Bencivenga, 1990: "Elea: problems of the relationship between city and territory, and of urban organization in the Archaic Period", in Jean-P. Descoedres (ed.) *Greek Colonists and Native Populations* (Oxford) 365-372.

TRIPP, Edward, 1970: *The Meridian Handbook of Classical Mythology* (New York).

TRUMP, David, 1966: *Central and Southern Italy before Rome. Ancient People and Places* 47 (New York).

VAGNETTI, Lucia, 1979: "Il Bronzo Finale in Puglia nei suoi rapporti con il Mediterraneo orientale", *Atti della riunione scientifica dell'Istituto Italiano di Preistoria e Protostoria* XXI: 537-549.

VAGNETTI, Lucia, 1980: "Mycenaean imports in central Italy", in E. Peruzzi (ed.) *Mycenaeans in Early Latium. Incunabula Graeca* LXXV (Rome) 151-167.

VAN EFFENTERRE, Henri, 1980: "La fondation de Paestum", *ParPass* 35: 161-175.

VAN EFFENTERRE, Henri, & RUZÉ, Françoise, 1994: *Nomina I. Recueil d'inscriptions politiques et juridiques de l'archaïsme grec. Collection de l'École Française de Rome* 188 (Rome).

VITA-FINZI, Claudio, 1969: *The Mediterranean Valleys* (Cambridge).

VITA-FINZI, Claudio, 1978: *Archaeological Sites in their Settings* (London).

VON VACANO, Otto-Wilhelm, 1960: *The Etruscans in the Ancient World* (New York).

VOZA, Giuseppe, 1962a: "Giacimento preistorico presso il tempio di Cerere-Paestum", in M. Napoli, B. d'Agostino, & G. Voza (edd.) *Mostra della preistoria e della protostoria nel salernitano* (Salerno) 13-38.

VOZA, Giuseppe, 1962b: "Necropoli del Gaudo", in M. Napoli, B. d'Agostino, & G. Voza (edd.) *Mostra della preistoria e della protostoria nel salernitano* (Salerno) 39-62.

VOZA, Giuseppe, 1962c: "Necropoli di Capodifiume", in M. Napoli, B. d'Agostino, & G. Voza (edd.) *Mostra della preistoria e della protostoria nel salernitano* (Salerno) 79-88.

VOZA, Giuseppe, 1963: "La topografia di Paestum alla luce di alcune recenti indagini", *ArchCl* XV: 223-232.

VOZA, Giuseppe, 1965: "Ultimi scavi della necropoli del Gaudo", *Atti della riunione scientifica dell'Istituto Italiano di Preistoria e Protostoria* IX: 265-274.

ZANCANI MONTUORO, Paola, 1950: "Sibari, Poseidonia e lo Heraion", *Archivio storico per la Calabria e la Lucania* XIX: 65-84.

ZANCANI MONTUORO, Paola, 1958a: "Altre metope scolpite dallo Heraion alla Foce del Sele", *AttiMGrecia* II: 7-26.

ZANCANI MONTUORO, Paola, 1958b: "Dossenno a Poseidonia", *AttiMGrecia* II: 79-94.

ZANCANI MONTUORO, Paola, 1960: "Lampada arcaica dallo Heraion alla Foce del Sele", *AttiMGrecia* III: 69-77.

ZANCANI MONTUORO, Paola, 1961: "Hera Hippia", *ArchCl* 13: 31-39.

ZANCANI MONTUORO, Paola, 1962: "Sibariti e Serdei", *Atti dell'Accademia Nazionale dei Lincei: rendiconti* XVII: 11-18.

ZANCANI MONTUORO, Paola, 1980: "Serdaioi?", *Schweizer Münzblätter* XXX: 57-61.

ZANCANI MONTUORO, Paola, & ZANOTTI-BIANCO, Umberto, 1951: *Heraion alla Foce del Sele* (Roma).

ARISTOTELES: *Politics* ed. H. Rackham (Harvard University Press; Cambridge, 1944).

ATHENAIOS: *The Deipnosophists* ed. C. B. Gullick (Harvard University Press; Cambridge, 1927).

DIODORUS SICULUS: *Bibliotheca Historica* ed. C. H. Oldfather (Harvard University Press; Cambridge, 1933).

DIONYSIOS HALIKARNASEOS: *Roman Antiquities* ed. E. Cary (Harvard University Press; Cambridge, 1937).

HERODOTOS: *History* ed. A. D. Godly (Harvard University Press; Cambridge, 1925).

HOMER: *Oddyssey* ed. A. T. Murray (Harvard University Press; Cambridge, 1919).

LIVIUS: *Ab Urbe Conditia* ed. F. G. Moore (Harvard University Press; Cambridge, 1949).

LUCILIUS: *Satirae* ed. E. Bolisani (Messaggero; Padova, 1932).

PLATON: *Laws* ed. R. G. Bury (Harvard University Press; Cambridge, 1926).

PLINIUS: *Naturalis Historia* ed. H. Rackham (Harvard University Press; Cambridge, 1938).

PLUTARKHOS: *Moralia* Ed. F. C. Babbit (Harvard University Press; Cambridge, 1927).

SILIUS ITALICUS: *Punica* Ed. J. D. Duff (Harvard University Press; Cambridge, 1927).

STRABON: *Geography* ed. H. L. Jones (Harvard University Press; Cambridge, 1923).

VIRGILIUS: *Georgicon* in ed. H. R. Fairclough *The Eclogues and Georgics* (Harvard University Press; Cambridge, 1929).

VITRUVIUS: *De Architectura* ed. F. Granger (Harvard University Press; Cambridge, 1931).

XENOPHON: *The Estate-Manager* in edd. H. Tredennick and R. Waterfield *Xenophon: Conversations with Socrates* (Penguin Classics; London, 1990).

Index of Peoples, Persons and Deities

Index of Places

Frontispiece: the study area

1. The Capodifiume survey: artifact density
2. The Capodifiume survey: prehistoric distribution
3. The Capodifiume survey: VI - V century distribution
4. The Capodifiume survey: IV - III century distribution
5. The Capodifiume survey: post-III century distribution
6. Sites discussed in Chapters 2 and 3
7. Geomorphic features of the southern Sele Plain
8. The Sele Plain in antiquity
9. The course of the Capodifiume east of Paestum
10. Poseidonia
11. Sites discussed in Chapters 4 and 5
12. Distribution of sites by century
13. Archaic cemeteries at Poseidonia and Athens
14. Prehistoric materials
15. Prehistoric materials
16. Archaic materials
17. Archaic and Classical materials
18. Classical and V - III century materials
19. V - III century and IV - III century materials
20. IV - III century materials
21. IV - III century materials
22. IV - III century materials
23. II - I century and 2nd - 3rd century
24. 2nd - 3rd century and Greco-Lucanian material
25. Greco-Lucanian material
26. Greco-Roman material
27. Indeterminate material
28. Indeterminate material
29. Indeterminate material
30. Indeterminate material
31. Indeterminate material

LIST OF PLATES

1. View of the upper Capodifiume from Capaccio Vecchia
2. View of Capaccio Vecchia from the Capodifiume
3. Survey unit CS-1
4. Detail of Hondius (1619), *Abruzzo et terra di Lavoro*
5. Detail of Anon. (1969), *Regno di Napoli*
6. Detail of Anon. (1791), *Naples and Sicily*
7. The temple of Hera I
8. The temple of Athena
9. The temple of Hera II
10. CS-4 material
11. CS-4 material
12. CS-4 material
13. CS-7 material
14. CS-7 material
15. CS-7 material
16. CS-9 material
17. CS-10 material
18. CS-11 material
19. CS-11 material
20. CS-12 material
21. CS-13 material
22. CS-15 material
23. CS-16 material
24. CS-18 material
25. CS-20 material
26. CS-30 material
27. Material from CS-30, CS-31, CS-35, CS-37 and CS-38
28. Material from CS-40 and CS-41
29. Material from CS-42, CS-43 and CS-44
30. CS-49 material
31. CS-50 material

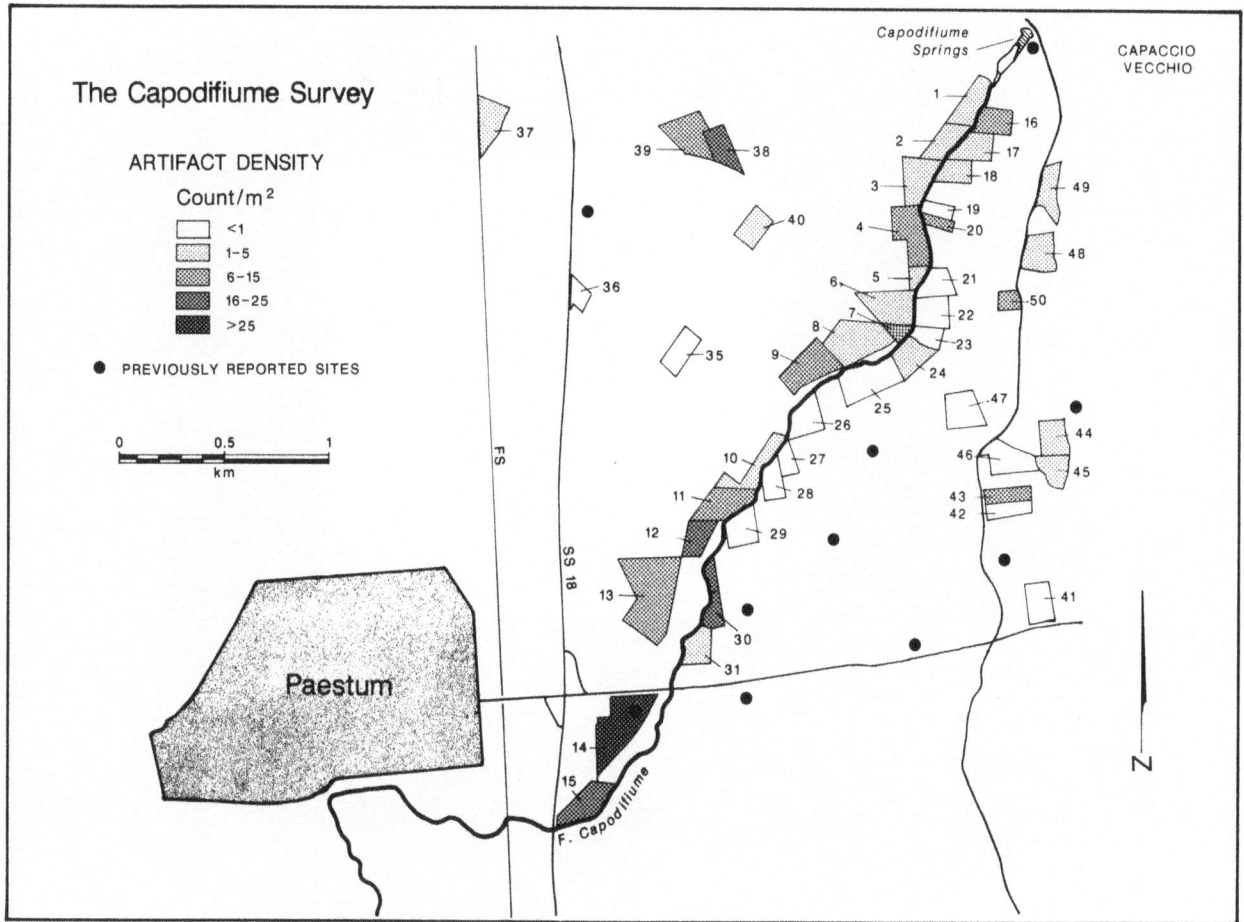

Figure 1. The Capodifiume survey: artifact density

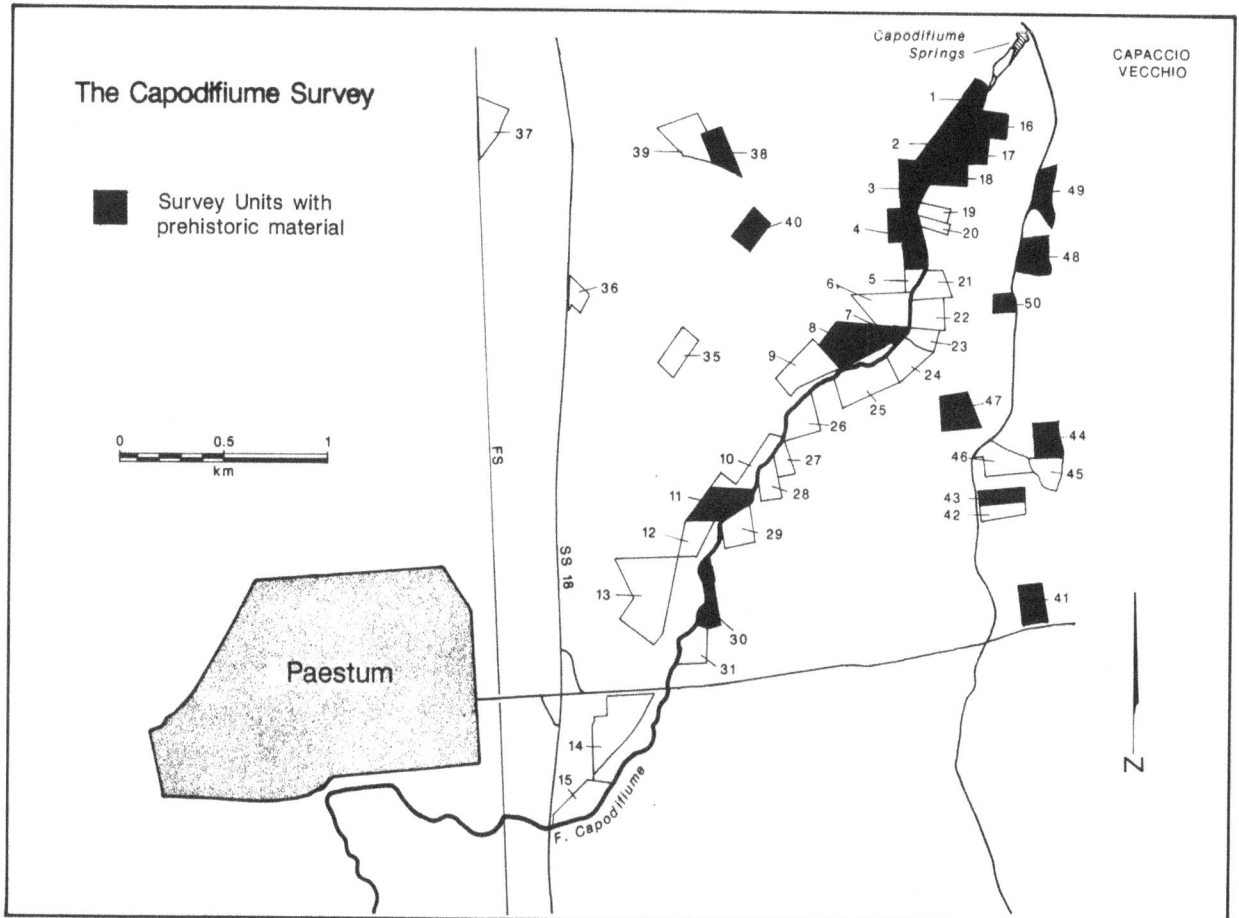

Figure 2. The Capodifiume survey: prehistoric distribution

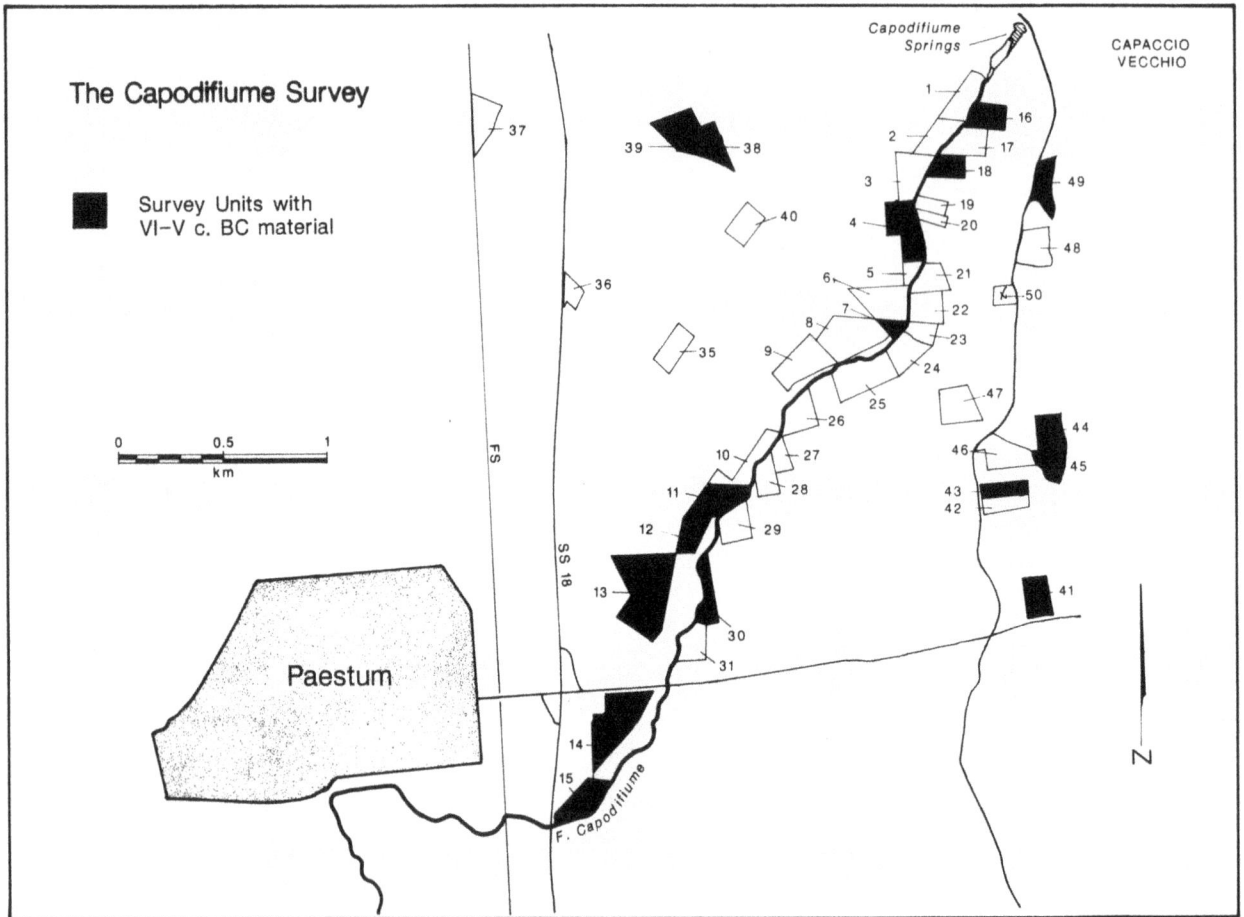

Figure 3. The Capodifiume survey: VI - V century distribution

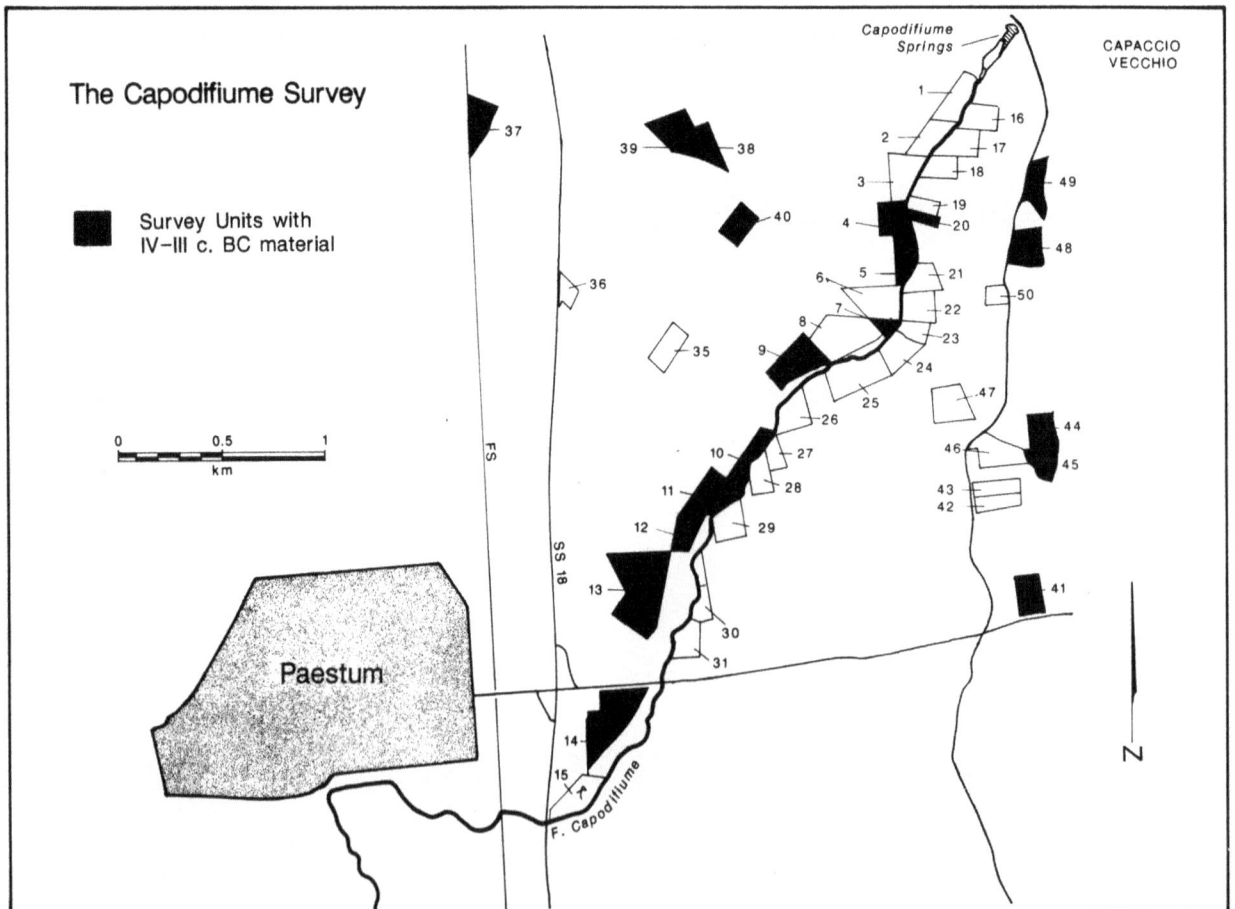

Figure 4. The Capodifiume survey: IV - III century distribution

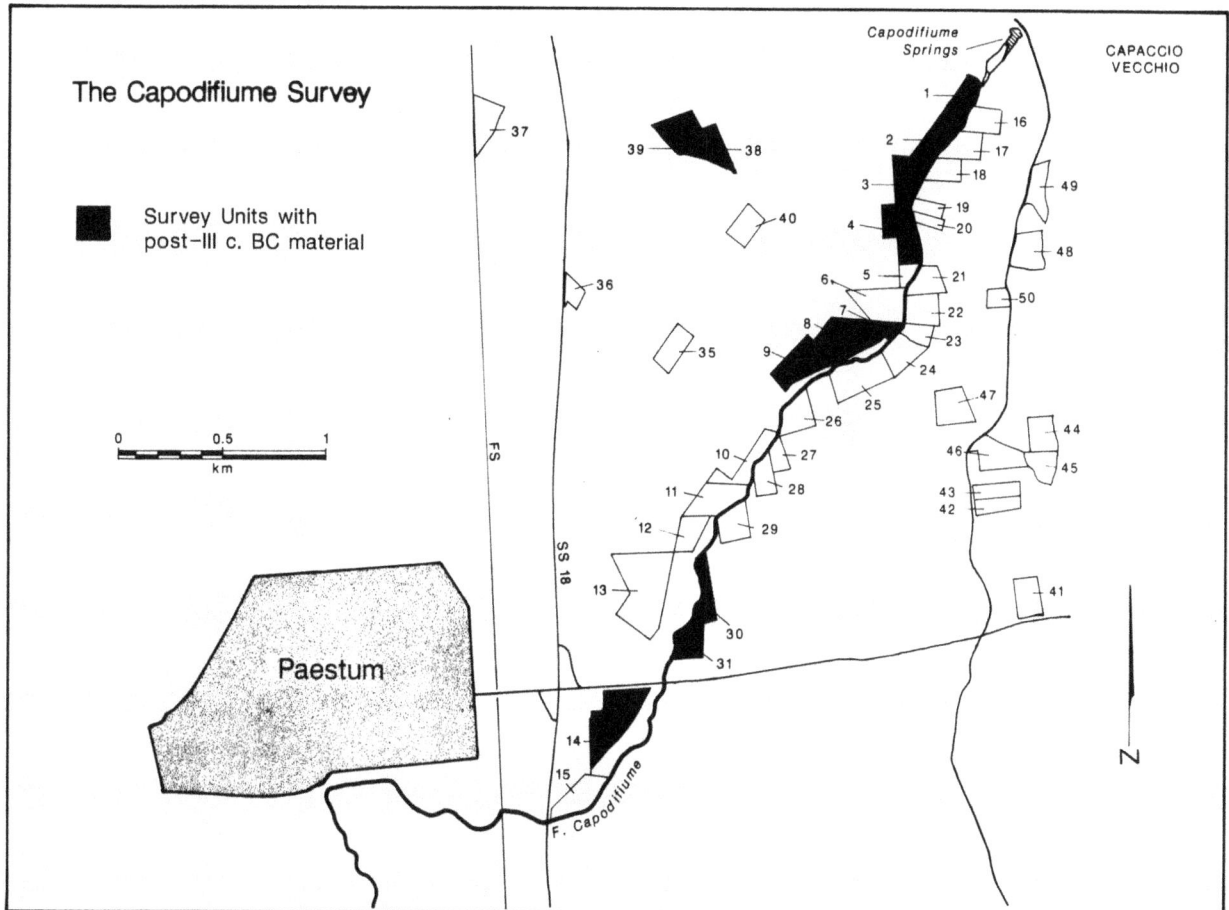

Figure 5. The Capodifiume survey: post-III century distribution

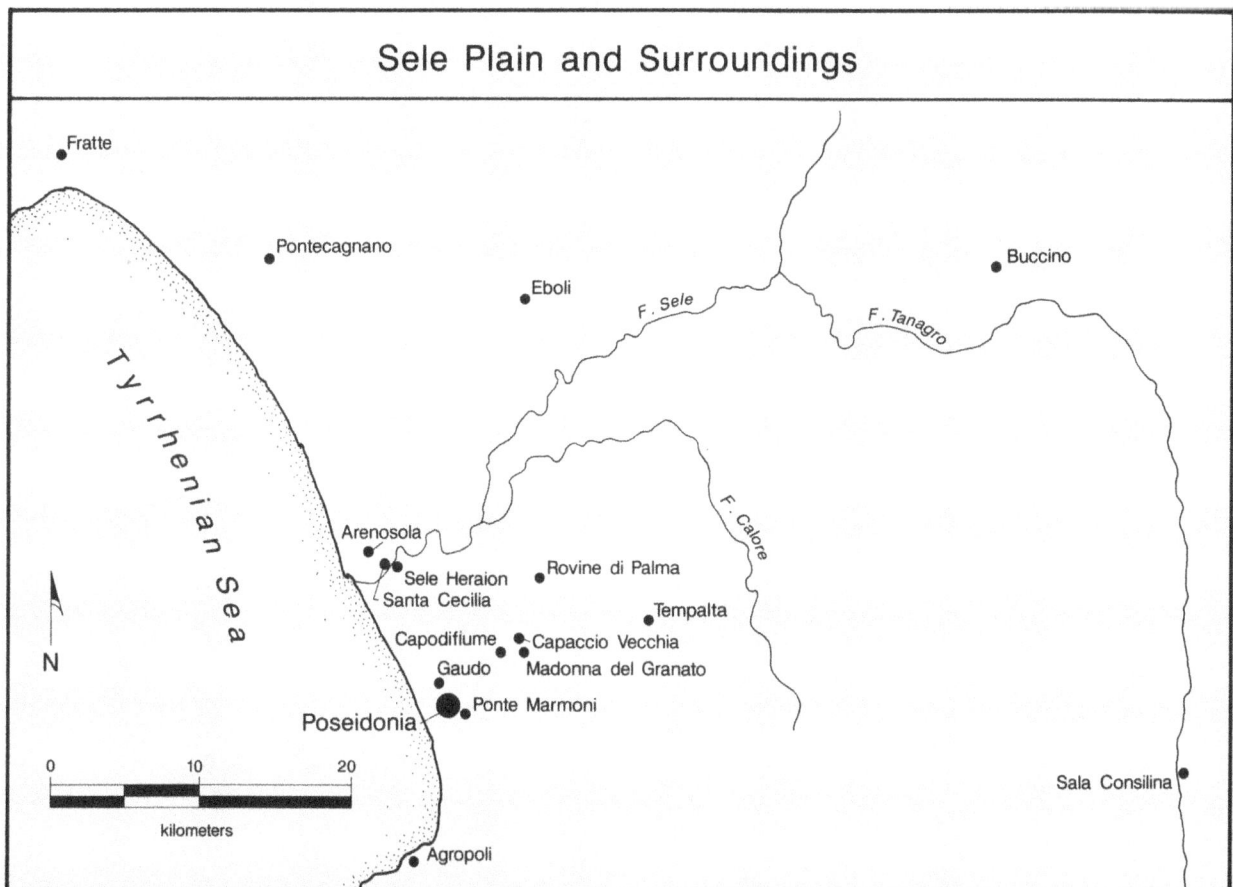

Figure 6. Sites discussed in Chapters 2 and 3

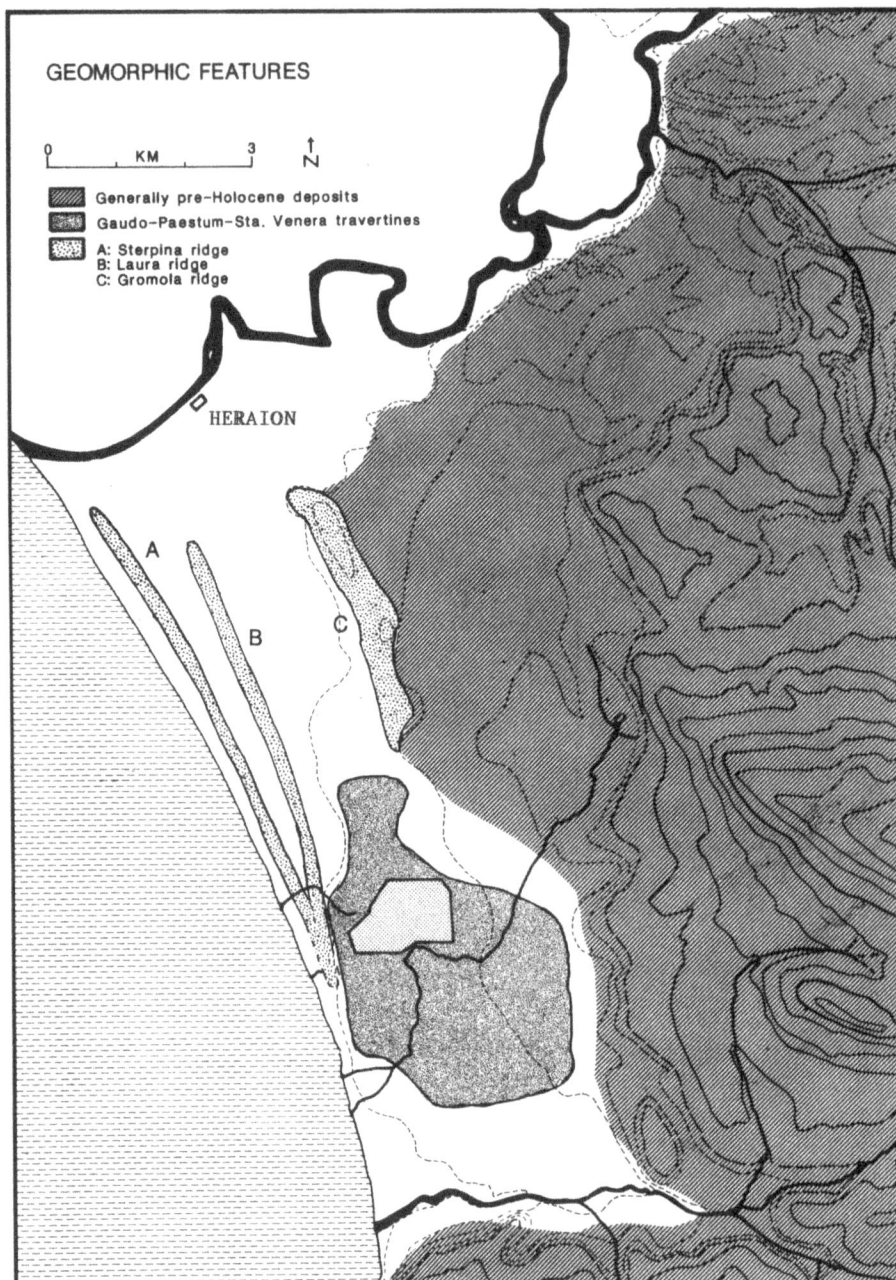

Figure 7. Geomorphic features of the southern Sele Plain

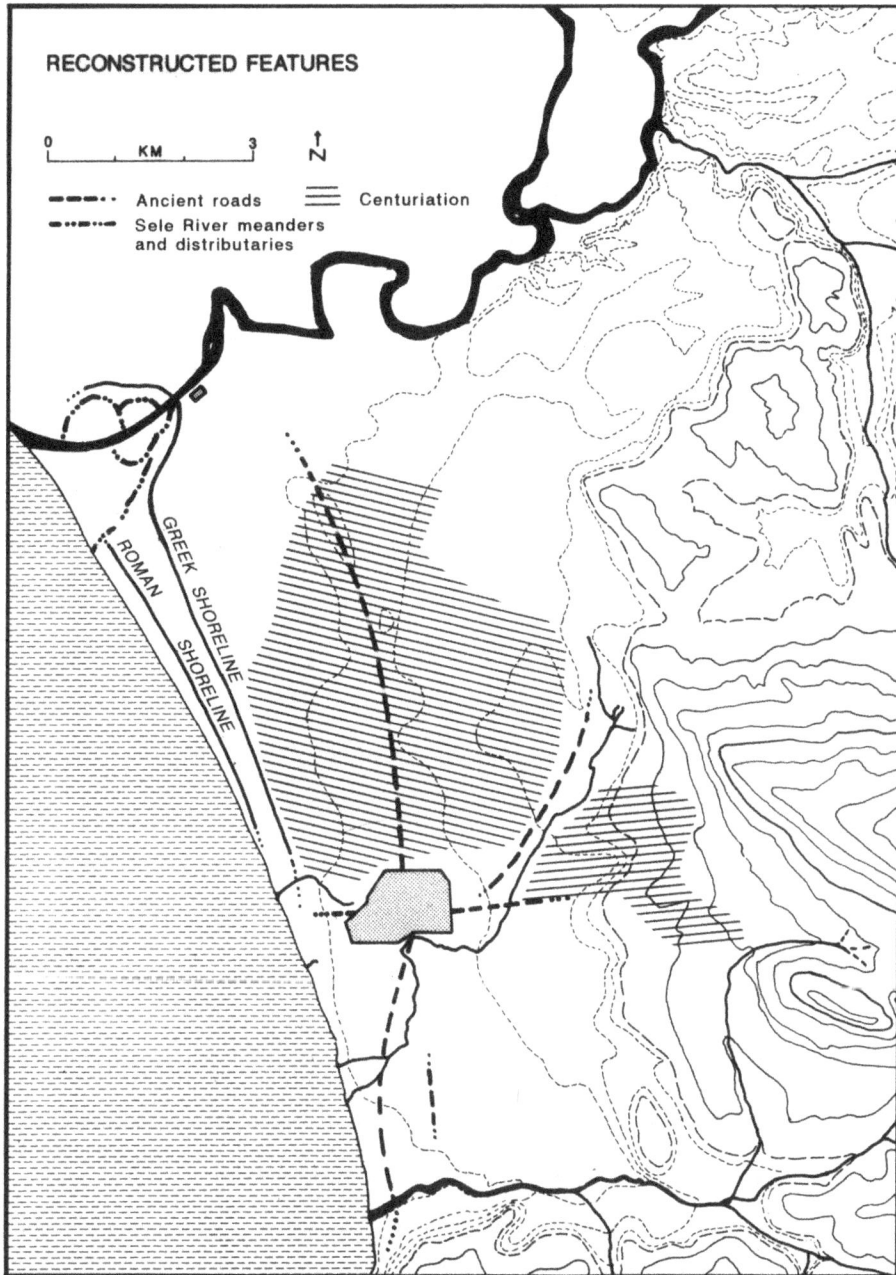

Figure 8. The Sele Plain in antiquity

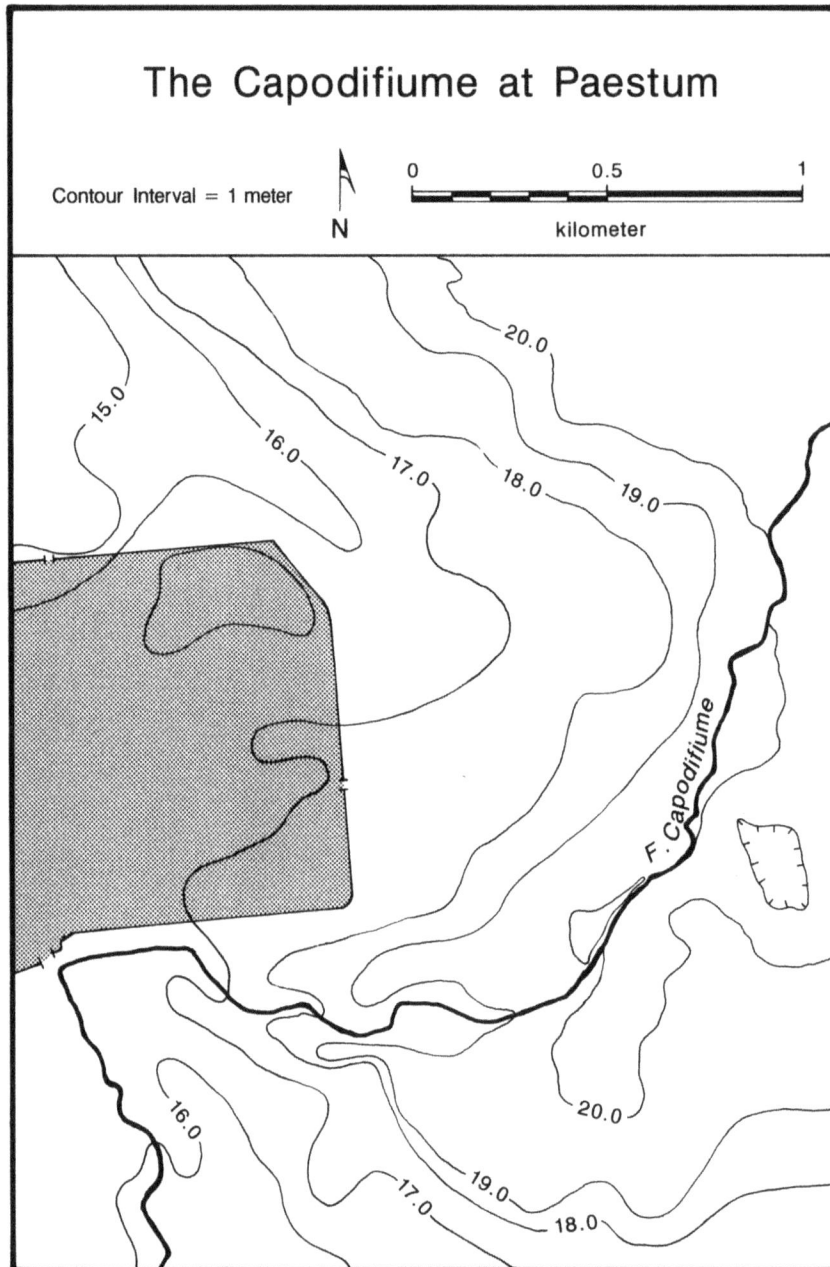

Figure 9. The course of the Capodifiume east of Paestum

Poseidonia

N

0   0.5   1
kilometer

Porta Aurea

Athena

Northern
Temenos

Porta Marina

Porta Sirena

Southern
Temenos

Hera II

Hera I

F. Capodiflume

Porta Giustizia

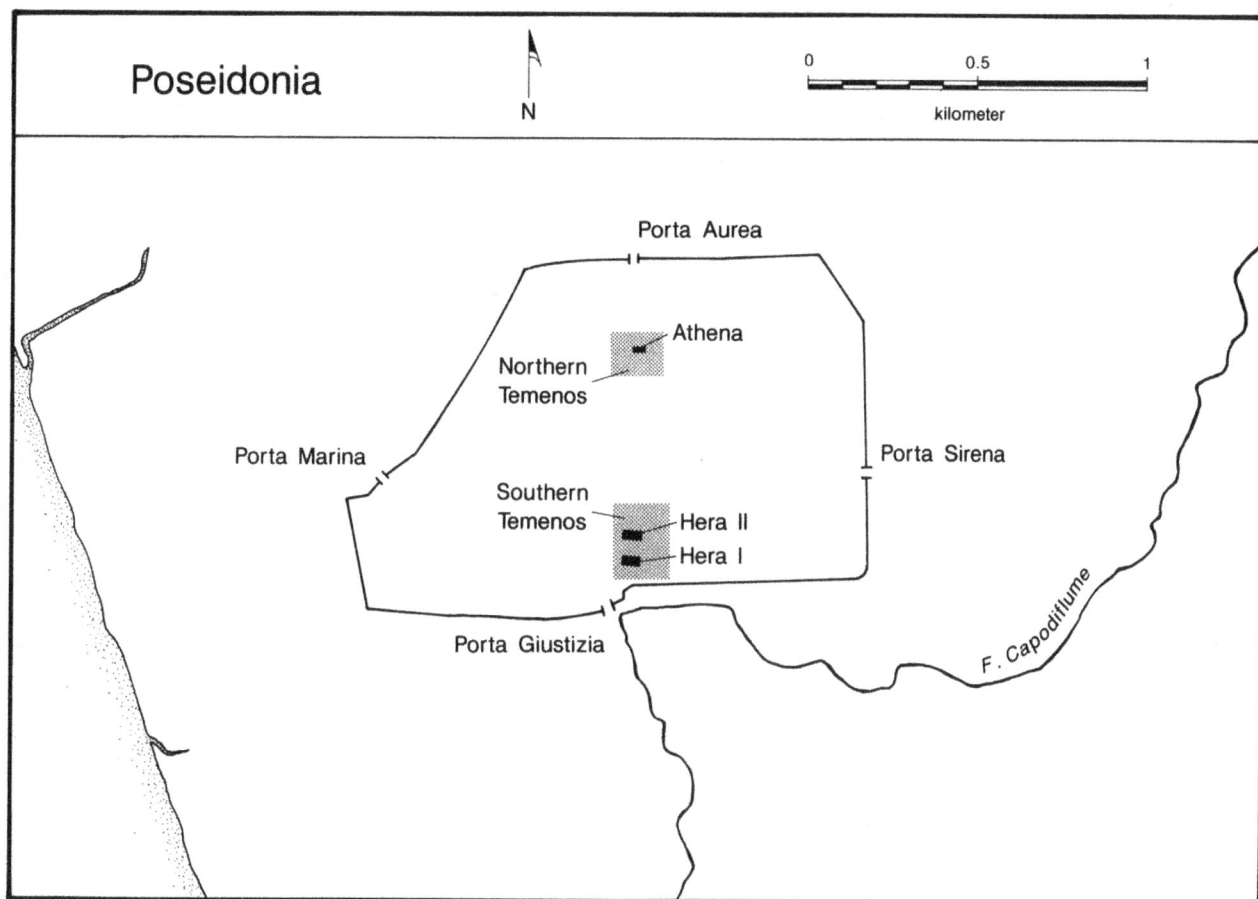

Figure 10. Poseidonia

The Plain of Poseidonia

1. Sele Heraion
2. Laghetto/Andriuolo
3. Arcioni
4. Gaudo
5. Spinazzo
6. Agropoli
7. Capaccio Vecchia
8. Capodifiume
9. Madonna del Granato
10. Getsemani
11. Acqua che Bolle
12. Lupata
13. Fravita
14. Rovine di Palma
15. Tempa San Paolo
16. Tempalta
17. Giungano
18. Trentinara
19. Linora
20. Santa Venera
21. Tempa del Prete
22. Contrada Cupa
23. Tempa del Lepre
24. Ponte di Ferro
25. San Nicola di Albanella
26. Parco Ogliastro
27. Boccalupo
28. Fonte di Roccadaspide

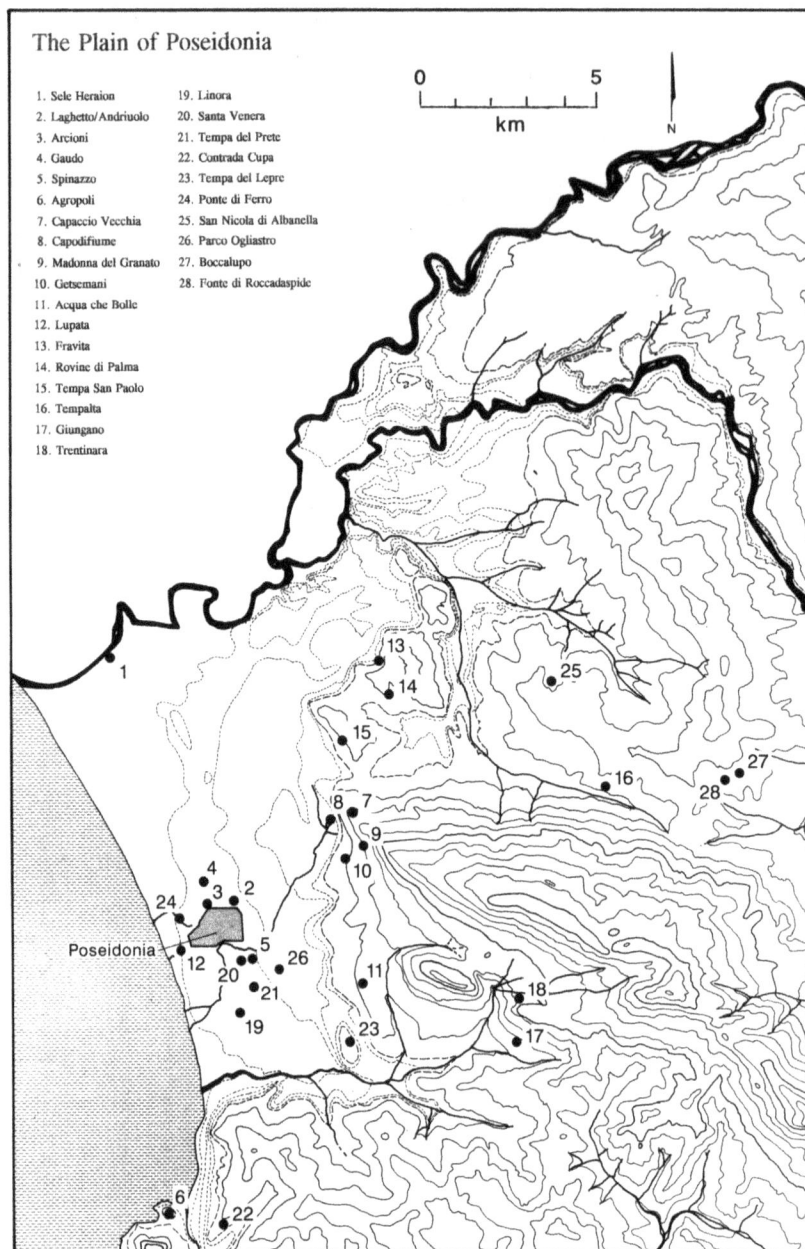

Figure 11. Sites discussed in Chapters 4 and 5

84

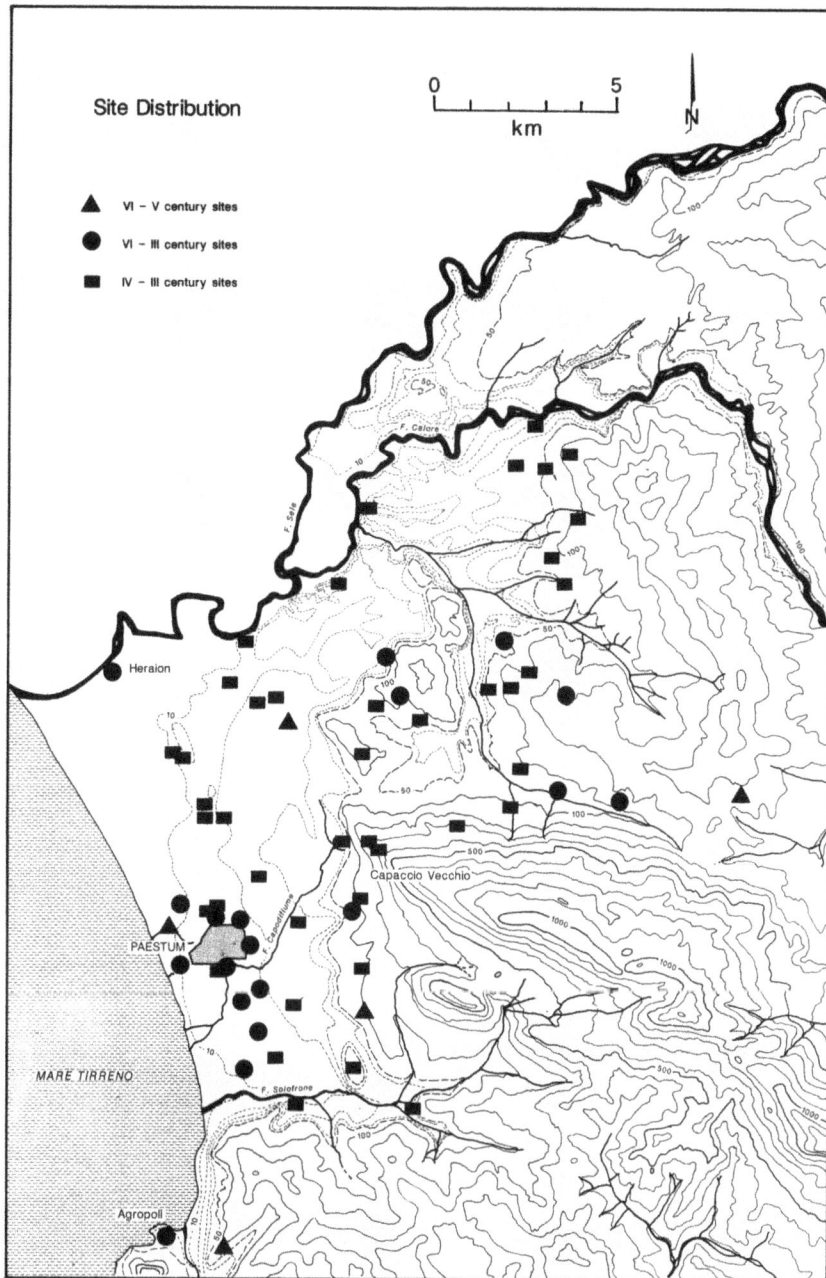

Figure 12. Distribution of sites by century

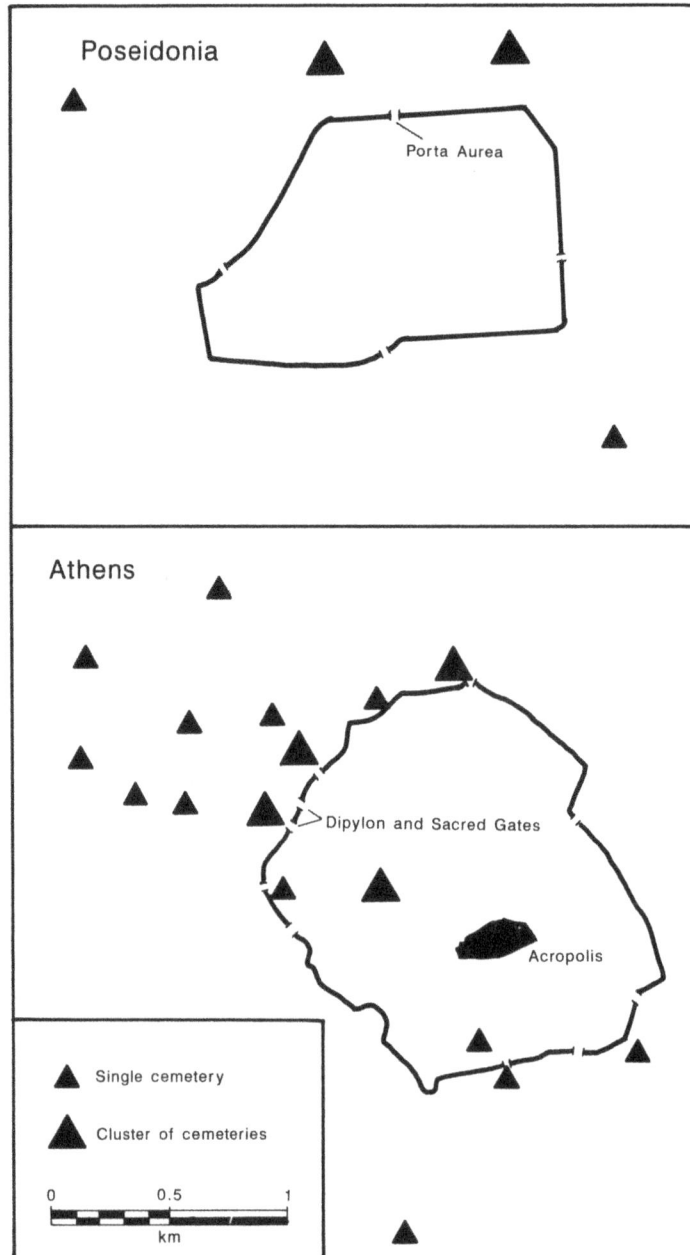

Figure 13. Archaic cemeteries at Poseidonia and Athens

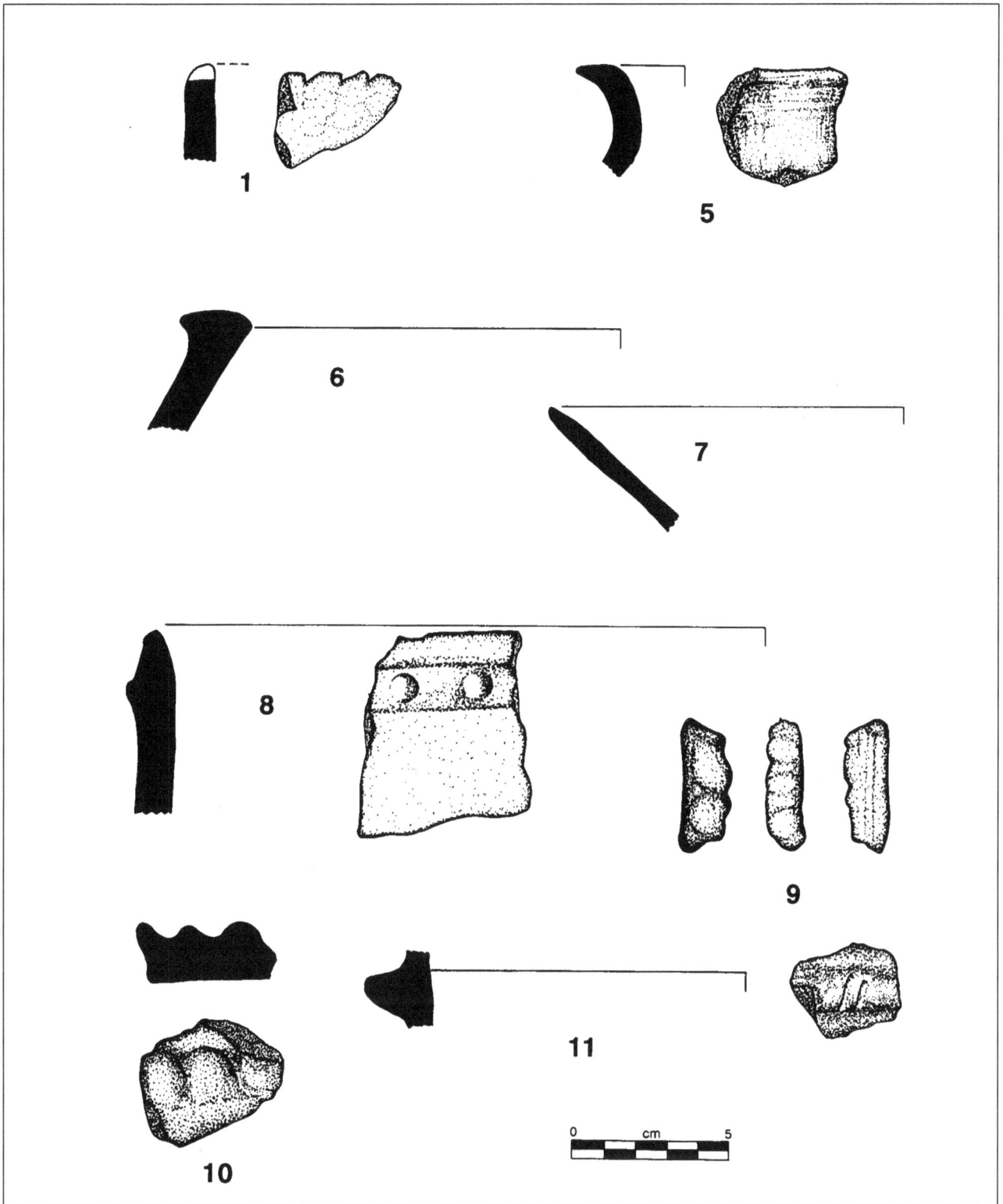

Figure 14. Prehistoric materials

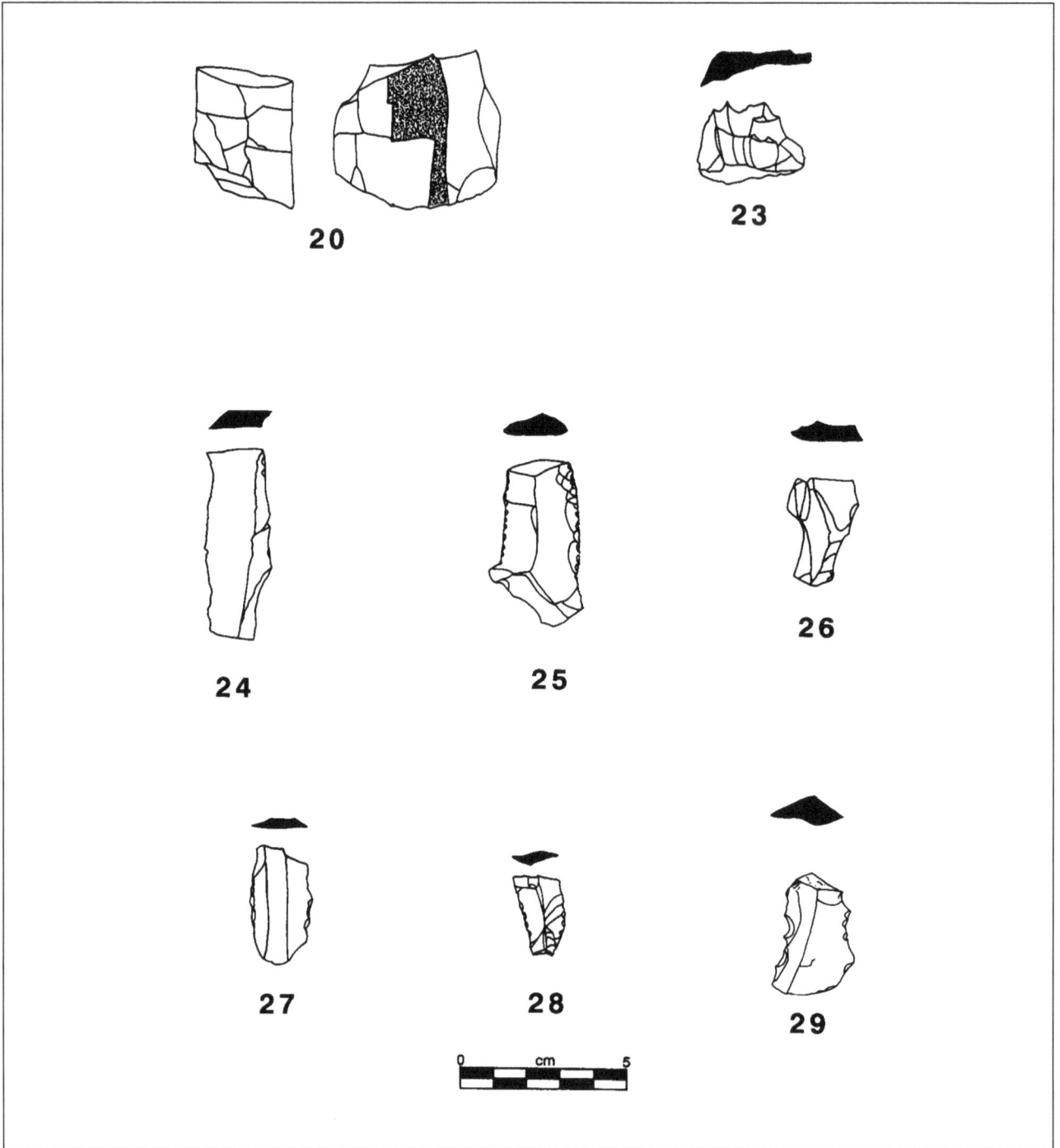

Figure 15. Prehistoric materials

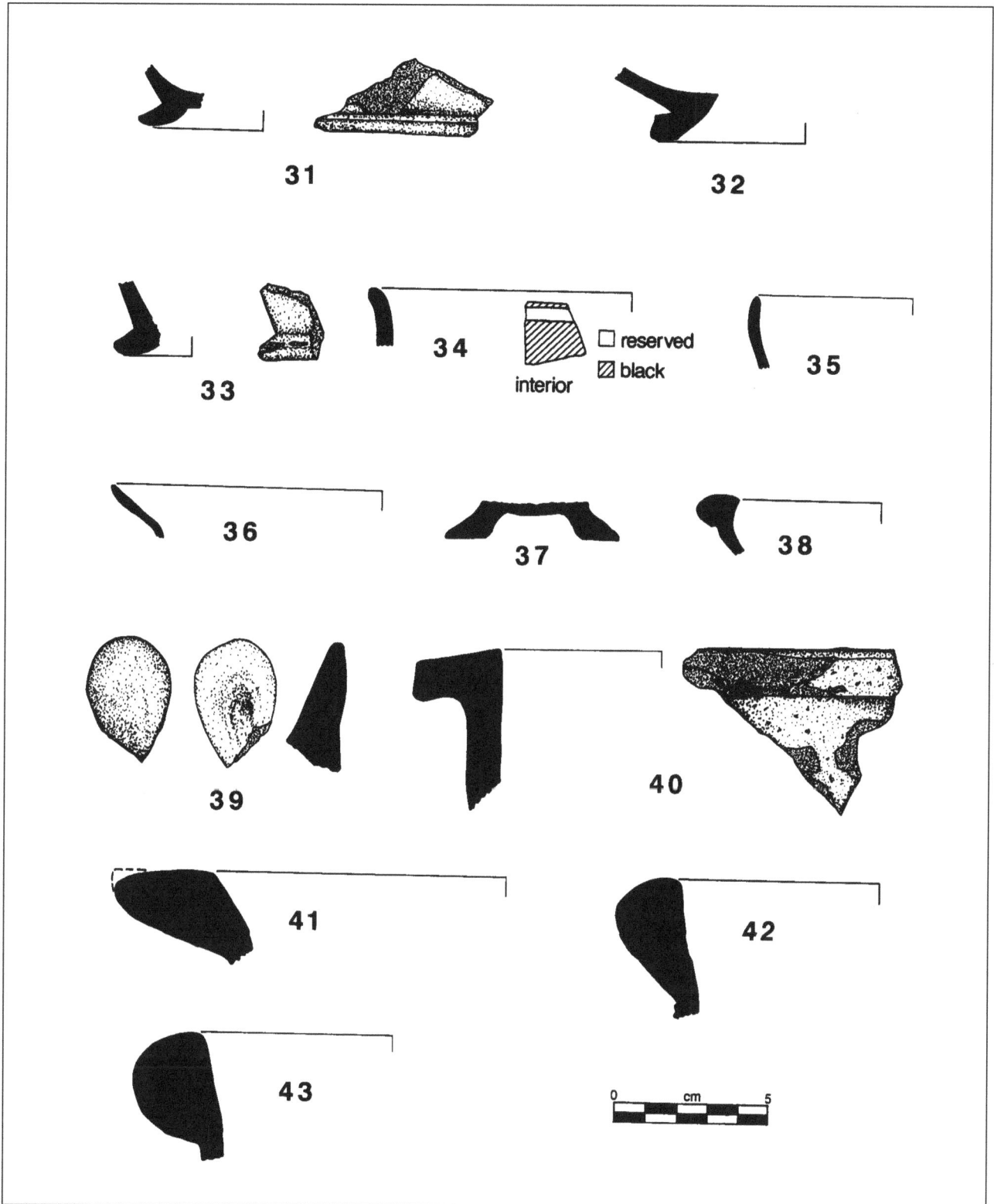

31

32

33

34

□ reserved
▨ black

interior

35

36

37

38

39

40

41

42

43

0   cm   5

Figure 16. Archaic materials

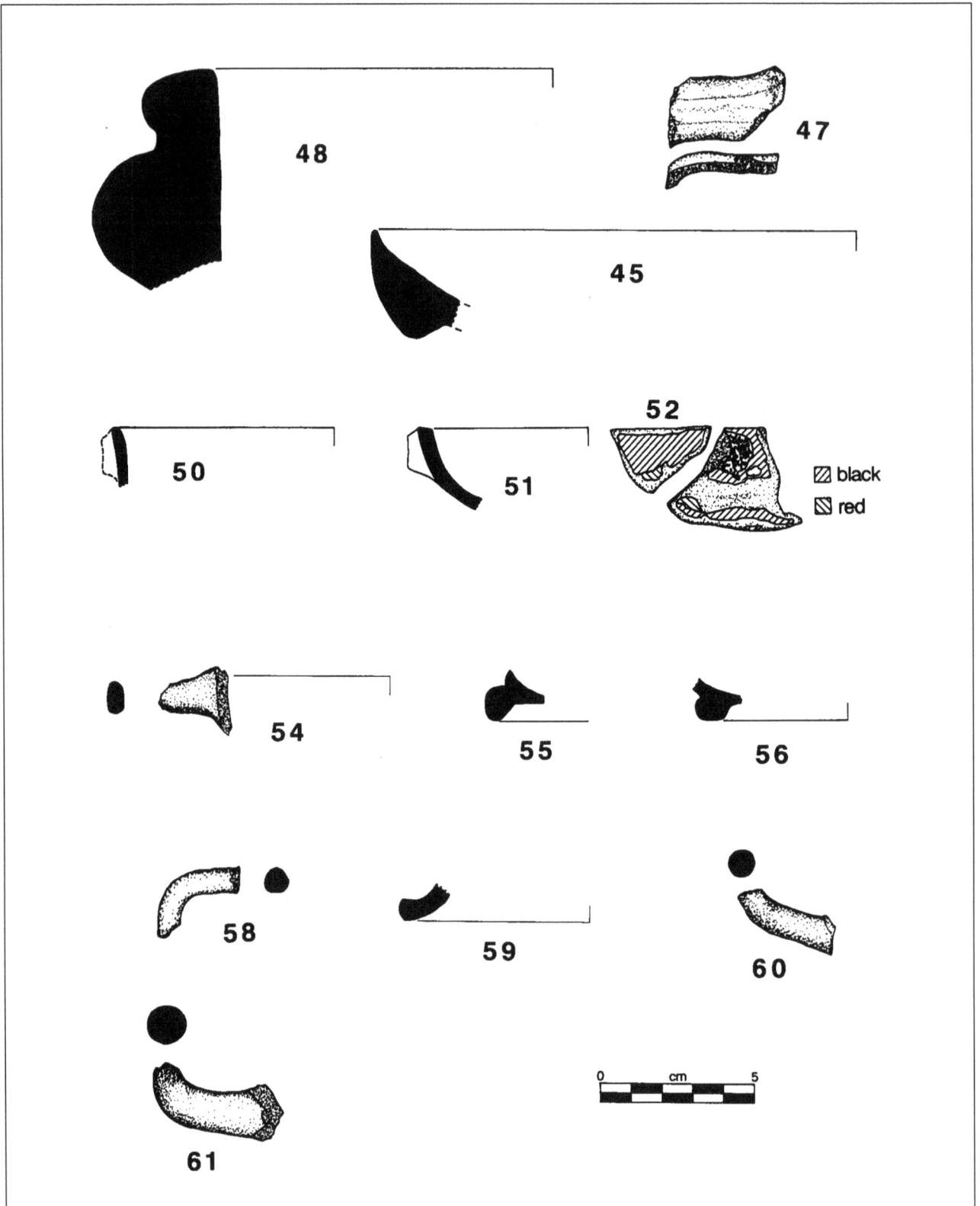

Figure 17. Archaic and Classical materials

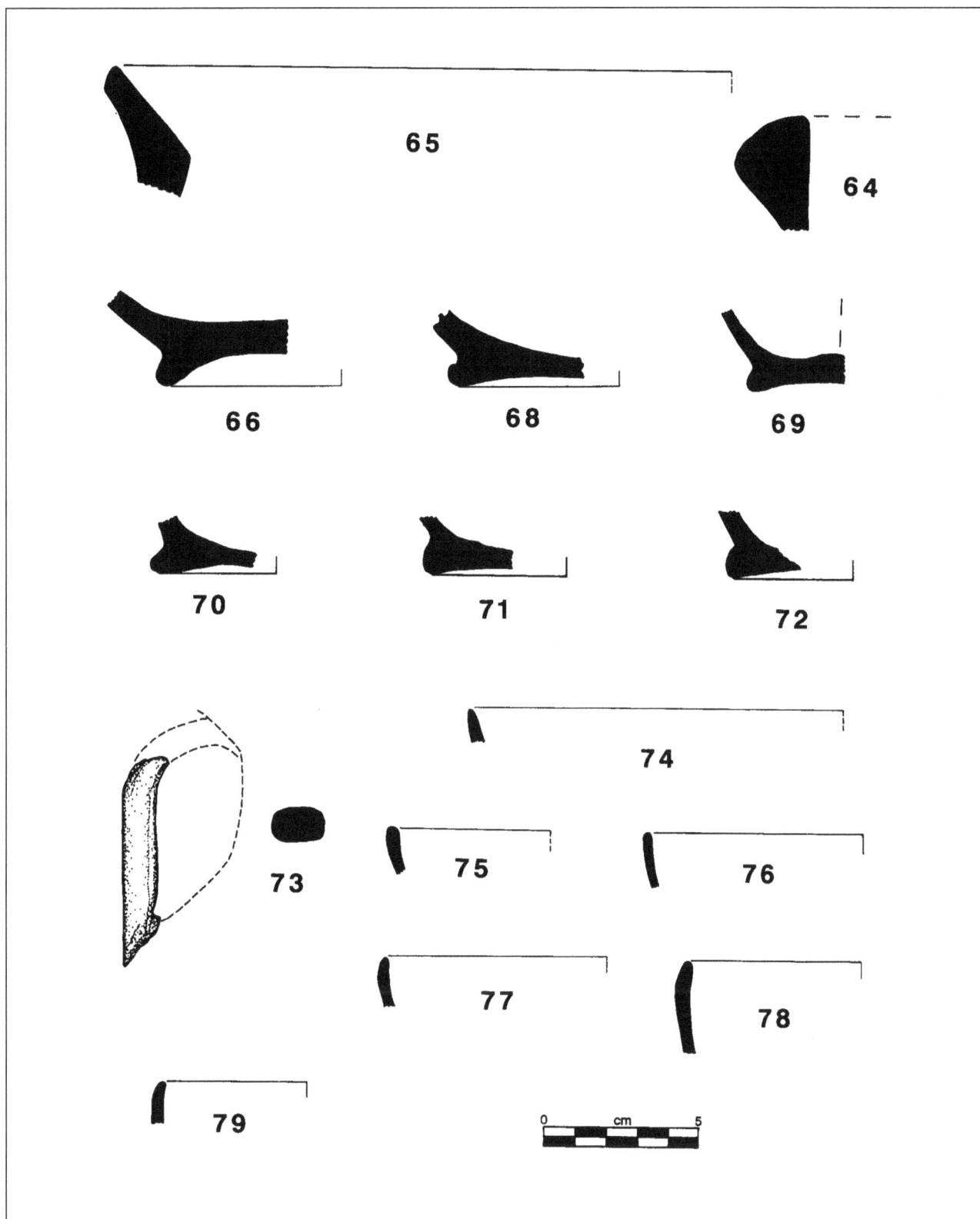

Figure 18. Classical and V - III century materials

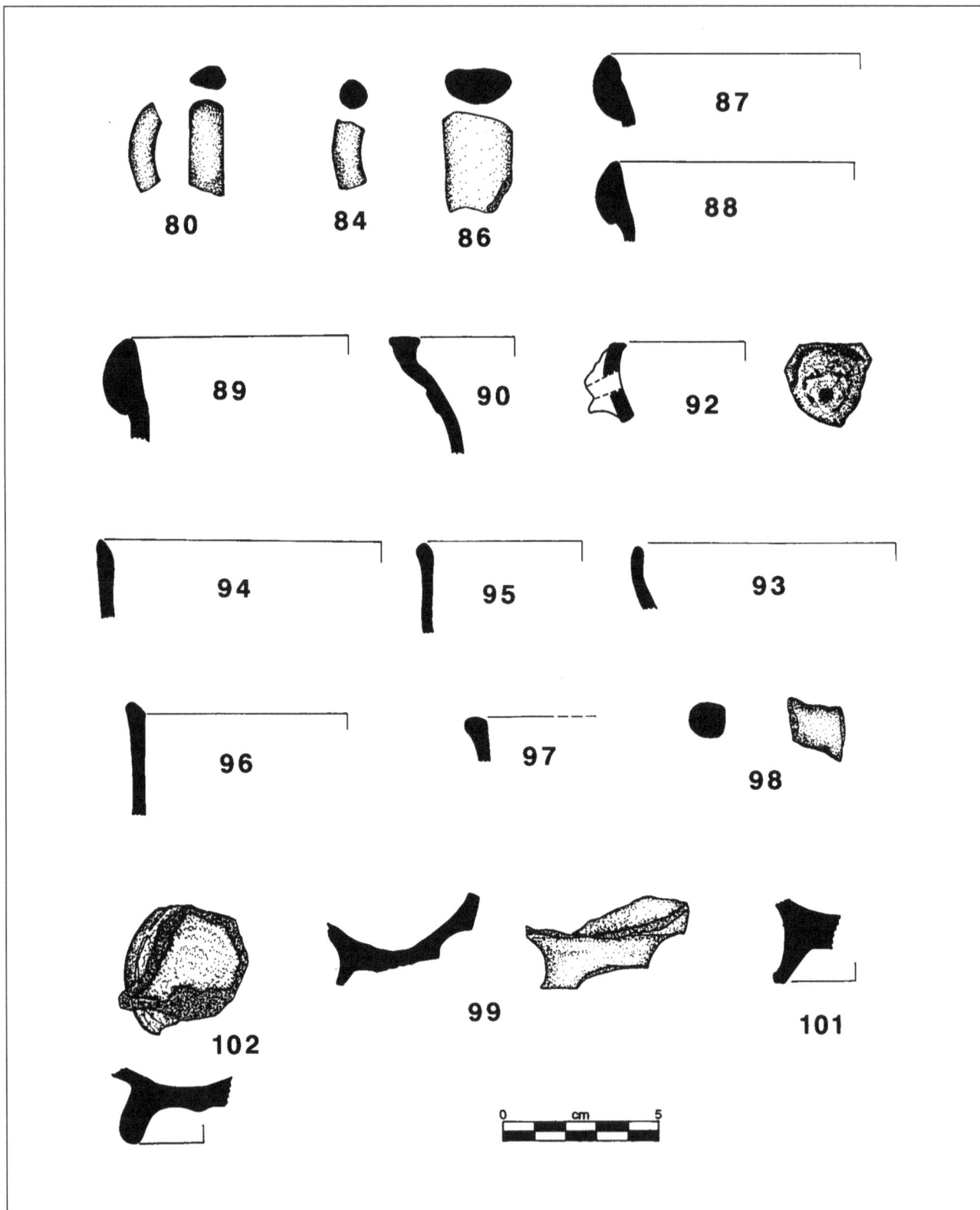

Figure 19. V - III century and IV - III century materials

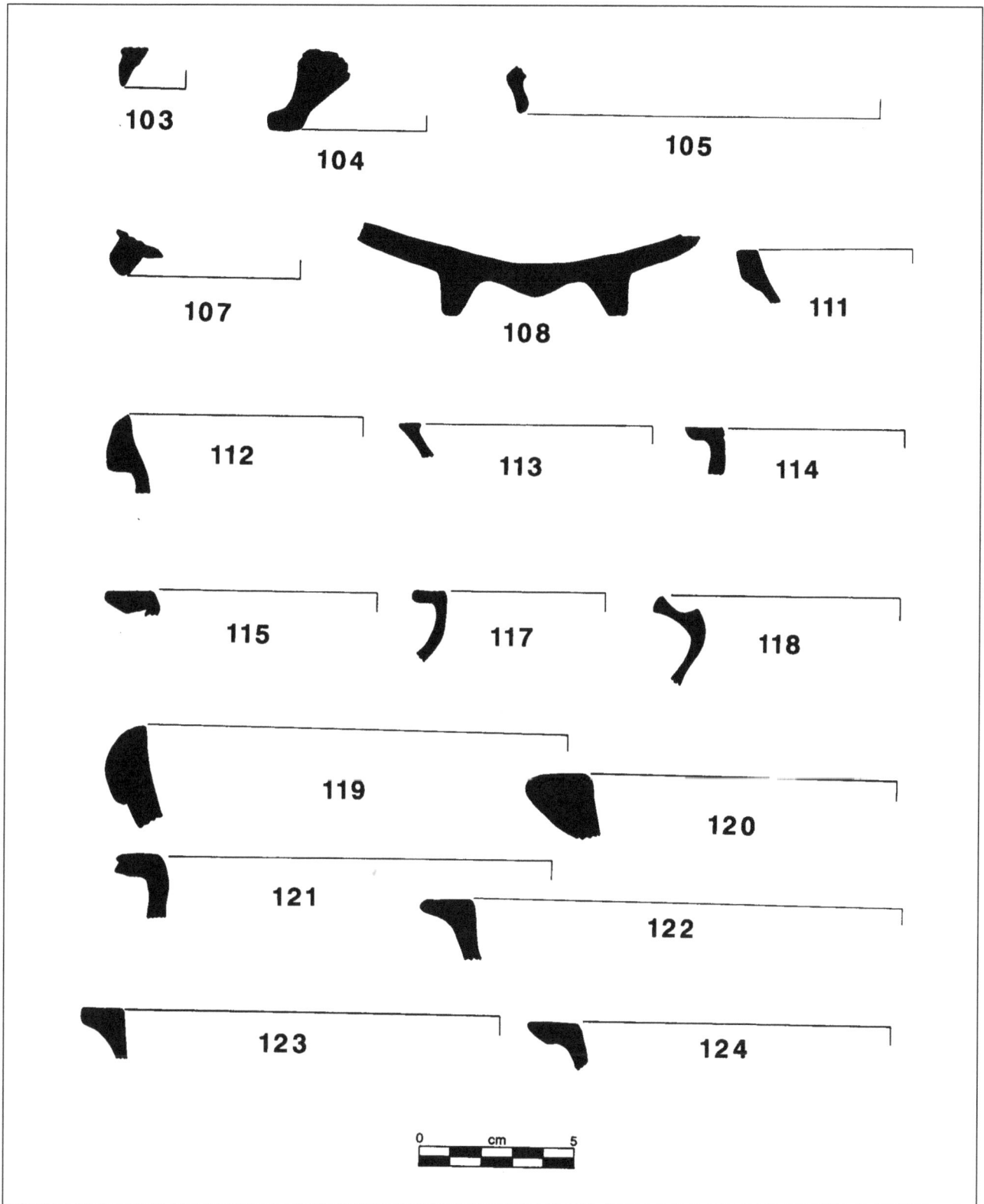

Figure 20. IV - III century materials

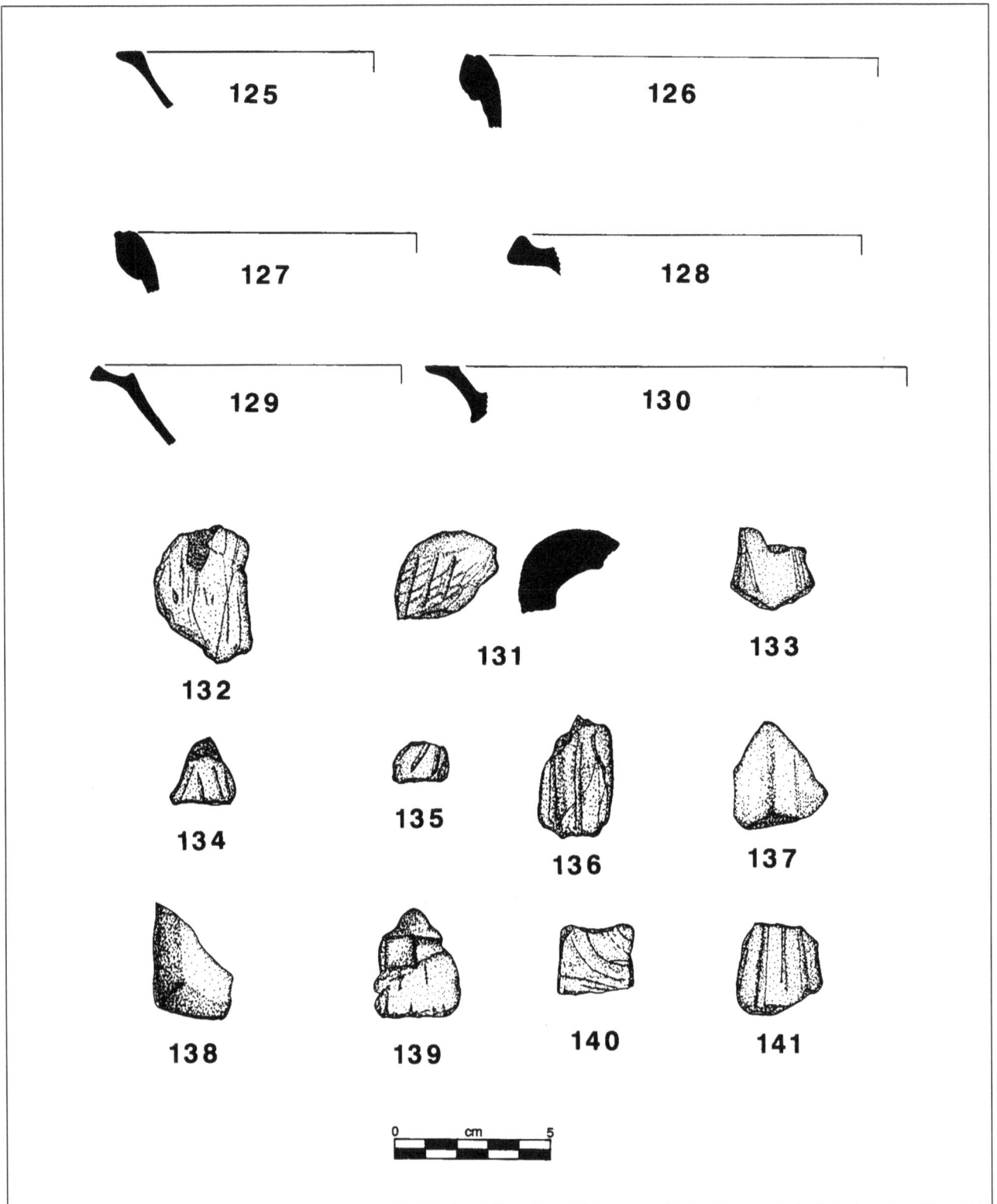

Figure 21. IV - III century materials

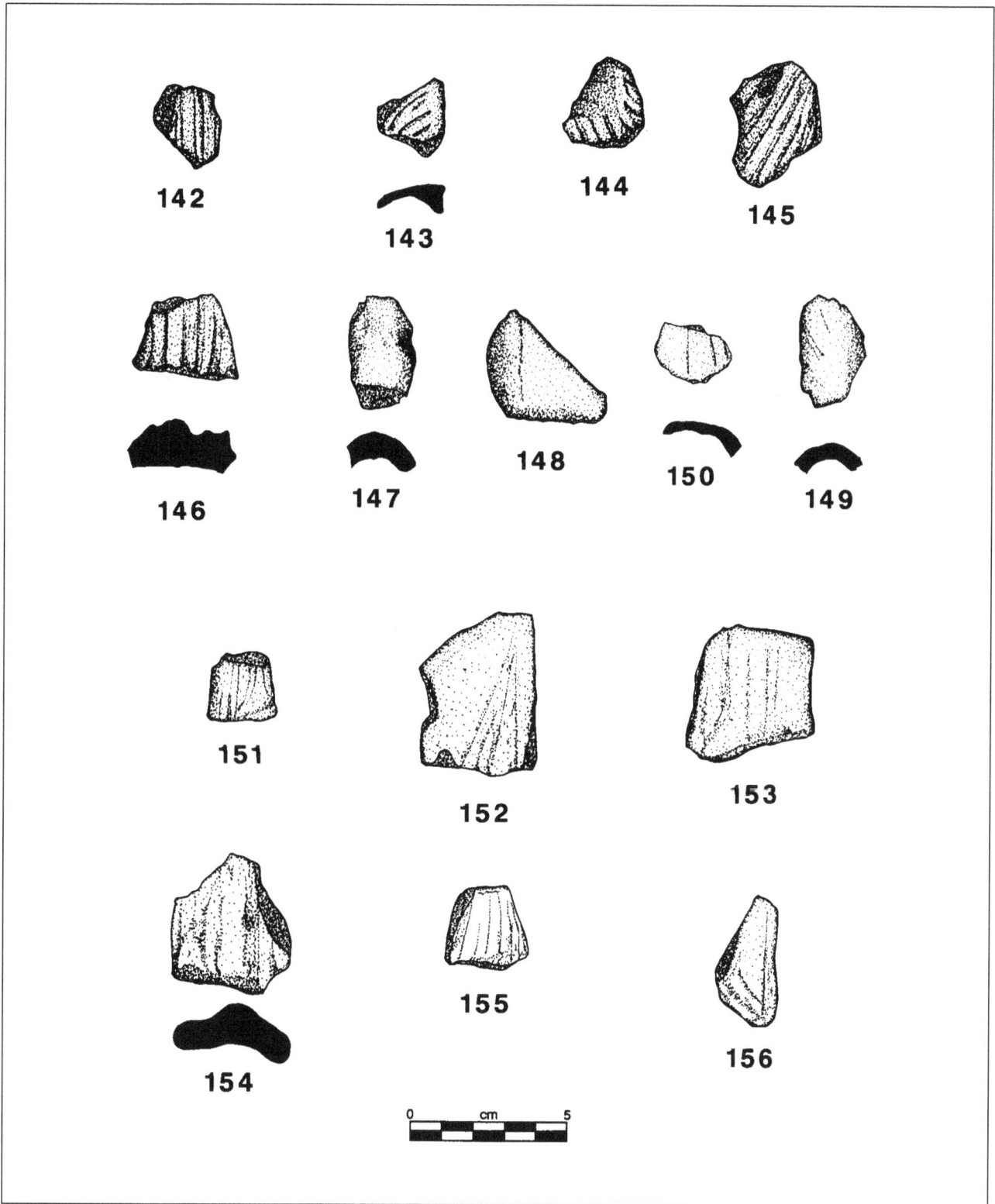

Figure 22. IV - III century materials

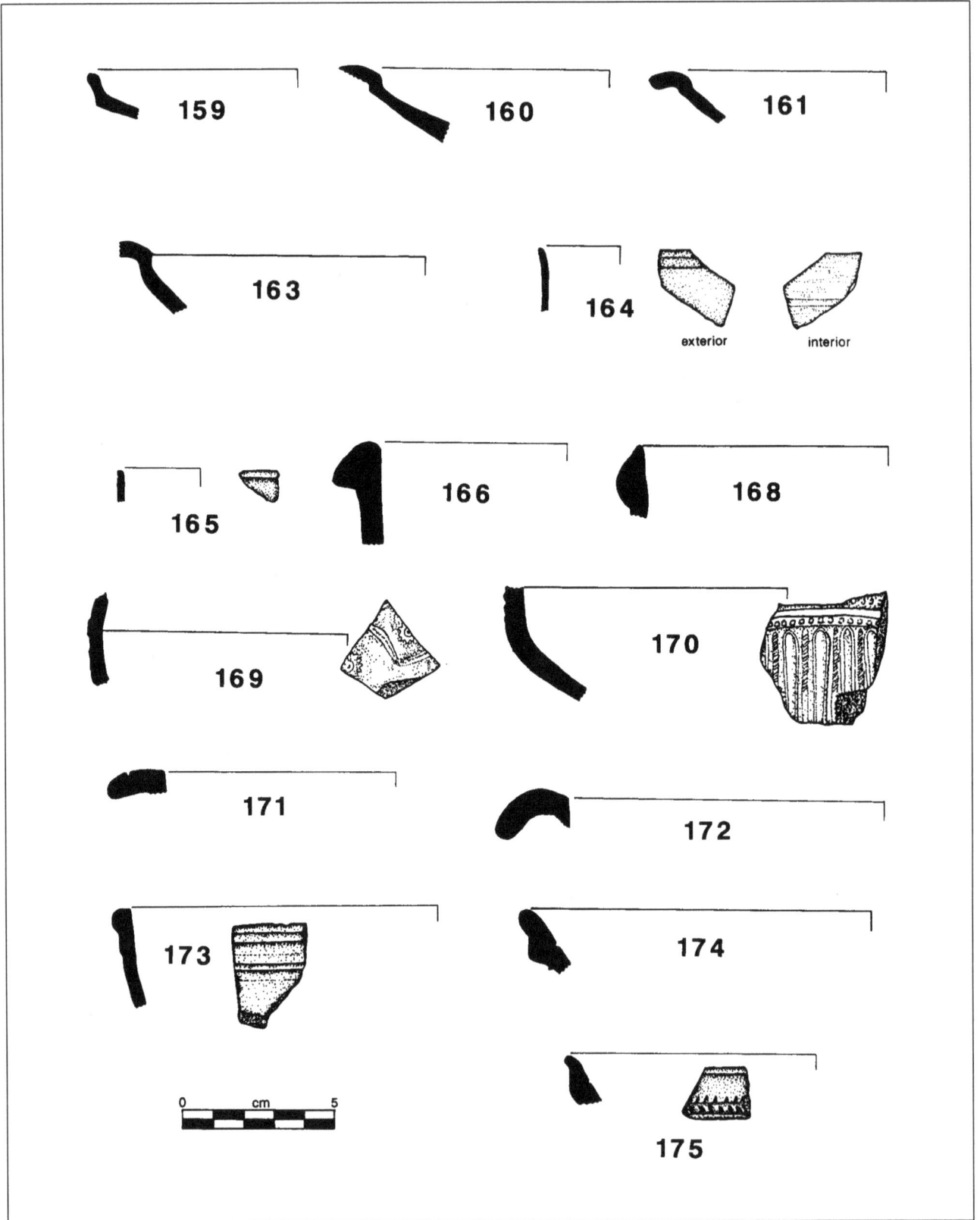

Figure 23. II - I century and 2nd - 3rd century

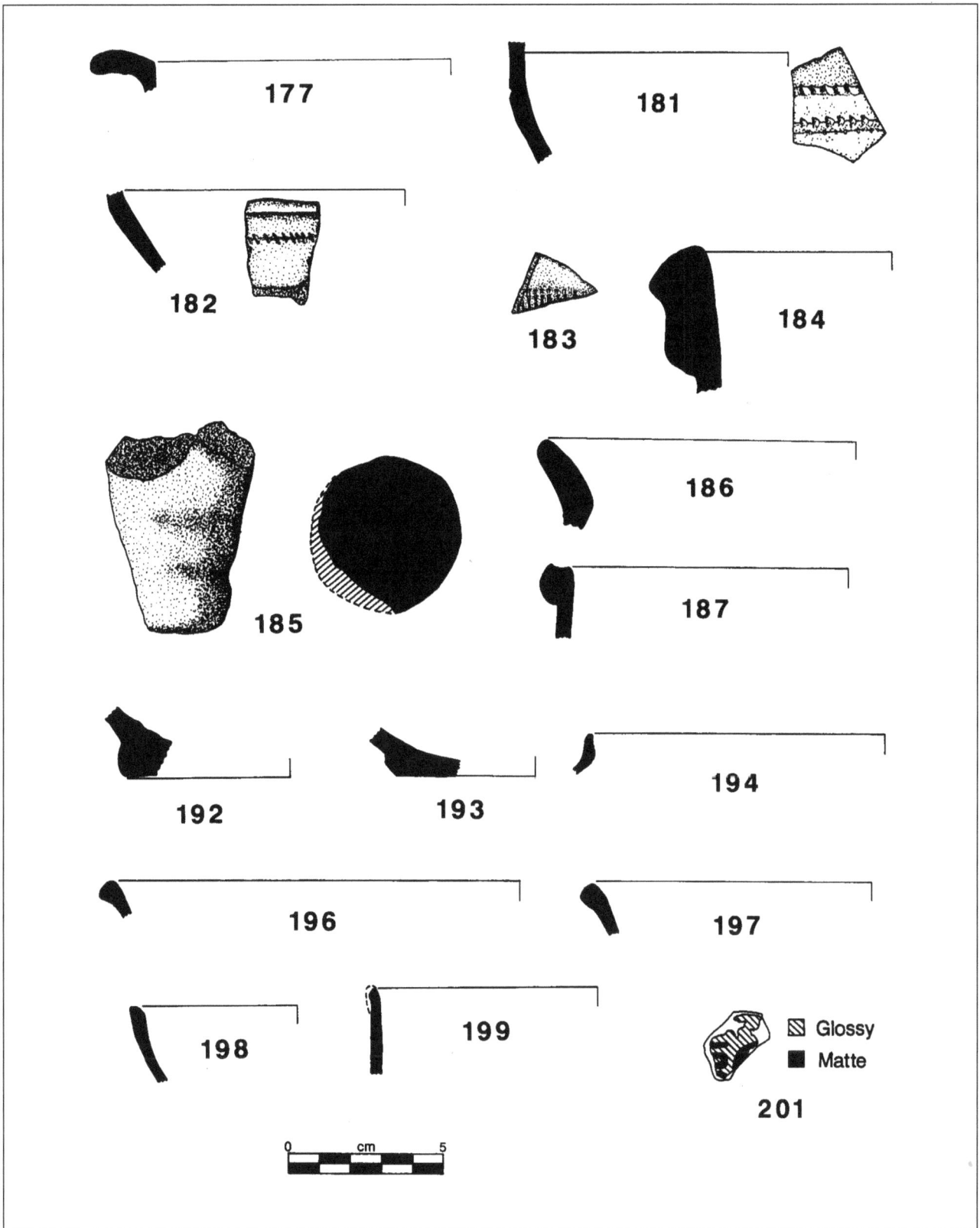

Figure 24. 2nd - 3rd century and Greco-Lucanian material

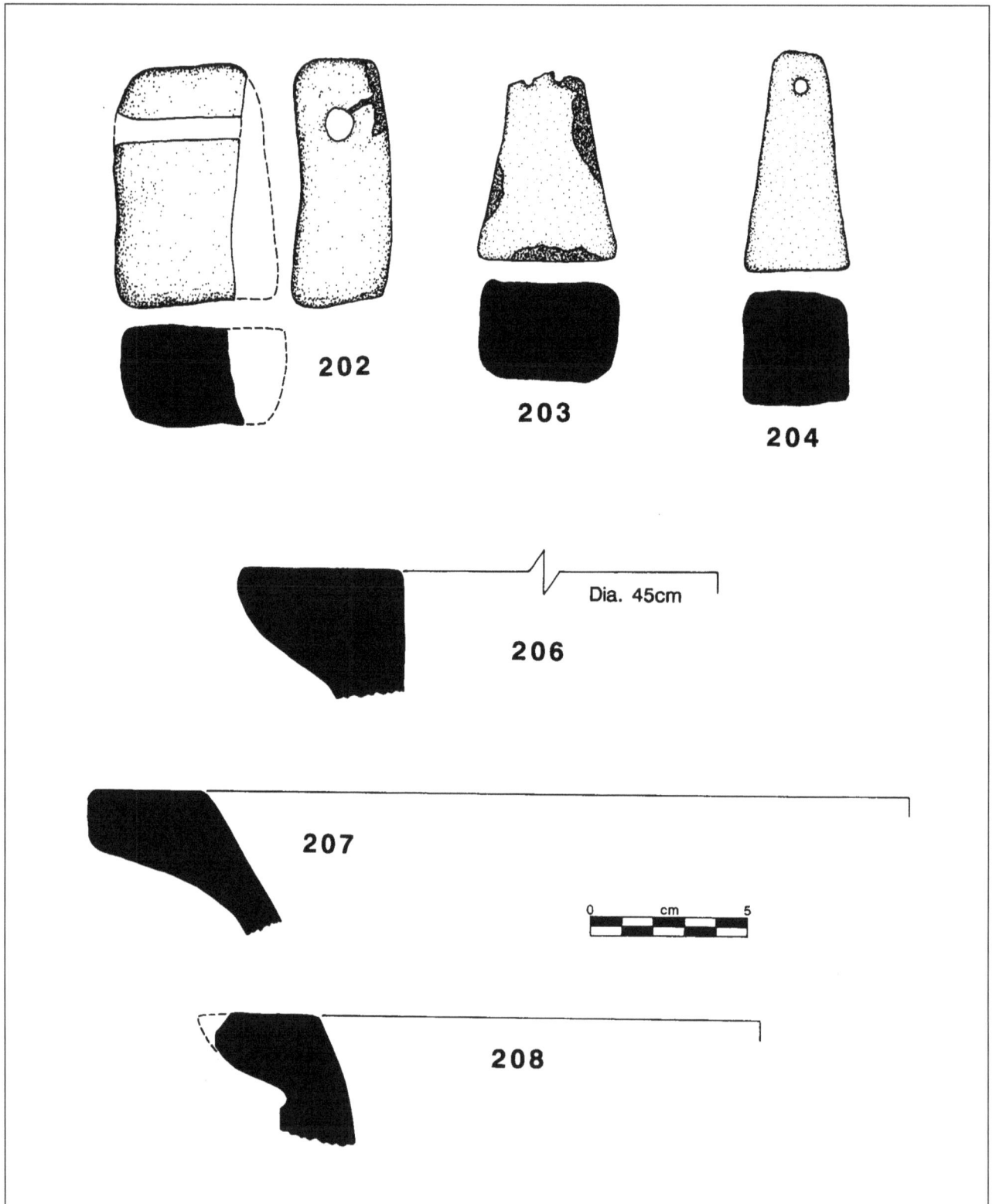

Figure 25. Greco-Lucanian material

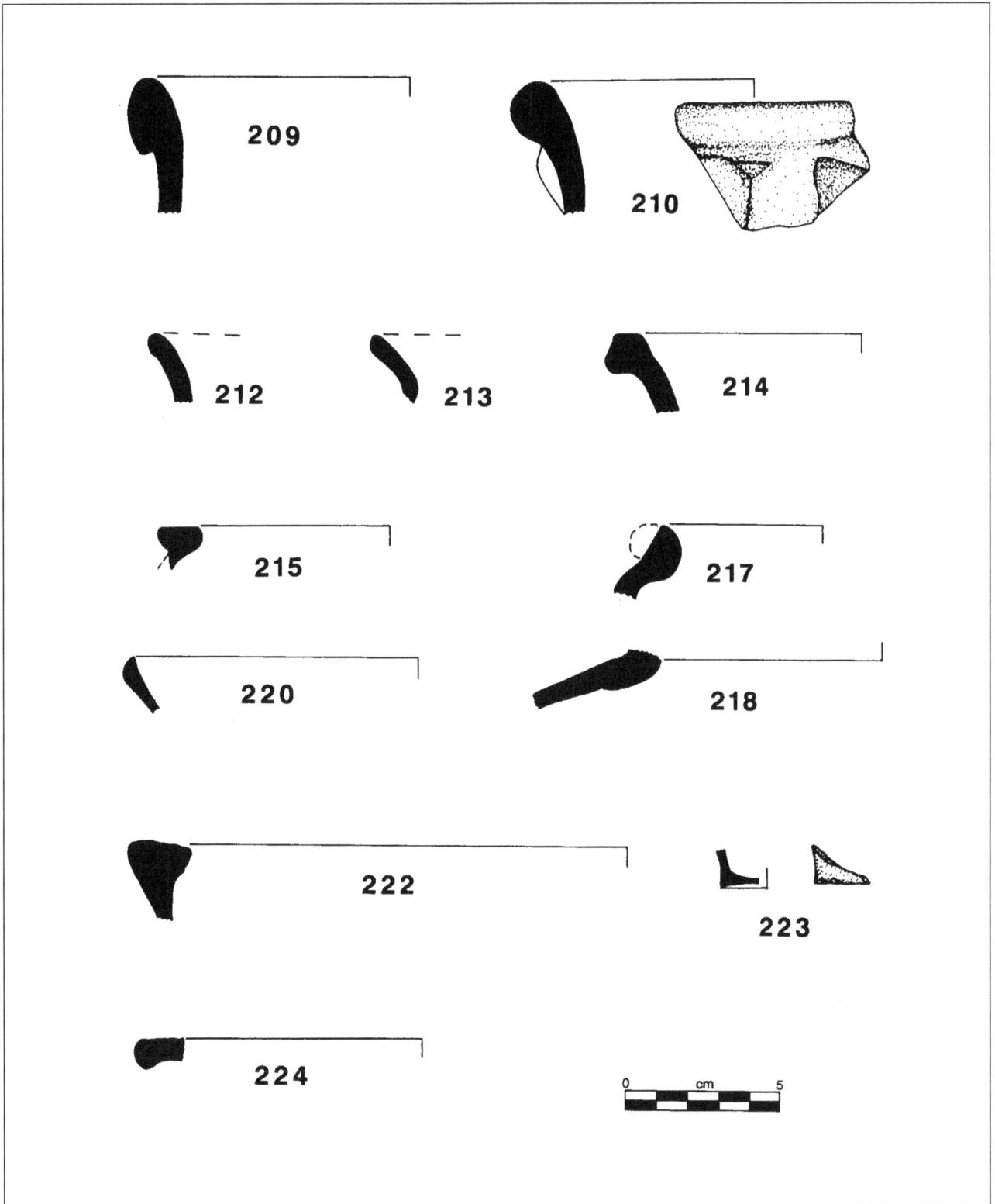

Figure 26. Greco-Roman material

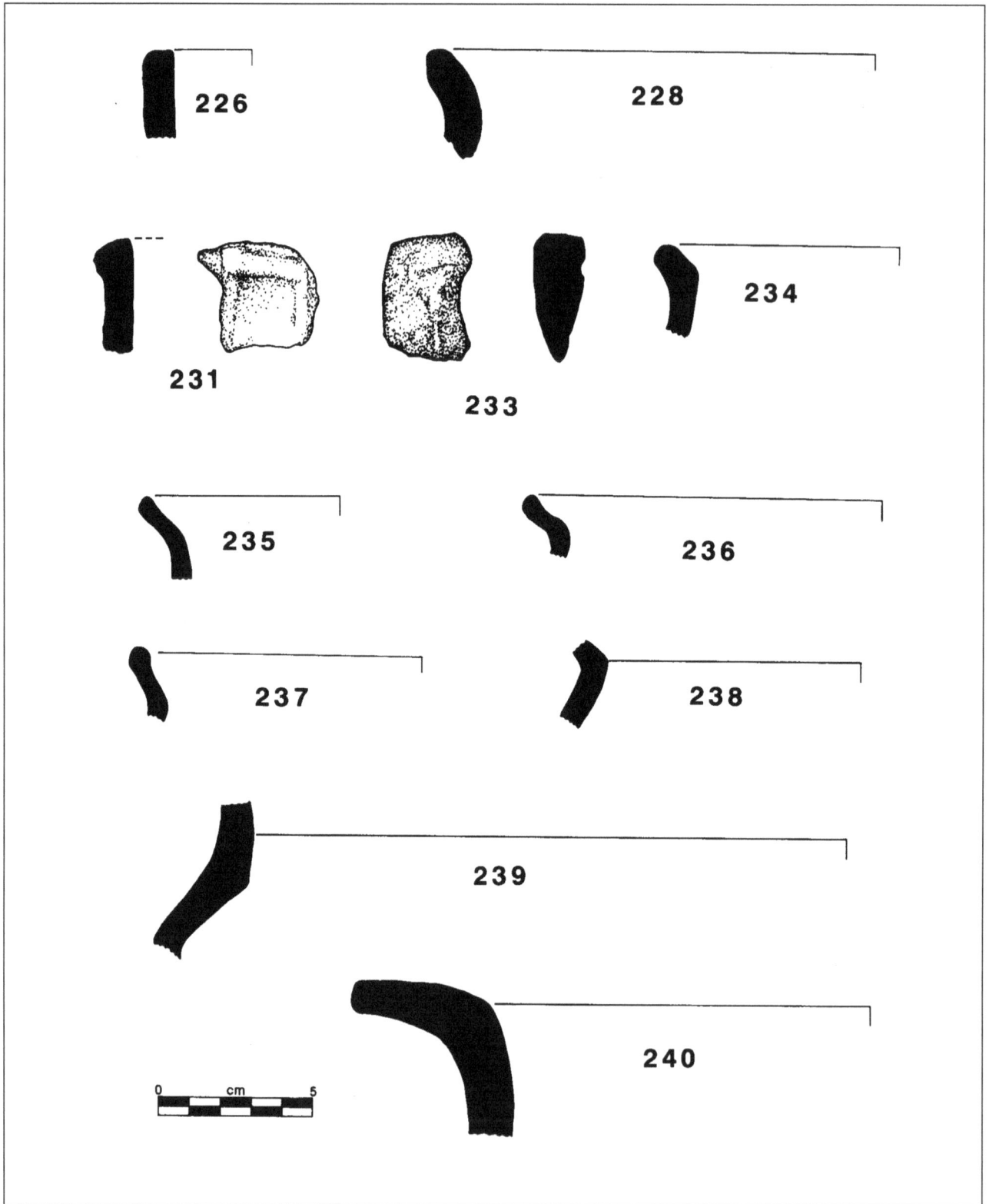

Figure 27. Indeterminate material

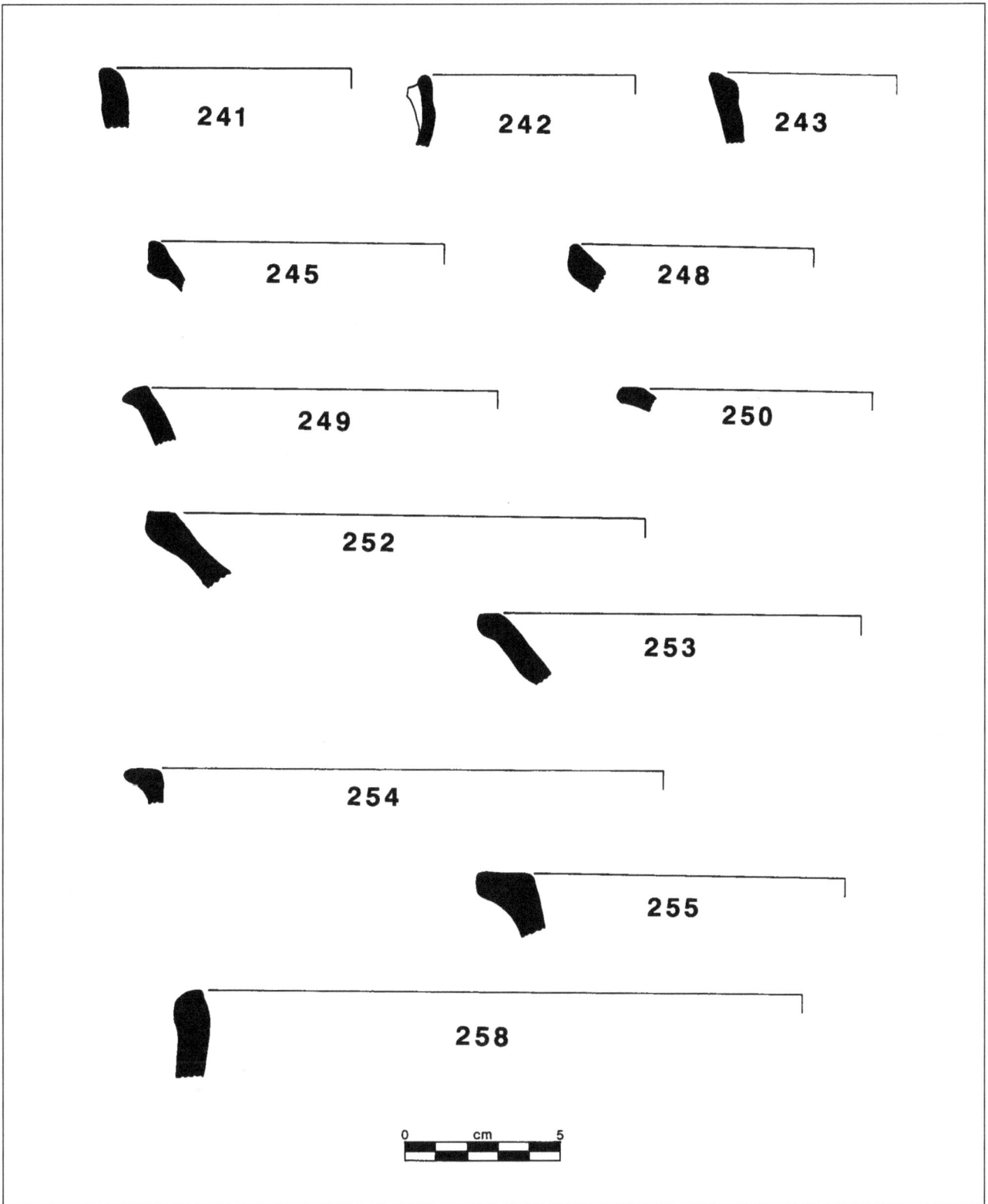

Figure 28. Indeterminate material

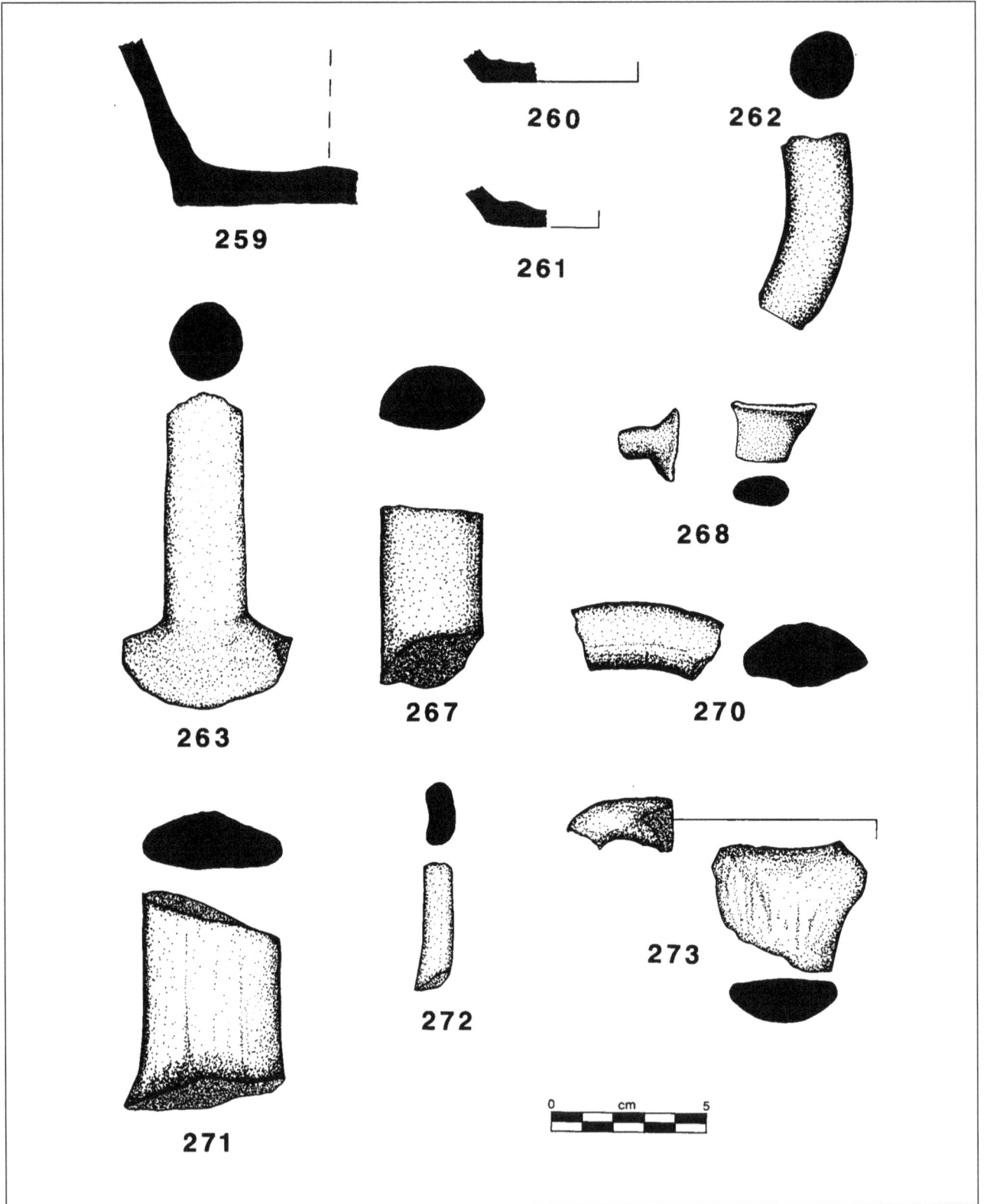

Figure 29. Indeterminate material

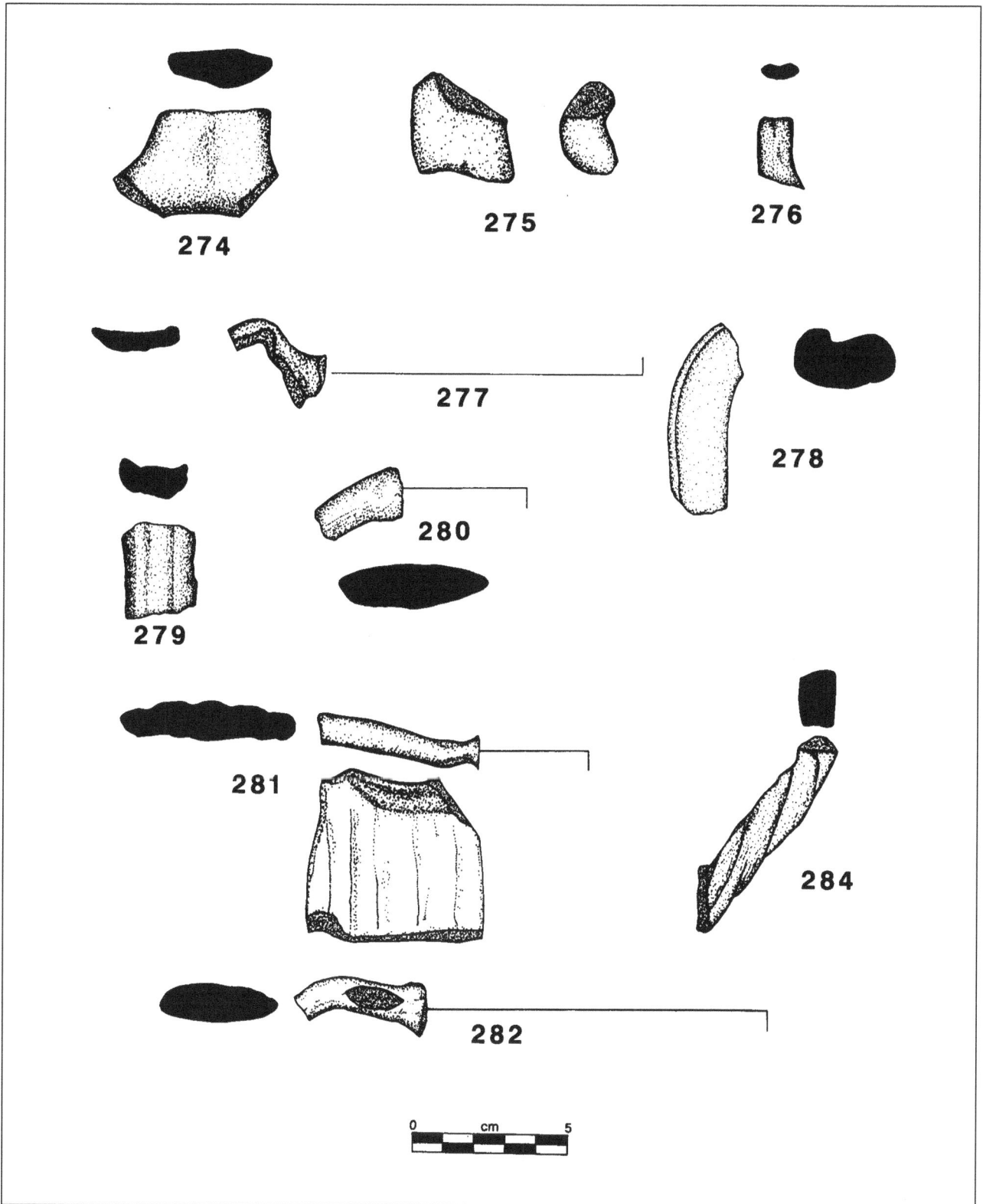

Figure 30. Indeterminate material

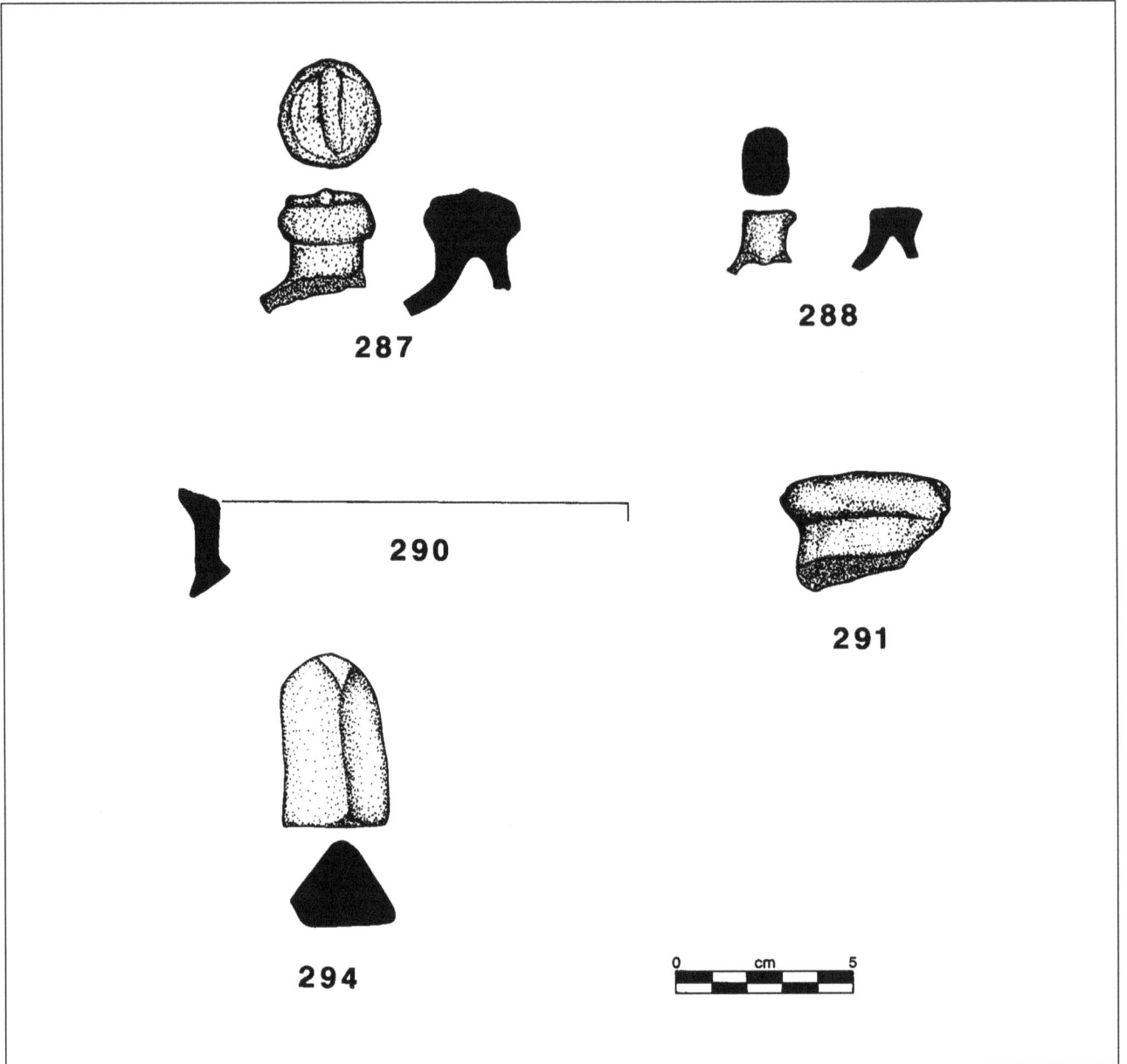

Figure 31. Indeterminate material

Plate 1. View of the upper Capodifiume from Capaccio Vecchia

Plate 2. View of Capaccio Vecchia from the Capodifiume

Plate 3. Survey unit CS-1

Plate 4. Detail of Hondius (1619), *Abruzzo et terra di Lavoro*

Plate 5. Detail of Anon. (1969), *Regno di Napoli*

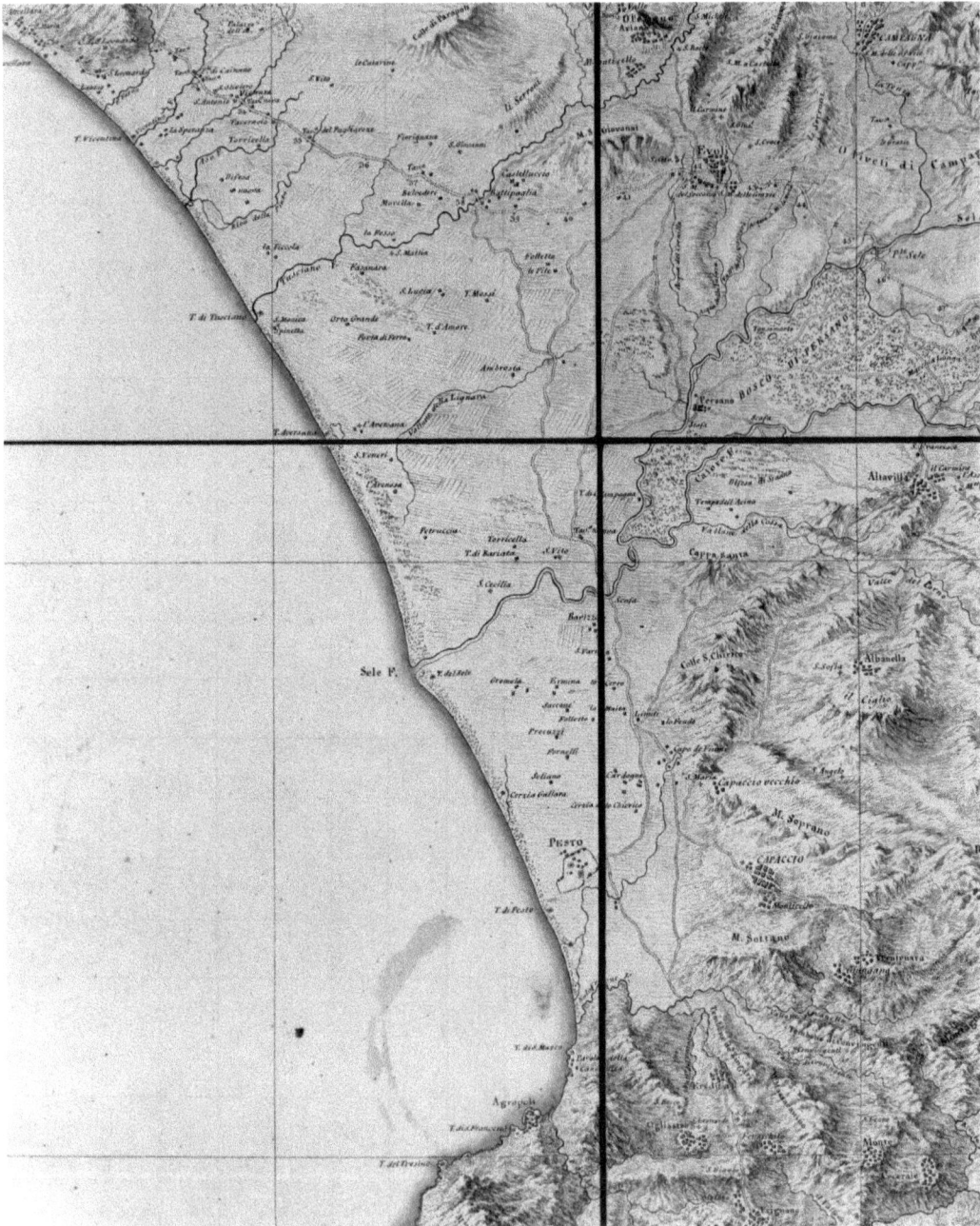

Plate 6. Detail of Anon. (1791), *Naples and Sicily*

Plate 7. The temple of Hera I

Plate 8. The temple of Athena

Plate 9. The temple of Hera II

Plate 10. CS-4 material

Plate 11. CS-4 material

Plate 12. CS-4 material

Plate 13. CS-7 material

Plate 14. CS-7 material

Plate 15. CS-7 material

Plate 16. CS-9 material

Plate 17. CS-10 material

Plate 18. CS-11 material

Plate 19. CS-11 material

Plate 20. CS-12 material

Plate 21. CS-13 material

Plate 22. CS-15 material

Plate 23. CS-16 material

Plate 24. CS-18 material

Plate 25. CS-20 material

Plate 26. CS-30 material

Plate 27. Material from CS-30, CS-31, CS-35, CS-37 and CS-38

Plate 28. Material from CS-40 and CS-41

Plate 29. Material from CS-42, CS-43 and CS-44

Plate 30. CS-49 material

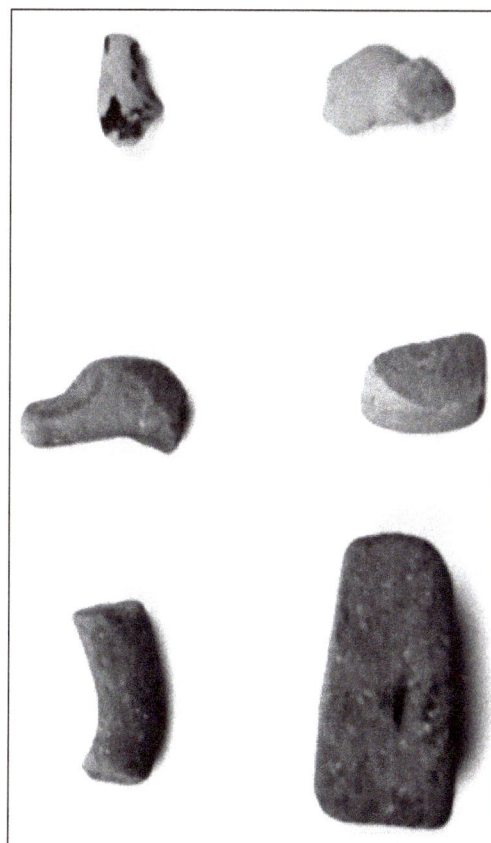
Plate 31. CS-50 material

www.ingramcontent.com/pod-product-compliance
Lightning Source LLC
Chambersburg PA
CBHW061004030426

42334CB00033B/3356